OATH KEEPERS

OATH KEEPERS

Patriotism and the Edge of Violence
in a Right-Wing Antigovernment Group

SAM JACKSON

Columbia University Press

New York

Columbia University Press
Publishers Since 1893
New York   Chichester, West Sussex
cup.columbia.edu
Copyright © 2020 Columbia University Press

Library of Congress Cataloging-in-Publication Data
Names: Jackson, Sam (Professor of social sciences), author.
Title: The Oath Keepers : patriotism and the edge of violence in a
    right-wing antigovernment group / Sam Jackson.
Description: New York : Columbia University Press, [2020] | Includes
    bibliographical references and index.
Identifiers: LCCN 2020011040 (print) | LCCN 2020011041 (ebook) |
    ISBN 9780231193443 (hardback) | ISBN 9780231193450
    (trade paperback) | ISBN 9780231550314 (ebook)
Subjects: LCSH: Oath Keepers (Organization) | Right-wing
    extremists—United States. | Militia movements—United States. |
    Radicalism—United States.
Classification: LCC HN90.R3 J375 2020 (print) |
    LCC HN90.R3 (ebook) | DDC 303.48/4—dc23
LC record available at https://lccn.loc.gov/2020011040
LC ebook record available at https://lccn.loc.gov/2020011041

Cover image: © William Campbell / Corbis via Getty Images
Cover design by Lisa Hamm

Contents

OATH KEEPERS

Introduction

n April 2015, Rick Barclay and George Backes received a letter from the Bureau of Land Management ordering them to stop work on the small Sugar Pine gold mine in southwestern Oregon. The government accused the two mine operators of violating regulations that required them to seek permission before building on the land around their mine.

Barclay and Backes disagreed with the BLM. They said that the nature of their claim to the mine meant they were exempt from the regulations they were accused of violating. The men filed an appeal with the Interior Board of Land Appeals, and they approached the Oath Keepers chapter in Josephine County, Oregon, with a request for help. They asked the chapter to provide security for their property to ensure that the miners' rights to due process were protected while they waited on the results of their appeal. Barclay and Backes said that the BLM had a habit of intimidating miners, even burning down cabins to force people off their land.

The Bureau of Land Management said that the men had the right to appeal the determination that their mine was in violation of regulations and that the agency had no plans to take any action before that appeal made its way through court. Despite this, the

Josephine County chapter of Oath Keepers,[1] led by a man named Joseph Rice, organized an around-the-clock security operation for Sugar Pine Mine. The national leadership took notice and issued a call to action: "We need hundreds of volunteers to help secure the mine."[2]

Dozens of Oath Keepers—perhaps even hundreds, according to Mary Emerick, the Josephine County Oath Keepers public information officer—responded to the call. They came from as far away as Alabama and Massachusetts.[3] Many of those who responded were eager to take up their firearms to protect the miners' rights. Perimeter security teams checked incoming vehicles for hidden bombs. Armed escorts accompanied members of the press at all times. The road up to the mine was blocked by a bulldozer and "three men armed with AR-15s and wearing tactical gear."[4] As Joseph Rice escorted a journalist up that road, the head of the security team, a former marine named Brandon Rapolla, detonated an explosive. Rice declined to answer the journalist's question about what had been blown up.[5]

Representatives of the Bureau of Land Management were confused by the security operation. A public affairs officer said that the miners had taken the right action to contest the stop-work order by appealing that order and that the government would do nothing until their appeal was decided by a judge.[6] Heavily armed men seemed out of place in a disagreement that consisted mainly of letters and legal filings.

In May, the Interior Board of Land Appeals told the miners that they could continue work while their appeal was considered. The miners declared victory, and Oath Keepers ended its operation.[7]

Despite the aggressive posture of the security operation at the mine, there was no direct conflict between Oath Keepers and the government—no members of law enforcement showed up to take action against the security operation or the miners. Barclay said he believed that the only reason the BLM hadn't burned down his cabin was because of the security operation. Bureau officials said the agency would not have taken any action until the ongoing legal process had concluded.[8] Whether because of or despite the security operation, the disagreement between the miners and the federal government stayed in the courtroom, away from the body armor and bullets.

Since its founding in 2009, the right-wing antigovernment group known as Oath Keepers has perceived a number of threats to the American people, most coming from the government. Its members have taken action around the country to mobilize support for the group, to push back against government actions it has deemed tyrannical, and to take up firearms in pursuit of its political goals. From Boston to Berkeley, from rural Oregon to the U.S.-Mexico border, from Tennessee to Missouri to Kentucky, the group has perceived threats to American lives and liberties and has worked to stop those threats. Some of these perceptions of threat led to hostile interactions between Americans and their government, but some—like the Sugar Pine Mine operation—never materialized in any meaningful sense.

Oath Keepers has been remarkably consistent (at least until mid-2016) in the ideas it promotes, the events it anticipates, and the behavior it advocates. For years, the group has warned that the federal government is preparing to attack its own citizens, and it urges Americans to prepare for that conflict by gathering supplies and engaging in paramilitary training. It has also warned that the global economy will soon collapse, and it urges Americans to prepare by stockpiling goods and retreating into small self-sufficient, community-based economies.

This perception of threats and the group's understanding of its members as patriots—even as model Americans—contain something of a contradiction. These Americans, who view themselves as patriots, believe that they may need to take up weapons to fight the government. In addition, Oath Keepers claims that many of its members are current and former military and police, yet it advocates for a set of political beliefs and actions that may lead those members to point their guns at the police and maybe even the military.

This is a book about this apparent contradiction, the tension among patriotism, antigovernment hostility, and the possible use of violence. Oath Keepers draws on American history and core political values to situate its goals and behavior, in particular by retelling the stories of moments of conflict and crisis from American history. Through these stories, the group helps its members and the wider American public make sense of the political situation in which they find themselves. These stories also teach Americans how to fight back against the threats the group perceives.

I build this argument across three core analytical chapters, beginning with the group's references to natural rights, a foundational idea in American politics; then moving to the group's references to the Revolutionary War, the foundational event in American history; and concluding with the group's references to the Branch Davidian standoff in Waco, Texas, in 1993 and the government's response to Hurricane Katrina in 2005, two moments of crisis from recent American history. Through this argument, I show how Oath Keepers and the broader patriot/militia movement of today—and radical political movements in general—make sense of their political context and pursue support from a less radical public.

This book also contains two appendixes. The first describes the data and methods used for this analysis. The second appendix contains one of the most important documents for Oath Keepers: its "Declaration of Orders We Will Not Obey." This document, which was written before the group officially launched in

April 2009, contains its guiding principles; prominent figures in the group have repeatedly referred back to it to explain the ideas and actions that Oath Keepers has considered most important throughout its ten years of existence.

The argument in this book comes from a close reading of thousands of texts (containing more than one million words) posted to the internet by Oath Keepers.[9] This project uses a sociological approach called framing analysis to examine Oath Keepers discourse about politics, history, and forms of political behavior. In other words, it is my attempt to understand how the group talks to its members and the public at large to convince both audiences that its political goals are just and its political actions justifiable.

All political actors talk about the issues that are important to them in ways that help them understand their context and build support for their cause. Scholars of social movements refer to this rhetorical activity as strategic framing (drawn from Erving Goffman's definition of frames as concepts that individuals use to make sense of the world).[10] Researchers have identified a number of different forms and functions of social movement frames, often following a motivation to explain social movement outcomes.[11] Rather than examining the group's strategic framing activity to explain broader outcomes for the group, though, this book instead is meant to provide a deeper understanding of how Oath Keepers makes sense of contemporary America. The methodological appendix gives more information about how I carry out this analysis.

The internet has become a central channel for the discursive work of making sense of the world. Therefore, those are the data this project examines—documents, images, and videos that Oath Keepers has shared online. These documents are all texts that the group has shared with a wide audience on platforms where it can control the content. I do not include data posted by others about

Oath Keepers, instead focusing on the documents that the group has decided to use to build its reputation online. These documents are an explicit attempt by the group to communicate to a large audience. This makes them excellent sources of data for my attempt to understand how Oath Keepers frames its political goals and behavior.

This book does not use interviews with individual members of the group as data. My interest is in how the group portrays itself to a wide public, not how the group's members talk in one-on-one conversations with a single academic. Additionally, as this analysis does not investigate whether the group's members believe everything they say or whether they agree with the group's talking points or actions, interviews would not provide me any additional analytical leverage.

The argument in this book focuses on the group from its founding in early 2009 through 2016. The 2016 presidential election campaign season was an inflection point for the group. Before the election, it consistently viewed government as the single greatest threat to Americans. But with Donald Trump's candidacy, many supporters of different factions of the far right in America found their man—and with him, a chance to reclaim electoral politics for their purposes. Gradually, Oath Keepers adopted this perspective. Though the group never formally endorsed Trump—and in fact was occasionally reluctant to trust him, particularly on issues like gun control—members of the group widely supported him.[12] And when it was clear that the general election would be a contest between Trump and Hillary Clinton, there was no question whom Oath Keepers would support.

With Trump's victory, the relationship Oath Keepers had to government changed dramatically. Now, it had a man in the Oval Office. The group had real hopes that Trump would pursue policies that aligned with its views on immigration, public land, economics, and more. For the first time in years, Oath Keepers could imagine government as a force for good.

At the same time, a new enemy emerged to take government's place: Americans who oppose Trump, his policies, and his presidency. "Antifa"—short for "antifascist" and commonly used to describe leftist activists who engage in a range of street action—has become the new boogeyman for Oath Keepers. Members of Oath Keepers (along with others on the far right) see these activists as the real fascists, as people who will use violence and intimidation to prevent other Americans from exercising First Amendment rights to speech and assembly. According to Oath Keepers, today government is not the greatest threat to Americans—other Americans are.

It remains to be seen whether this change will last. I return to this question in the conclusion, but this book is not meant to forecast the future of Oath Keepers. Instead, it is an investigation into how the group perceives and presents itself. This presentation can justify its goals and behavior, even when these don't seem to fall within the range of acceptability in contemporary America. In doing so, the book will accomplish two things. First, it will provide a richer understanding of this important group—one of the most prominent far-right groups of the past decade. And second, it will explore how radical groups work to make themselves appear less radical, thereby gaining more popular support.

Some readers might ask why this group warrants a book devoted to exploring its ideas and rhetoric, particularly since Oath Keepers may have never had more than five thousand active members at any single point in time (despite claims from 2014 through 2016 that there were as many as 35,000 dues-paying members). But this group, whose size is negligible when compared with the population of the United States, has been involved in several tense situations where firearms were openly carried and violence between

Oath Keepers and law enforcement was narrowly avoided (such as the Bundy Ranch standoff in 2014). Since 2016, Oath Keepers has engaged in violent conflicts with left-leaning activists, including in Berkeley and Boston. More broadly, Oath Keepers exemplifies a style of American politics that views violence as a legitimate means to achieve political goals, at least under certain conditions. As I discuss throughout this book, that legitimate violence may come in a number of different forms and may be used in a number of different contexts. No matter how it is used, though, those who consider violence to be an illegitimate form of political behavior should learn about those who disagree with them, to understand why some people think of violence as legitimate.

Before presenting this argument about how Oath Keepers uses core political ideas and important moments of conflict and crisis to justify its goals and actions, the next three chapters provide background on right-wing extremism in the United States and on Oath Keepers.

1

Understanding Right-Wing Extremism in the United States

The United States is no stranger to contentious political activity that can be understood as political extremism, that is, activity that seeks to change fundamental features of the American political system. Indeed, the nation was founded out of attempts to fundamentally alter the political system, replacing distant monarchical government with (relatively) local, (relatively) democratic government. Some of this contentious political activity is right-wing extremism, an amorphous category that includes conservative or regressive forms of extremism based on a desire to preserve existing political structures or return to previous structures. This chapter provides a brief history of right-wing extremism, which will contextualize how Oath Keepers fits in with the far right in the United States.

Observers of American politics often talk about the right wing versus the left wing. Though this single-dimension spectrum is dramatically reductive and ignores much of the diversity in American political thought, it is still useful for understanding trends in U.S. politics. Following many other authors, I use "right wing" as a label for political thought or actors who aim to preserve or restore traditional politics.[1] Put differently, right-wing politics is a response to a perception that changes in structures of authority, privilege, or wealth unjustly hurt people who have traditionally enjoyed authority, privilege, or wealth. Different factions of the political right focus on different things. Social conservatives wish to maintain the influence of tradition or religion in public life, often playing out in opposition to gender and sexual equality, nonarchetypal families (that is, anything other than a man married to a woman, particularly where families include children), and access to abortion. Fiscal conservatives wish to revert to a time with less government involvement in the economy, a massively reduced welfare state, and maximum independence from the global economy. Libertarians wish to return to a golden age of minimal government and maximum independence. Isolationists wish to see the nation restored to the principle of minimal international involvement in issues where the United States does not have strong self-interests, rooted in George Washington's wish that the nation "steer clear of permanent alliances with any portion of the foreign world."[2]

However, the traditions that right-wing movements aim to preserve or restore may not have actually ever existed. Arguably, the United States never embraced isolationism, given early expansionist efforts like the Louisiana Purchase and the annexation of the Southwest. And traditional Christianity was never as dominant as social conservatives claim, given the heterodox religious beliefs of those who wrote the nation's foundational legal documents.

Put most simply—perhaps reductively—right-wing politics sees its ideal political community somewhere in the past (or sees its ideal community as a new embodiment of past political values), whereas left-wing politics sees its ideal political community somewhere in the future. Oath Keepers, like other far-right actors, seeks to restore an imagined past golden age.

The concept of "extremism" is not new. The German political scientist Uwe Backes traces the term back to "the ancient Greek ethics of moderation." He argues that it became part of contemporary political discourse after the Russian Revolution of 1917 and that for some time "extremism" was used overwhelmingly in reference to the far left.[3] By the middle of the twentieth century, though, the term was also used to discuss right-wing politics. One of the most well-known invocations of "extremism" in the United States comes from Barry Goldwater's speech accepting the Republican Party's nomination for the presidency in 1964: "I would remind you that extremism in the defense of liberty is no vice."[4] As Goldwater's statement suggests, extremism has long been used as a description for people whose politics we don't like, whose actions or beliefs we view as beyond the realm of acceptable action or belief.

Since 2000, some scholars have adopted the term and offered various definitions. Some definitions focus on the use of violence or the violation of human rights.[5] Others situate extremism as fundamentally opposed to democracy or specific democratic values.[6] Though not explicit in these definitions, each seems to focus implicitly on identifying actors whose actions or beliefs are deemed unacceptable.

I have argued elsewhere for a non-normative scholarly understanding of extremism that is deeply contextual and facilitates comparison among different actors, actions, and ideas. In short, I define political extremism as "purposeful disruptive political behavior" that "aims to change fundamental features of a particular political system."[7] With this definition, any actor who seeks to change fundamental features of their political system—whether I support or oppose those changes—falls into the category of extremists. Some right-wing extremists in the United States have tried to draw parallels between themselves and the civil rights movement; this definition takes that comparison seriously at the level of behavior and goals without suggesting any moral equivalence.[8]

Other scholars have objected to this definition of political extremism. For example, J. M. Berger, who defines extremism as "the belief that an in-group's success or survival can never be separated from the need for hostile action against an out-group," objects to my definition of political extremism in part because, as a result of being deeply contextual and defined in opposition to what is dominant in any political context, my definition results in supporters of the Nazis while the NSDAP was in power in Germany not being considered extremists, as they were supporting the dominant political ideas and actors in their political context.[9]

If we combine these two definitions—the right wing as political thought or actors who aim to preserve or restore traditional politics and extremism as purposeful disruptive political behavior that aims to change a political system fundamentally—then right-wing extremism is activity that, in reaction to perceptions of negative change, aims to revert fundamental features of the political system to some imagined (though not necessarily imaginary) past state.[10]

In other words, right-wing extremism seeks to restore a perceived past "golden age."[11] Different forms of right-wing extremism pursue different imagined golden ages—perhaps when white men had more power, perhaps when Christianity was more dominant, perhaps when government was smaller and less involved in different facets of daily life. And certainly not all movements based in political nostalgia are extremist. The term only applies to movements that seek to change fundamental features of the current political system, such as separation of church and state or the involvement of the government in regulating a wide range of industries. Though many other scholars use other definitions of right wing and right-wing extremism (often centered on race and violence), my definition attempts to distill the principle that underlies the more concrete (but also more contextually specific) definitions used by others.[12]

Several examples are perhaps useful at this point. White supremacy is a form of right-wing extremism in that it seeks to change the American political system to consider racial identity in a way that it currently doesn't. Though it is certainly true that racism is endemic in U.S. politics, white supremacists aim to make that form of bigotry more central and explicit. Black nationalism is not a form of right-wing extremism in the United States: it does not seek to restore a golden age when black Americans held more power. Likewise, Islamist extremism in the United States is not right-wing extremism, as it does not seek to restore a lost state where political Islam was dominant in this country. But Islamist extremism in other contexts, perhaps in Turkey, Iran, or Egypt, does meet the definition of right-wing extremism, in that such extremists hope to restore the historical political power of Islam in their country.

Contemporary right-wing extremism in the United States contains three primary categories: racist extremism, nativist extremism, and antigovernment extremism (see figure 1.1). In practice, there is substantial overlap between the categories, and distinguishing among them is sometimes difficult or even impossible. But recognizing these three categories as analytically distinct helps researchers develop more nuanced and accurate understandings of different right-wing extremists in the United States.

There are also other forms of right-wing extremism that don't fall into any one of these categories. For example, some forms of male supremacy identify feminism in any form as a threat to

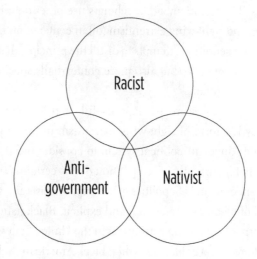

Figure 1.1 Right-wing extremism in the United States

This figure illustrates the overlap between the different categories of right-wing extremism. The blurred boundaries of each category can make it hard to determine whether certain cases belong to a particular category. The relative size of each circle in this figure is not meant to indicate the relative size of the different types of extremism. Nor is the amount of overlap between different circles meant to indicate the actual size of overlap between different categories (Jackson, "A Schema of Right-Wing Extremism in the United States.").

traditional gender roles and power structures.[13] Some observers have argued that male supremacy is a sort of gateway drug for other forms of right-wing extremism.[14] Some scholars argue that at least some forms of male supremacy cut across different forms of extremism, including left-wing extremism and jihadi extremism. Thus, perhaps some forms of male supremacy, for example the "incel" movement—men who describe themselves as "involuntarily celibate" because women refuse to have sex with them— should be thought of as their own form of extremism.[15]

Some of the forms of right-wing extremism that don't fit neatly into one of these categories were previously more common than they are now. In the 1990s and 2000s, antiabortion extremism spawned acts of violence across the United States, including Eric Rudolph's bombing of abortion clinics in Georgia and Alabama and the murder of Dr. George Tiller in 2009.[16] This form of extremism doesn't fall under the categories of racist extremism, nativist extremism, or antigovernment extremism, though some antiabortion extremists were also involved with one of the three primary forms of right-wing extremism in the United States: for example, Eric Rudolph was involved in the rabidly antisemitic and racist Christian Identity movement.[17] Opposition to abortion is also common among antigovernment extremists, but it is not a necessary characteristic of antigovernment extremism.

Of the three primary forms of right-wing extremism in the United States, racist extremism has received the most attention from both scholars and the public. Some scholars even define the extreme right as only those who are white supremacists or antisemitic.[18] More precisely, this form of extremism is explicitly organized around perceptions of racial identity. The classic examples of right-wing extremism—the so-called alt-right,[19] the KKK, and neo-Nazis—fall into this category: they organize in defense of a particular understanding of "whiteness" that they believe to be threatened by other racial groups or by multiculturalism and pro-diversity initiatives.[20] Race here is a constructed identity, meaning that its definition is based on perceptions and negotiations that may shift over time, and different understandings of a single racial identity may exist at the same time. For example, white supremacists throughout American history have disagreed about whether Jews are "white."[21] Thus, the racial enemies identified by racist right-wing extremists have varied over time and across different actors.

A close cousin of racist right-wing extremism is nativist extremism.[22] This form of extremism is organized around a perception that foreign people, organizations, and ideas are a threat to Americans. What counts as "native" or "foreign" is often not clear, but nativism centers on a sense that "foreign" people, organizations, and ideas are in conflict with what is native. Ultimately, nativists believe that the foreign seeks to replace the native. Some of the most common categories identified as foreign threats by nativist right-wing extremism movements are immigrants (or a subset of immigrants); non-Christian (or non-"Judeo-Christian") religions, in particular Islam; and political systems that are seen as incompatible with capitalism and democracy, particularly communism. Nativist right-wing extremism can be seen in the John Birch Society (most active in the 1960s, though it still exists today), anti-Islam groups like ACT for America, and civilian paramilitary groups like Arizona Border Recon that patrol the U.S.-Mexico border with the self-professed goal of deterring illegal immigration. These examples illustrate that right-wing extremist activity is often constitutionally protected in the United States.[23]

While nativist and racist right-wing extremism overlap substantially, the category of antigovernment extremism is more distinct.[24] This form of extremism manifests in several sets of ideas, but the core principle is that the federal government and perhaps even state governments are illegitimate and must be resisted by any means necessary.[25] Antigovernment extremism contains two main subcategories: sovereign citizens and the patriot/militia movement.

Sovereign citizens believe that, as sovereign individuals, they are not bound by the authority of any government.[26] They often use arcane legal theories to justify this belief—for instance, that the Articles of Confederation are still the basis of authority for the federal government, rather than the Constitution; that the Four-teenth Amendment, which guarantees citizenship to all individu-als "born or naturalized in the United States," created an artifi-cial second-class form of citizenship from which individuals can opt out; and that filing certain legal documents using very spe-cific language can free individuals from the jurisdiction of all laws, including requirements for driver's licenses and paying state and federal income taxes.[27] In 2014, researchers affiliated with the National Consortium for the Study of Terrorism and Responses to Terrorism (START) surveyed law enforcement officers from across the country, asking whether officers viewed different types of extremists as a "serious terrorist threat." The respondents believed that sovereign citizens posed a greater threat than "Islamic Extremists/Jihadists," neo-Nazis, or any other category of extrem-ist actor.[28]

The second subcategory of antigovernment extremism is the patriot/militia movement. Others refer to this set of ideas and actors as the "patriot movement," the "militia movement," or the "constitutional militia movement." Those inside the movement also refer to it as the "liberty movement" or the "freedom move-ment."[29] I use the clunky term "patriot/militia movement" rather than these other terms for two reasons. First, "patriot" carries a strong positive connotation in the United States: to call someone a patriot is to compliment them. I do not wish to imply—however slightly or incidentally—that those who are part of this move-ment are admirable patriots. Second, not all of the individuals and groups in this movement are militias in the sense of being hierarchical paramilitary organizations that deliberately imitate militaries, though some certainly are. Some, like Oath Keepers, encourage and engage in paramilitary or vigilante action without adopting the pseudoformal characteristics that militias typically adopt, such as military-style uniforms and ranks.

The patriot/militia movement believes that the federal government poses the greatest threat to the life, liberty, and happiness of Americans and that all true Americans should prepare themselves for an inevitable conflict with the government. That preparation means learning paramilitary skills; becoming self-sufficient in basic needs like nutrition, medicine, and energy; and finding like-minded neighbors with whom they can stand against any tyrannical force that comes knocking. Supporters of this movement regularly argue that the United States has forsaken the political system created by the Founders and that many of the nation's problems could be solved by returning to that system.[30]

It is important to recognize the substantial overlap between these categories of right-wing extremism. This is most apparent with the two categories of nativist extremism and racist extremism. It could even be argued that these two categories are better understood as two subtypes of xenophobic extremism rather than as discrete primary categories. Both of these categories operate on the basis of separating insiders from outsiders. Perhaps the primary difference between racist right-wing extremism and nativist right-wing extremism lies in whether the extremists think that outsiders can "convert" to insider status. In many (though not all) forms of nativism, outsiders can reject what makes them outsiders, assimilating and adopting the characteristics that would make them insiders.[31]

Consider, for example, extremist understandings of Muslim identity.[32] Some right-wing extremists adopt a seemingly biological understanding of Muslim identity, arguing that no Muslim person can ever leave it behind. This leaves no room for a person perceived as Muslim to ever be recognized as non-Muslim. Other right-wing extremists understand Muslim identity as primarily religious, arguing that the Muslim faith is incompatible with "American values." This understanding allows Muslims to convert if they reject Islam in a way that those who perceive them as Muslim find credible.

This conceptual overlap between racist and nativist right-wing extremism complicates attempts to place particular actors and incidents precisely. A prime example of this is the case of a militia group in Kansas who plotted to bomb a mosque and apartment community that housed Somali immigrants.[33] One of the plotters, Patrick Stein, described Muslims as "cockroaches."[34] During a trial in which the defendants were ultimately convicted, prosecutors argued that the men had considered a number of targets before deciding on the mosque and apartments. The common feature of all of the potential targets was that they supported immigrants.[35] Referring to people as animals (particularly pests) has long been a practice associated with racism. The use of this language here suggests that Stein held a racial understanding of Muslim identity, but this alone does not provide decisive evidence about whether his anti-Muslim bigotry is best understood as racism or nativism.

As this example suggests, there is also overlap between antigovernment extremism and the two xenophobic forms of right-wing extremism. If one takes their ideas seriously, similarities between antigovernment extremism, on the one hand, and nativist or racist extremism, on the other, is perhaps surprising—many organizations and actors who can be understood as antigovernment extremists (including Oath Keepers) explicitly condemn bigotry attached to race, ethnicity, or religion. But overlap does exist, despite any protestations to the contrary.

One reason for the overlap lies in the history of ideas that animate antigovernment extremism, some of which were developed by racist and nativist actors.[36] The foremost example of this is the Posse Comitatus movement (not to be confused with the Posse Comitatus Act, which places restrictions on the use of federal military personnel within the United States).[37] Posse Comitatus (Latin for "power of the county") emerged in the 1970s. William Potter Gale—a prominent member of the antisemitic Christian Identity religious movement—played a critical role in developing and spreading the movement's ideas. Its supporters believed that the county is the most powerful level of government in the United States and that "the only valid law enforcing power was the sheriff's posse."[38] The movement adopted a number of uncommon political theories. For example, Gale argued that the Articles of Confederation were still in force, and, because of the provisions of that document, a federal income tax and the IRS were unconstitutional.[39]

Gale was a minister with Christian Identity, and he argued that Jews were literal descendants of Satan.[40] Members of the Posse Comitatus movement promoted a conspiracy theory that "Jews, Catholics, [and] blacks" were partially responsible for an economic crisis that had devastated Midwestern farmers in the 1980s.[41]

Today, many of the ideas previously articulated by Posse Comitatus adherents are promoted by antigovernment extremists (though often without the explicit racism), and some scholars argue that certain elements of antigovernment extremism developed directly out of Posse.[42] For example, the contemporary Constitutional Sheriffs and Peace Officers Association (CSPOA) argues that "the county sheriff is the one who can say to the feds, 'Beyond these bounds you shall not pass.' This is not only within the scope of the sheriff's authority; it's the sheriff's sworn duty."[43] The organization emphasizes "State Sovereignty and local autonomy,"[44] framing these ideas as a defense of individual liberty against tyranny. The CSPOA has encouraged county sheriffs to issue ultimatums to IRS officials and the U.S. Marshals Service, suggesting that they should threaten to use their powers of arrest to prevent the enforcement of federal laws and court orders that the CSPOA views as unconstitutional.[45] Despite the ideas it shares with Posse Comitatus, the CSPOA does not organize around a perceived racial identity, and the organization is not antisemitic. These ideas of radical localism are prevalent within the patriot/militia movement with or without the racism that was baked into the original formulations of radical localism.[46]

Besides inheriting core ideas from explicitly racist predecessors, antigovernment extremists of various flavors engage in activities that suggest affinity with contemporary racist extremists. For example, throughout 2016 and 2017, members of antigovernment militia groups acted as de facto security for the so-called alt-right.[47] These militia members stressed that they undertook their "security operations" to defend the rights of white supremacists to assemble peaceably and express their constitutionally protected political beliefs—but not to support those beliefs. But they have not undertaken any similar activity to protect the First Amendment rights of those widely understood as left-leaning or liberal.

The contemporary overlap between nativist extremism and antigovernment extremism is even more pronounced. Much of the patriot/militia movement, for example, is anti-Islam or anti-immigrant (though these individuals more commonly say they are anti-*radical*-Islam or anti-*illegal*-immigrant).[48] For example, Oath Keepers has supported paramilitary action on the U.S.-Mexico border to stop what it describes as an "invasion" of "illegals."[49] Members of the organization were also present at rallies organized by ACT for America in June 2017. These "March Against Sharia" events were held in twenty-eight cities around the country, bringing together people who think that Muslims are working to replace the American legal system with sharia law.[50] According to Oath Keepers, rally organizers invited the group to provide "security" to "defend free speech" and protect rally-goers from an alleged violent threat posed by leftists opposed to the Islamophobic theme of the event.[51]

Despite the common overlap between these three primary categories of right-wing extremism in the United States, this typology draws attention to different sets of ideas and actors that can all be understood as right-wing extremists. The short discussion of the categories provided here is meant to set the stage for the remainder of the book, which is a detailed investigation of Oath Keepers, perhaps the most prominent organization within the patriot/militia movement, which in turn belongs to the antigovernment extremist category.[52] Before refocusing on Oath Keepers, though, a short history of the patriot/militia movement is warranted.

The patriot/militia movement emerged in the early 1990s. Most scholars identify 1994 as the year the movement began.[53] In the first few years, the two most prominent groups in the patriot/militia movement were the Michigan Militia and the Militia of Montana.[54] The historian Robert Churchill has argued that these two groups illustrate the two main tendencies within the movement. The constitutionalists like the Michigan Militia believed that public, organized political activity could "act as a deterrent against further government abuse." The millenarians like the Militia of Montana believed that organizing into militias was "the only way to survive an imminent invasion by the forces of the New World Order."[55] Churchill's categories, like the categories of right-wing extremism presented here, are useful analytic categories that draw attention to important distinct sets of ideas; at the same time, the constitutionalist and millenarian trends overlap substantially, and to describe any single actor as solely constitutionalist or millenarian, with no hints of the other trend, is rarely accurate.[56]

Information about the size of the patriot/militia movement in this first incarnation is difficult to come by. The historian D. J. Mulloy reports that estimates of the number of individuals who were part of militias ranged from 7,000 to 300,000, and estimates of the number of supporters and potential supporters of the movement ranged from 5 million to 12 million individuals.[57] As he notes, militia organizations "have a vested interest in overstating their own significance" and size, and outside organizations (including government agencies and watchdog organizations) face substantial difficulties in gathering reliable information on this question, particularly given legal restrictions on law enforcement investigation without some reasonable sense that the organizations were involved in illegal activity.[58]

Some organizations, most notably the Southern Poverty Law Center (SPLC), tracked the number of militia groups rather than the number of individuals affiliated with them. The SPLC reported 224 militias in thirty-nine states in 1995, growing to 441 militias in all fifty states by 1996.[59] As the scholar J. M. Berger has observed, though, the SPLC lists of antigovernment organizations and of hate groups can be problematic.[60] Among other issues, counting organizations doesn't tell us anything about the size of those organizations: an organization with five members counts the same as an organization with a thousand members.

Regardless of the size of the movement, militia groups burst into public awareness after Timothy McVeigh bombed the Murrah Federal Building in Oklahoma City on April 19, 1995. McVeigh would later reveal that part of his motivation for the bombing—which killed more than 150 people, including fifteen children—was the federal government's actions at Ruby Ridge in 1992 and at the Branch Davidian compound in Waco, Texas, in 1993. In both cases, armed standoffs between Americans and law enforcement led to the death of scores of people.[61] McVeigh viewed these two incidents as the opening shots in a war between Americans and their government—actions that he believed justified his use of indiscriminate violence against the government. The American citizens who died were, in his view, collateral damage.[62]

Some scholars and watchdog organizations have argued that these groups declined in popularity immediately after the Oklahoma City bombing, given widespread beliefs that McVeigh was connected to this new patriot/militia movement. Others argue that the increased attention that militias received from major media outlets led to a short-term spike in movement numbers for the next several years.[63] What is certain is that the patriot/militia movement was far larger and more influential in the 1990s than in the early 2000s. After failed predictions that Y2K would cause societal collapse hurt the credibility of many prominent voices in the movement and after al-Qaeda's attacks on September 11, 2001, shifted attention away from potential domestic threats to liberty and toward international threats to security, membership in militias declined.[64] Rather than seeing the federal government as a threat to liberty, Americans across the political spectrum rallied around the flag in support of military intervention against foreign terrorism.

Attention remained focused on the threat posed by violent jihadi terrorism for much of the first decade of the twenty-first century. The wars in Iraq and Afghanistan were controversial, but these conflicts did not seem to lead to a resurgence of the patriot/militia movement. Certainly, the movement was not dead, but it remained mostly dormant for much of George W. Bush's presidency.

That would change in 2008 and 2009. With the financial crisis and government responses to that crisis, the election of Barack Obama as America's first black president, and the explosive growth of the Tea Party, the stage was set for an active, angry resurgence. Oath Keepers formed in 2009, after Stewart Rhodes (who had recently worked for the congressman Ron Paul) and some friends decided in 2008 that they would form an organization mobilized around a perception of imminent tyranny. Mike Vanderboegh, a long-time activist in the movement, began a blog called Sipsey Street Irregulars in November 2008, which became one of the early homes for the burgeoning Three Percenters Movement recently founded by Vanderboegh.[65] In 2009, the Southern Poverty Law Center declared that this resurgence amounted to a "second wave" of militia groups.[66]

Rhodes, Vanderboegh, and other prominent figures in the patriot/militia movement found much to like about the Tea Party movement, even going so far as to speak at Tea Party events. But they were not content to participate in rallies and town halls, write letters to elected representatives, and donate money to political candidates. They believed that the government in general—particularly the federal government—was so corrupt that these normal forms of political activity would likely prove insufficient. Rhodes and others in this movement encouraged like-minded Americans to prepare for more direct confrontation with the government.

This trend continued throughout Barack Obama's presidency. The patriot/militia movement was quick to voice opposition to any and all policies proposed by the Obama administration. It was also quick to explain events around the world as driven by a conspiracy of hidden actors working in secret to benefit themselves at the expense of most people. Harking back to the communist conspiracy theories prevalent during the Cold War, many in the patriot/militia movement today still argue that there is a communist—or socialist, Marxist, progressive, collectivist, statist, or globalist—conspiracy to erode American sovereignty and end individual liberty.[67] These conspiracy theories manifest in opposition to policies around gun control, environmental regulations, public health initiatives, police militarization, and immigration.

This conspiracism also influenced how those in the patriot/ militia movement viewed the 2016 presidential election. The movement was already anticipating crisis, given the strong candidacy of Hillary Clinton. Since the 1990s, antigovernment extremists of all stripes have viewed Hillary and Bill Clinton as major enemies willing—perhaps even eager—to violate Americans' rights at any turn for their own benefit. A convergence of other factors (including Russian disinformation, some of which was aimed at the far right) exacerbated the movement's concern about the election.[68] Groups like Oath Keepers pounced on information provided by Project Veritas—a conservative activist group known for conducting manipulative video stings of progressive organizations—that allegedly documented organized attempts by Democrats to rig the election.[69] Oath Keepers anticipated wide-scale voter fraud during this election, and the group warned of catastrophic consequences if that happened.

In the end there was no evidence of systematic voter fraud, and Donald Trump won the presidency despite losing the popular vote. Trump had energized the far right throughout his campaign, and the patriot/militia movement was no exception. He enjoyed enthusiastic support throughout the movement, in part because of his opponent in the election, in part because of his intense opposition to anything related to Barack Obama, and in part because of his vitriolic rhetoric about Muslims and immigrants.

After his election, the movement made clear their ongoing support for Trump. Members of Oath Keepers traveled to Washington, DC, to serve as informal security during Trump's inauguration. The group fixated on the alleged threat posed by anti-Trump activists, especially antifa (short for antifascist) groups that Oath Keepers interpreted as a fascist threat to America. In a short period of time, the patriot/militia movement pivoted: no longer was the federal government the primary threat of the American people and the American way of life; now it was those who oppose Donald Trump.

Members of the patriot/militia movement have long objected that they are not antigovernment. Instead, they argue that they are opposed to bad government or overbearing government. And indeed, their support for Donald Trump's presidency affirms that they do not oppose all government. Yet the label "antigovernment" is still valuable, as one of the defining characteristics of the patriot/militia movement in general is a perception that the government poses the greatest threat to the lives and liberties of Americans. This is certainly true for Oath Keepers.

2

Introducing Oath Keepers

On April 19, 2009, members of Oath Keepers gathered outside of Boston, Massachusetts, on Lexington Common, the site of the opening battle of America's War for Independence from Great Britain. In this, the group's first public event, several dozen Oath Keepers from around the country met on the 234th anniversary of the Battle of Lexington to reaffirm their oaths to "support and defend the Constitution against all enemies, foreign and domestic, so help us God."[1] According to the group, "The principle [sic] mission of Oath Keepers is to prevent the destruction of American liberty by preventing a full-blown totalitarian dictatorship from coming to power."[2]

Oath Keepers formed in March 2009. Today, it consists of a national leadership along with state, county, and local chapters in all fifty states.[3] The national leadership, centered on a board of directors led by Stewart Rhodes, the group's president and founder, controls the group's primary website and social media presence. Rhodes and other leaders periodically issue calls to action and release official organization statements. Much of the on-the-ground activity of Oath Keepers is left to the group's chapters. Local and state leadership organize meetings, demonstrations, and training exercises. Occasionally, a chapter will become involved in an issue that gains public attention, and national leadership then calls for supporters from across the country to mobilize and support the local chapter. This organizational structure means that national leadership is primarily responsible for developing the reputation of Oath Keepers writ large, despite much of the activity being driven by local affiliates.

Since the group's beginning, Stewart Rhodes has been Oath Keepers' most visible member. He is its founder and president, though in a speech Rhodes noted that several others had been involved in the group's formation.[4] His status is even written into the group's bylaws, which state that he is president of the group for life, unless he resigns or is found incompetent.[5]

At the age of eighteen, Rhodes joined the army. He served as a paratrooper for several years until he was injured in a night jump exercise. After leaving the military, he worked as a congressional staffer in Washington, DC, for Ron Paul. In the early 2000s, he graduated from Yale Law School. Though Oath Keepers is part of a large antielite milieu that targets higher education as a threat to America, Rhodes touts his education at Yale and is quick to point out that a paper he wrote on "enemy combatant status"—a controversial legal status used to detain Americans without trial as part of the War on Terror—won the Judge William E. Miller Prize for best paper on the Bill of Rights.[6] Most recently, Rhodes practiced law in Montana; he was disbarred in December 2015. The process that led to his disbarment in Montana started with accusations of professional misconduct filed by a federal judge in Arizona.[7] The Southern Poverty Law Center reports that Rhodes increasingly neglected his legal practice as he spent more of his time with Oath Keepers.[8]

In 2014, Rhodes told the *St. Louis Post-Dispatch* that his group had approximately 35,000 dues-paying members across the nation. The Anti-Defamation League and the Southern Poverty Law

Center both estimate actual membership to be less than 5,000.[9] According to the group's bylaws, "full membership" in Oath Keepers is reserved for retired and currently serving military members and first responders. Those with no such experience are welcomed as "associate members." There seems to be no substantive difference between these two categories of membership.[10]

To accomplish the group's mission, Oath Keepers seeks to "reach, teach, and inspire" (RTI) Americans to recognize the threats they face (especially threats from the government) and prepare to defend themselves.[11] This RTI effort involves recruiting new members to join Oath Keepers, and it also more generally consists of "reach[ing] out to both current serving and veterans to remind them of their oaths, to teach them more about the Constitution they swore to defend, and to inspire them to defend it."[12]

Rhodes has said that Oath Keepers wants to recruit those with military service to serve as the "tip of the spear" if the federal government were to use the military to infringe on Americans' rights. This would leave the government with fewer members of the military to carry out such orders, and it would give Oath Keepers more members with the skills to actively resist the government.[13] In 2009, he wrote, "We are in a battle for the hearts and minds of our own troops. To win that battle, Oath Keepers will use written and video testimony of active duty military, veterans (especially combat vets), and peace officers to reach, teach, and inspire our brothers in arms in the military and police to fulfill their oaths and stand as guardians of the Republic."[14] Later, in a radio interview, he said of current and former military and first responders:

> That's the message to the military and police is, you need to make a real hardcore decision right now. Look inside your soul. What are you? Are you just an enforcer for the power that, the illegitimate powers that be? Are you going to crap all over the American

Revolution and our Bill of Rights? Or are you going to do the right thing? . . . You have to make a decision right now, going down in history. How will you go down in history? As a traitor to your own country and the Bill of Rights? Or as a defender of the Constitution you swore an oath to defend? We're at that point now. We have to make a decision. I made my choice a long time ago. I know many others have also. We will not be like Nazi Germany, because this country, there will be another revolution. Whether we'll be successful or not if we have to do that will also depend largely upon the police and military, on whose side will you be on?[15]

In an interview with Alex Jones (the notorious conspiracy theorist and far-right provocateur), Rhodes was more succinct: "I'm talking to the military out there especially. Either you are a son of the republic and you will defend the Bill of Rights and the Constitution or you are a traitor to your country and you are nothing but a lowly dog, an obedient dog to the powers that be. Choose now whom you shall serve."[16] And in another video, he said, "This Republic cannot fall without their consent, without [the military] going along and obeying unlawful orders. We are confident that when we reach them and teach them more about the Constitution, they will do what's right."[17]

By recruiting current and former police and military, Oath Keepers hopes to reach, teach, and inspire those who legally participate in government-sponsored violence. Having allies in these institutions may reduce the likelihood of violent conflict between Oath Keepers and the government, and it may reduce the likelihood of any law enforcement response to Oath Keepers activity.

Yet this attempt to reduce the chances of violence does not completely remove a paradox for the group: Oath Keepers describes its members, many of whom are veterans, as patriots, but if the expected conflict with government indeed happens, its members will aim their firearms at police and military.

Oath Keepers describes itself as a nonpartisan organization.[18] It believes that tyrants and corrupt politicians come from both parties. Rhodes has argued that Americans "have a heritage of defeating any tyrant that tries to put his boot on the back of our neck, I don't care if it's a left boot or a right boot."[19] He has also said that he decided to start the organization before Barack Obama won the 2008 presidential election. In fact, John McCain, the Republican who ran against Obama in 2008, was a recurrent target of Rhodes's ire.[20] Members of Oath Keepers almost never support the Democratic Party, but they occasionally (or perhaps even regularly) support the Republican Party. Though Oath Keepers likes to present itself as independent and willing to work with all Americans to improve the country, the group's claim to be nonpartisan rests on the premise that neither of the two major political parties is sufficiently conservative, in the sense of conserving a fixed political system established by eighteenth-century politicians. In no sense is Oath Keepers centrist or moderate.

Oath Keepers adamantly rejects any accusations that it is racist, white supremacist, or associated with the so-called alt-right, a white supremacist movement that emerged from obscurity during the 2016 presidential election.[21] The group's bylaws bar anyone "who advocates, or has been or is a member, or associated with, any organization, formal or informal, that advocates discrimination, violence, or hatred toward any person based upon their race, nationality, creed, or color" from joining.[22] Rhodes has scoffed at the idea that he personally is a racist: "I'm a quarter Mexican, so it's kind of hard for me to be a white supremacist."[23] The group is also fond of highlighting its minority members: for several years, the homepage of its website featured a video interview with a member named David Berry, an African American navy veteran.

Specific demographic information about the group is not available, but images from the group's public events show that most of its members are white. Members of Oath Keepers think of themselves as rejecting racism, yet they and allied groups have served as de facto security for neo-Confederate and alt-right groups.[24] In other words, like most of the contemporary patriot/militia movement, the group is not organized around a perceived racial identity, but neither is it as free of racism and bigotry as it likes to claim.[25]

Oath Keepers has also repeatedly made vocal statements attacking so-called illegal immigrants. The group has featured interviews with leaders of informal volunteer paramilitary border patrol groups, such as Tim Foley of Arizona Border Recon (AZBR), and has encouraged its members to give time or money to groups like AZBR who patrol the border. In 2019, the group encouraged Donald Trump to declare a national emergency to fund his proposed border wall, and the group organized a security operation on the border in Texas.[26] Some videos about these groups and interviews with people who live in border communities assert that criminal organizations (like MS-13) and terrorist organizations (like ISIS) take advantage of inadequate security to enter the United States illegally.[27] This form of bigotry is better described as a form of nativism than as racism.

The organization's bylaws also reject discrimination on the basis of "creed" (which presumably means religion). Yet the group frequently describes a threat that America faces stemming from jihadi terrorism, and the rhetoric used to describe this threat sometimes slips into Islamophobia. Posts on the Oath Keepers website also recommend content from well-known Islamophobic websites, such as *Gates of Vienna*. For example, after the Pulse nightclub shooting in Orlando, Florida, in June 2016, Stewart Rhodes directed readers to a *Gates of Vienna* post by Matt Bracken called

"Tet Take Two: Islam's 2016 European Offensive."[28] This form of bigotry has translated into on-the-ground action. For example, members of the organization provided "security" for demonstrations organized by ACT for America in the summer of 2017 to protest what ACT sees as a threat of sharia law being implemented in the United States.[29] Clearly, despite its claim that Oath Keepers does not discriminate on the basis of religion, the organization is part of a broad segment of the American population that sees Islam as incompatible with American values and is unwilling to grant Muslims freedom to their religious beliefs. Oath Keepers is best understood as belonging to the antigovernment category of right-wing extremism, but it certainly exhibits some characteristics of nativist right-wing extremism as well.

The group's incomplete rejection of bigotry is further complicated by its frequent engagement with conspiracism (that is, a tendency to understand events in the world as caused by secret alliances of nefarious actors). Many conspiracy theories supported by other far-right American political actors are imbued with racism, antisemitism, or religious bigotry.[30] Conspiracy theories supported by Oath Keepers carry many of the same themes from these bigoted conspiracy theories but (at least on the face of things) remove the bigotry. For example, a frequent target of Oath Keepers' wrath is the global financial elite; sometimes Oath Keepers specifically names entities such as the Bilderbergers and the Rothschilds as the primary culprits behind economic crises.[31] In other contexts, conspiracy theories about the financial elite—and especially about the Rothschild family—are antisemitic, portraying these elites as greedy, manipulative Jews.[32] For Oath Keepers, though, the salient aspect of the identity of these financial elites is their elite status, not their race or religion. This repeated promotion of conspiracy theories is one of many features that Oath Keepers shares with earlier patriot/militia movement groups.[33]

Financial elites are not the only subject of conspiracy theories endorsed by Oath Keepers. Many of the conspiracy theories the group engages with focus on ideas of gun control or confiscation. Oath Keepers perceives any attempt at gun control as an attempt by a powerful elite to cripple potential resistance to that elite's authority. As with others in the patriot/militia movement, this group argues that gun-control proposals are not actually about reducing gun violence or gun crime; instead, they are attempts to consolidate governmental power and make it harder for Americans to defend themselves and their rights against tyranny and abuse.

Again following a line of thought common in the patriot/militia movement, Oath Keepers has repeatedly argued that the Federal Emergency Management Agency (FEMA) is an organization meant to facilitate the implementation of martial law. Stewart Rhodes has said that federal budget appropriations to FEMA for emergency relief are actually intended to be used to identify, round up, and intern political dissidents. Specifically, he has suggested that FEMA emergency relief camps are "dual use": the government states their public use is emergency relief, but their covert purpose is to intern Americans.[34]

Engaging with yet another conspiracy theory common among antigovernment extremists in the patriot/militia movement, Oath Keepers has worried about the United Nations being a vehicle for tyranny. The group warns about the potential use for foreign troops under UN command[35] and about the United Nation's Arms Trade Treaty being a "de facto repeal of the Second Amendment."[36] A particular issue of interest for Oath Keepers is the UN's Agenda 21, a nonbinding sustainable-development plan that Oath Keepers interprets as an attempt to violate America's sovereignty by dictating land-use policy based on lies about climate change and sustainable development—or perhaps even an attempt to "seiz[e] total control of everyone on the planet, in every aspect of your life."[37] As has been the case for many supporters of the patriot/militia movement since its earliest days, the United Nations is a particularly prominent threat for Oath Keepers, embodying its fears about tyranny, internationalism, and the loss of American sovereignty.[38]

In response to all of these threats, Oath Keepers encourages local groups to prepare for crises. The group wants to see Americans be ready to provide for themselves in emergency situations, rather than relying on help from the government. Oath Keepers promotes a version of self-reliance that harks back to motifs of independent homesteaders on the western frontier. The perceptions of threats and the belief that Americans should solve problems for themselves with minimal help from the government can be seen in many of the activities that the group has engaged in.

Oath Keepers has been one of the most prominent and important actors within the far right in the United States since 2009, though its importance has perhaps waned since November 2016. Oath Keepers is best understood as an organization that is part of the patriot/militia movement, placing it within the antigovernment category of right-wing extremism. Some of the group's members have engaged in extremist activity that is clearly racist or nativist, but the group itself denounces bigotry. And though those claims that Oath Keepers does not tolerate bigotry are not entirely persuasive, the group is not organized around the defense of imagined racial identity—the defining feature of racist extremism. Instead, the group is much closer to the category of nativism: it believes that foreign ideas and actors pose a threat to America and American values. But since 2009, the core theme of Oath Keepers ideas and actions has been that the single greatest threat to American lives and liberties comes from the U.S. government.

3

An Operational History of Oath Keepers

ath Keepers' muster on Lexington Common on April 19, 2009, was the group's first public event. Oath Keepers posted a series of videos from that event on its YouTube channel. The day's events centered around a number of speeches that described a range of threats that America faces, many of which feature prominently in the group's "Declaration of Orders We Will Not Obey," which they read out during the event: citizen disarmament, military tribunals, martial law, foreign troops, and citizen internment. Stewart Rhodes spoke about the need for the people to reassert their sovereignty, in particular by supporting state sovereignty.[1]

Later that day, a former Arizona sheriff named Richard Mack argued that another way for the people to claim their sovereignty would be to elect a "constitutional sheriff" who would refuse to enforce tyrannical laws and would prevent others from enforcing them.[2] Mack gained some measure of notoriety in the 1990s when, as a sheriff in rural Graham County, Arizona, he sued the federal government over a provision of the Brady Bill that required state law enforcement officers to approve of firearm transfers on an interim basis while the federal government's National Instant Criminal Background Check System was created. Mack's case made its way to the Supreme Court, where it was combined with a similar lawsuit filed by Jay Printz, a sheriff from Montana. The Supreme Court found that the interim provisions of the Brady Bill that required state law enforcement officers to take action to enforce federal law violated the anticommandeering doctrine implicit in the Tenth Amendment.[3] Though limited in its actual effects (the National Instant Criminal Background Check System was up and running the year after the Supreme Court's decision in *Printz v. United States*), Mack interpreted the Supreme Court's ruling as a validation of his interpretation of the Constitution—in particular, his understanding that dual sovereignty places dramatic limitations on the federal government.[4]

Retired Navy Lt. Commander Guy Cunningham also spoke during the Oath Keepers "muster" on Lexington Common. While a student at the Naval Postgraduate School in 1994, Cunningham conducted a notorious survey that asked Marines whether they would submit to orders issued by the United Nations and whether they would carry out orders to confiscate firearms owned by Americans, using lethal force if necessary.[5] At Lexington, Cunningham explained that he had asked those questions because he was concerned that President Bill Clinton would order U.S. military personnel to follow orders issued by non-American military officers or to enforce the Assault Weapons Ban portion of the Violent Crime Control and Law Enforcement Act of 1994.[6] Though some in the patriot/militia movement took this survey as proof that the federal government intended to use the military to disarm American citizens, Cunningham revealed that he intended for his survey to identify the extent to which Marines were ignorant of the Constitution: those who would be willing to fire on Americans while attempting to disarm them demonstrated a lack of knowledge about their obligations as service members, he said.[7]

The Lexington muster was the first public opportunity for supporters of Oath Keepers from around the country to gather together, and it illustrated the group's tendency to draw historical parallels—here between contemporary America and Revolution-era America—to frame its goals and motivations. Oath Keepers would spend its first few years spreading its message and recruiting new members. Just a few days before, Stewart Rhodes spoke at a Tea Party rally in Knoxville, Tennessee, on April 15, 2009. While there, he led the crowd of several thousand people in an oath-swearing ceremony, in which they promised to support and defend the Constitution against all enemies, foreign and domestic.[8] But the group's muster on Lexington Common was a dramatic and public moment that it would not repeat for some time.

For the next several years, Oath Keepers existed in relative obscurity, only gaining attention in the news when a member was arrested. The Anti-Defamation League reports a number of examples of Oath Keepers members committing crimes of varying severity.[9] David M. Phillips, an Oath Keeper in Massachusetts, was convicted of firearms charges and sentenced to two and a half years of jail time. In 2010, Matthew Fairfield, an Ohio Oath Keepers leader, was indicted on ninety-seven charges, including illegal possession of explosives, possession of stolen property, and child pornography. The same year, Darren Huff was convicted of a firearms charge after traveling from Georgia to Tennessee to put government officials under citizen's arrest for refusing to indict President Obama. Charles Dyer was arrested in 2010 on charges related to sexual assault of a child and possession of an explosive device; he was later sentenced to thirty years in prison. Before he was arrested, Dyer had been a rising star in Oath Keepers. While serving in the Marines, he posted a number of videos to YouTube under the pseudonym "July4Patriot." In these videos, a masked Dyer railed against the government, threatening to use his military training against it. He attended the Lexington muster on April 19, 2009, and the Oath Keepers blog announced that year that Dyer would "represent Oath Keepers at the July 4 Tea Party in Broken Arrow, Oklahoma."[10] After his arrest, Rhodes released a statement that Dyer never actually joined Oath Keepers; the post mentioning Dyer is no longer on their blog.[11]

Outside of this criminal activity, Oath Keepers as a group did not receive much attention from the public through 2013. During this time, they participated in several protests in Arizona. On Memorial Day, 2011, the group held an event to protest the killing of the Marine veteran Jose Guerena by a SWAT team in Tucson, Arizona, and to support his family.[12] Earlier that month, a heavily armed SWAT team burst into Guerena's house to execute a search warrant. Thinking that the commotion was a home invasion, Guerena grabbed his rifle and prepared to defend himself and his family. When SWAT officers saw Guerena with his rifle, they opened fire, shooting him dozens of times in just a few seconds.[13] Oath Keepers decried this as a terrible tragedy caused by police militarization and the overuse of SWAT teams. In speeches by Stewart Rhodes, Richard Mack, and local Oath Keepers leaders, the group denounced the Pima County Sheriff's Office, which had conducted the raid, and expressed their hope that this shooting would lead to police reform.[14]

Later in 2011, Oath Keepers participated in a day of demonstrations and speeches in Quartzsite, Arizona, to support local police officers who had refused to follow orders issued by their police chief. The tiny town had jumped into national attention in June when a local activist named Jennifer Jones was handcuffed and escorted out of a town council meeting. A video of the event made the rounds on the internet, leading national media figures such as Keith Olbermann to condemn Jones's treatment.[15] Quartzsite's chief of police, Jeff Gilbert, announced that Jones had been arrested "because she refused to leave when the council voted to have her removed" after Jones continued to speak after her allotted time had expired.[16] According to a report in the *New York Times*, most of the town's police officers had appeared at a council meeting two weeks prior to "complain about the chief," but the council declined to hear the officers' statement because there was an open investigation by the state into Gilbert.[17] Adding to the tumult, Quartzsite's mayor, Ed Foster, had made allegations of a conspiracy involving financial misconduct by members of the town council, and Foster was a vocal opponent of Gilbert.[18] Foster had filed lawsuits against the town, the town council censured him twice, and Gilbert had arrested him for disorderly conduct.[19]

In August, Jennifer Jones organized an event to protest the town council and to support Mayor Foster. Oath Keepers traveled to Quartzsite to join the protest along with two state representatives, Judy Burges and Carl Seel.[20] In a speech he delivered to the crowd, Stewart Rhodes pointed out other groups with representatives in attendance: the Greater Phoenix Tea Party Patriots, the Sons of Liberty Riders, and the Campaign for Liberty. Rhodes said that besides protesting against the police chief, Oath Keepers also wanted to honor the police officers who had tried to file complaints against Chief Gilbert. The group gave each of those ten officers a silver Oath Keepers challenge coin as a "token of appreciation." These officers, Rhodes said, "did the right thing and kept their oath, listened to their conscience, and refused to follow unlawful, unconstitutional orders." The group gave Mayor Foster a silver challenge coin, too, since he had "stepped up and kept his oath." As for Jennifer Jones, Rhodes said she provided a model "of what we the citizens should be doing . . . get the oath breakers out of office, replace them with oath keepers." Oath Keepers gave her a bronze challenge coin.[21] After this day of speeches, Quartzsite did not remain prominent in the memory of Oath Keepers for long.

Unlike some other events (especially the first event on Lexington Common), the group does not refer to the Quartzsite event in posts to its website or in YouTube videos posted in later years.

After the events in Arizona in 2011, the next two years remained fairly quiet for Oath Keepers. Then, in October 2013, Oath Keepers announced the launch of its CPT program. This "Community Preparedness Teams" initiative—originally called "Civilization Preservation Teams"—encouraged Americans to form armed neighborhood-watch teams modeled on Special Forces teams.[22] Rhodes argued that Americans must be prepared to respond to disasters, natural or otherwise. Guidance for CPTs indicates that each team should have individuals focused on emergency medicine, communications, engineering, and security. Rhodes encouraged these teams to train together to respond to threats: "Whether it is a husband and wife, father and son, or neighbors, you need to know how to move, shoot, and communicate as a team. Bad guys, like MS-13 or ISIS, attack in teams."[23]

Rhodes encouraged Oath Keepers to use the model of the Community Emergency Response Teams (CERT) program run by the Federal Emergency Management Administration to gain wider support for their CPT teams: "whatever it takes to get your neighbors off their butt." More explicitly, he suggested using the CERT program as cover for the CPT program: neighbors might see that as a seal of approval from the government and thus be more likely to get involved. According to Rhodes, the CPT program works equally well as preparation for a conflict with ISIS or with the "secret police."[24] This initiative is one that the group seems to view as core to its identity: in the six years since it launched, Oath Keepers has pointed back to it multiple times and has continued to engage in activities related to the CPT program.

That October, the group also participated in less controversial public activity. Ongoing disagreement within Congress about the

Affordable Care Act led to a federal government shutdown that began on October 1 and ended October 17.[25] During the shutdown, the National Parks Service furloughed most of its employees and closed all of the parks and memorials that it administered—including the World War II Memorial in Washington, DC.[26] This particular closure gained national attention when media reports showed that elderly veterans who had traveled to Washington to visit the memorial could not enter the grounds and were forced to stand outside barricades erected along its perimeter.[27]

By October 16, several members of Oath Keepers had traveled to Washington, DC, to visit the memorial, including Stewart Rhodes and Warren Bodeker. Bodeker was a veteran of World War II who later passed away in 2015. He was there as part of a trip through Honor Flight, a nonprofit organization that arranges trips for veterans to visit military memorials in Washington, DC, that correspond to the conflicts in which they served.[28] Oath Keepers posted videos online showing members of the group removing barriers that were blocking entry to the World War II Memorial.[29] After Rhodes and Bodeker carried a barrier across the street, they were approached by several police officers. Though the audio of the conversation between the officers and Oath Keepers is mostly inaudible, the few moments of clear speech reveal Bodeker telling the officer that visiting the memorial was important to him. The officer asked him and the others to stop removing the barriers and not to move them again if the barriers were replaced, but Bodeker told the police officer that he would make no promises.[30]

This was not a particularly high-drama moment for Oath Keepers, but it served as a way for the group to engage in activity that would be less controversial with the American public at large. By accompanying an aging veteran to a war memorial, the group visibly identified itself with someone representing the most venerated type of person in the nation—a member of the Greatest

Generation who had fought in a global war against tyranny. As with much Oath Keepers activity in the first four years of its existence, though, this event would not be a central theme in the group's memory of itself.

The following year, 2014, would be much more important for Oath Keepers. In April, several members of the group traveled to Bunkerville, Nevada, to support Cliven Bundy in his conflict with the federal government. For approximately twenty years, Cliven refused to pay fees to graze his cattle on public land, eventually accumulating debts to the federal government that totaled more than $1 million.[31] The rancher defied multiple court orders to pay the grazing fees. Finally, in 2014, the Bureau of Land Management began the process of enforcing a recent court order by confiscating some of Bundy's cattle in lieu of his unpaid fees.[32] In response, Bundy issued a national call to action for Americans to help him resist the BLM at his ranch.[33] Hundreds of people from around the country came to Bunkerville to support him, including Stewart Rhodes, Richard Mack, and Jerry Delemus, an Oath Keeper from New Hampshire.[34] Many of those who came to support Bundy brought their weapons, anticipating a possible shootout with federal employees. Richard Mack revealed that Bundy's supporters had even made plans for a gun battle: "We were actually strategizing to put all the women up at the front. If they are going to start shooting, it's going to be women that are going to be televised all across the world getting shot by these rogue federal officers."[35] After just a few days of this armed activity, the Bureau of Land Management decided to stop its operation over concerns about the safety of its employees. Bundy and his supporters declared victory and reclaimed his cattle. A video posted by Oath Keepers shows Stewart Rhodes helping to remove a temporary fence separating Bundy's supporters from the cattle.[36]

Several of the Oath Keepers stayed at the Bundy Ranch for weeks after the BLM operation stopped on April 12.[37] Rhodes believed that Oath Keepers needed to remain at the ranch to prevent the federal government from returning to confiscate cattle after Bundy's supporters left. He called on members of the group to travel to the ranch "not because there is any great emergency, but [as] a preventative measure—sort of like doing a rotation on the DMZ."[38] By April 27, Oath Keepers claimed to have received credible intelligence that Eric Holder, then the U.S. attorney general, had authorized a drone strike against those at the ranch. After attempting to vet the intelligence, Rhodes and other Oath Keepers leaders on site decided to warn the Bundy supporters to either leave the camp or create fortified positions.[39] When the Oath Keepers left, other militia members who stayed at the ranch called them cowards and deserters.[40] Shortly after, Oath Keepers posted a lengthy video defending their decision to leave and describing their activities throughout the standoff; they also used that opportunity to attack other Bundy supporters.[41]

Despite the conflict with some of Bundy's other supporters, Oath Keepers and many others in Bunkerville viewed the standoff at Bundy Ranch as a major success in resisting the federal government. Since 2014, it has become one of the events that the group consistently refers to, a case of how American patriots can defeat a tyrannical federal government.[42]

Though the group has typically focused on identifying, preparing for, and responding to threats posed by the government (especially the federal government), it has also identified threats posed by other Americans. A prominent example of this can be seen in the group's actions in Ferguson, Missouri, in November 2014 through August 2015. The city of Ferguson was experiencing substantial unrest as local residents and activists from around the country gathered night after night in the city's streets to protest the death of Michael Brown, a young African American man who was shot by an on-duty police officer under unclear and controversial circumstances. These protests grew into larger protests about racial injustice and police militarization and were one of the key episodes in the explosive growth of Black Lives Matter, a social movement that aims to raise awareness of racial injustice in the American legal system.[43]

Police mounted an aggressive, heavily armed response to these protests, which Oath Keepers argued was both ineffective and a violation of the rights of the protestors. The group said that this example of police militarization could "only anger and frighten the people and reinforce the perception that it is 'the police vs. the people' rather than the police vs. a small number of criminals."[44]

By November 2014, some self-identified members of Oath Keepers—including John Karriman, an instructor at a Missouri police academy, and Sam Andrews, a weapons engineer who claimed to have worked as a government security contractor and police trainer—appeared in Ferguson.[45] They did not come to protest the police response, though; they came to defend local businesses after hearing reports of burglary and arson.[46] Dramatic images appeared in a number of media outlets, showing Oath Keepers standing on the roofs of businesses, clothed in camouflage, some with covered faces, all with long guns.[47] After a few days of confusion, local police ordered the members of Oath Keepers to leave their rooftop posts, threatening them with arrest for operating as security without a license. They initially complied but resumed their security operation just a few days later, saying that, as volunteers, they did not need a license.[48]

While in Ferguson, Oath Keepers provided security for four local businesses. Three were minority owned, a fact the group has mentioned repeatedly, arguing that it demonstrates that the group is not racist. In an interview with *Al Jazeera*, Stewart Rhodes said "we have black members, and we're guarding a black lady's bakery . . . So why would we do that if we're some kind of racist organization?"[49]

The streets of Ferguson would be filled with protests off and on for months to come, and Oath Keepers would be present in the city through the summer of 2015. In the meantime, the events at the Bundy Ranch inspired other Oath Keepers activity that pitted its members against various governmental authorities.

The first of these was the so-called security operation at the Sugar Pine Mine in Josephine County in southwestern Oregon. In April 2015, the Bureau of Land Management issued a stop-work order to two miners because of a dispute over the miners' claim.[50] In response, Rick Barclay, one of the miners, approached the Josephine County Oath Keepers, asking that chapter to provide security for his property while he and his mining partner appealed the BLM's order. Though the BLM said that the agency had no plans to take any action before the miners' case was heard by a judge, the leader of the Josephine County Oath Keepers, Joseph Rice, organized an around-the-clock security operation at the mine. His group released calls to action asking for volunteers, and dozens responded, traveling from around the country to this rural part of Oregon to join the operation.[51] Armed men provided security, one volunteer served as camp cook, and Mary Emerick served as a spokesperson as national media gathered to cover the events.

Emerick claimed that at least seven hundred volunteers participated in the operation, which ended in late May when the miners were allowed to continue to operate their mine while waiting for the resolution of their court case.[52] As at the Bundy Ranch, Oath Keepers claimed victory. According to the group, the security team at the mine protected the miners from anticipated acts of aggression by the BLM, and their presence forced the government to honor the miners' due process rights, which Oath Keepers expected the government would have violated otherwise.

Throughout the spring, some Americans fretted over what they saw as a bigger potential threat posed by the federal government: a military exercise called Jade Helm 15.[53] More than one thousand troops—mostly belonging to the U.S. Special Operations Command—were to engage in training operations throughout the Southwest. Conspiracy theories about Jade Helm grew prominent enough that Greg Abbott, the governor of Texas, ordered the Texas State Guard to monitor the exercise to ensure that "Texans know their safety, constitutional rights, private property rights and civil liberties will not be infringed."[54]

Oath Keepers was among those who promoted conspiracy theories about the exercise. Documents shared by the group about Jade Helm range from the cautiously suspicious ("Nothing about Jade Helm 15, in my opinion, looks good")[55] to the apoplectic ("If we do not stop Jade Helm 15 there may be no future for our children").[56] Some leaders in the group (for example, Elias Alias, a Vietnam War veteran who was the editor of the group's website until November 2016) thought that Jade Helm was an elaborate "psy-op" (psychological operation), part of an information war meant to make the American people more likely to go along with violations of their rights.[57] Others (like Rhodes) thought it was more likely that the operation wasn't a direct effort to wage war on Americans but a chance for the government to practice implementing martial law and gauge the public's reaction.[58] Either way, Oath Keepers urged Americans to recognize the threat this military exercise allegedly posed, to see it as proof of the government's intention to implement tyranny and steal Americans' rights. Later, the Jade Helm exercise was carried out with little fanfare, and after it began, Oath Keepers published no further articles about it.[59]

Perhaps part of the reason why Jade Helm received little attention from Oath Keepers once it began was the shooting of military recruiters in Chattanooga, Tennessee, on July 16, 2015. A Kuwaiti-born American shot and killed four Marines and a Navy sailor at a recruiting center and a Navy Reserve center in Chattanooga before police intervened and shot him.[60] Regulations prohibited military personnel from carrying firearms at recruiting centers, leaving most of those near the shootings unarmed.[61]

In response, several state chapters of Oath Keepers began organizing armed volunteer security at recruiting centers. On July 21, the group's national leadership put out a call to action, expanding the volunteer security teams—now called "Operation Protect the Protectors"—nationwide. In a statement announcing the operation, Stewart Rhodes encouraged Oath Keepers across the country to contact local military installations and offer to provide them with armed protection "until the DOD [Department of Defense] changes its idiotic policy of insisting that recruiters go unarmed."[62] Rhodes argued that unarmed military recruiters were in just as much danger as if they were to "walk unarmed, but in uniform, down the streets of Baghdad. The exposure is the same because any jihadist can simply look in the local phone book and find unarmed military service members to attack."[63] Oath Keepers chapters around the country—along with other organizations affiliated with the Three Percenters (III%)—visibly stood guard at recruiting centers.[64]

This operation highlights one of the fundamental tensions in the Oath Keepers identity: while Oath Keepers saw itself on the other side of the conflict from military and law enforcement during events at the Bundy Ranch and in Ferguson, Missouri, it aligned itself with military and law enforcement in the aftermath of the Chattanooga recruiting center shooting—without acknowledging any apparent contradiction or inconsistency in its actions.

In August 2015, the group's attention returned to Ferguson. Since the previous November, Sam Andrews, one of Oath Keepers' local leaders, had been trying to organize an open-carry march for local residents, most of whom would be black, alongside Oath Keepers, most of whom would be white. In his early interactions with some of the African Americans who lived in the area, Andrews learned that they did not believe that they could safely openly carry weapons in their streets, even though Missouri state law allows open carry. They believed that they would quickly be shot by police no matter what precautions they took to demonstrate that they were carrying firearms in accordance with the law.[65] Andrews decided that Oath Keepers should organize a march in which black locals would be surrounded by black and white members of Oath Keepers from the area and from around the country—all of them openly carrying long guns.

Others in Oath Keepers expressed reluctance. Steve Homan, then the national vice president, told Andrews that Stewart Rhodes would need to sign off on the march and that he (Homan) thought providing firearms training would be a better idea than a march. Later, John Karriman told Andrews that the national board of directors had decided not to go forward with the march.

Infuriated, Andrews left the group, started his own organization, and moved forward with his march.[66] He accused Rhodes and Oath Keepers of a "racist double standard." Rhodes, he said, "was perfectly willing to 'confront the cops' at Bundy Ranch, but is unwilling to say that when it is black people arming themselves to 'confront the cops.'"[67] In response, Oath Keepers posted a YouTube video in which Rhodes claimed to have court records that would reveal Andrews to be abusive, "potentially unstable and potentially very violent."[68] Rhodes and the other Oath Keepers leaders in the video urged the group's members to distance themselves from Andrews. In the end, Andrews organized a march for November 16, but fewer than twenty participants showed up.[69]

Meanwhile, Oath Keepers looked to repeat its victories at Bundy Ranch and the Sugar Pine Mine with another operation, this time in Montana. In August, the group began "Operation Big Sky" near Lincoln, Montana, again in support of miners who believed that the federal government (this time through the U.S. Forest Service) was violating their rights.[70] Even from Oath Keepers, though, this operation received much less attention than the Bundy Ranch standoff or even the Sugar Pine Mine operation. Like the BLM in Josephine County, Oregon, the USFS denied that it had plans to take aggressive action against the mine. A spokesperson for the Forestry Service even stated that the organization was working with the miners to reach a resolution that would allow the miners to continue working.[71] Though Oath Keepers issued a request for volunteers on their website, it seems there was never a large presence at the mine or in Lincoln. By September 18, the group published an after-action report from one volunteer to its website, and the operation received little mention after that.[72]

Like with Jade Helm 15, one of the reasons that Operation Big Sky did not receive sustained attention from Oath Keepers might be that a more pressing situation captured the group's attention. In late August and early September a county clerk in Rowan County, Kentucky, named Kim Davis gained national notoriety when she refused to issue same-sex marriage licenses. This refusal came after the Supreme Court had decided in *Obergefell v. Hodges* that the Constitution guarantees the fundamental right to same-sex marriage under the Fourteenth Amendment.[73] On September 3, 2015, a federal judge found her in contempt of court for refusing to comply with the Supreme Court decision and sent her to jail.[74] On September 8, Davis was released from jail after her deputies began issuing licenses to same-sex couples. The judge instructed the deputies to continue to do this and warned Davis that any interference would bring additional sanctions.

In response, Oath Keepers offered to protect Davis from what the group considered to be unlawful imprisonment. Stewart Rhodes argued that the judge "grossly overstepped his bounds and violated Mrs Davis' due process rights, and in particular her right to a jury trial." He declared that this was an example of America's "imperial judiciary that not only legislates from the bench but is attempting to expand their 'contempt' power to likewise swallow up our Bill of Rights and circumvent jury trial."[75] Rhodes planned to travel to Rowan County as part of an armed security team that would protect Davis from U.S. marshals or any other law enforcement officers attempting to jail her. During a conference call that Oath Keepers later posted to YouTube, Rhodes, John Karriman (one of the leaders of Oath Keepers' activity in Ferguson), Denny Peyman (a former Kentucky sheriff), and Allen Larderi (West Virginia's Oath Keepers leader) decided that the group would approach the Rowan County sheriff to "educate" him about his right and responsibility to prevent anyone from violating the Constitution in his county, even federal judges and law enforcement officials.[76]

National media outlets quickly picked up on this plan and began publishing stories about Oath Keepers.[77] However, when Davis's legal team learned of the group's offer, they turned it down quickly.[78] In response, Oath Keepers canceled its security operation, insisting that it "always seek[s] the full consent and cooperation of anyone we protect, and we must respect their wishes if they decline that protection."[79] Its members could choose as individual citizens to go to Kentucky and protest on Davis's behalf, but Oath Keepers urged them instead to save their resources for the next security operation.

They would not have to wait long. Just a few months later, those in the patriot/militia movement began paying close attention to the case of Dwight and Steven Hammond, in rural Burns, Oregon. The Hammonds, father and son, were local ranchers who were convicted of arson in 2012 after burning brush on federal land to clear it for cattle grazing. Though there is a five-year minimum sentence for that crime, the judge in the Hammonds' case issued substantially shorter sentences of less than a year. The Department of Justice appealed the sentencing in 2015, and an appeals court agreed that the Hammonds had to serve the minimum sentence. By the time the appeals court issued its decision, the two men had already served their original sentences and returned home. After the decision, they were ordered to return to prison in January 2016 to serve the remainder of their sentence.[80]

Many people in the patriot/militia movement—and even observers outside of antigovernment extremism—interpreted this as double jeopardy. Overlooking the details of the case (namely, that there was no second trial, just an appeal of the sentence imposed in the only trial), they claimed that this resentencing amounted to two convictions for the same crime.[81] Ammon Bundy, one of Cliven Bundy's sons, became a vocal leader of a group of people who took interest in the Hammonds' case.[82]

In November and December 2015, dozens of supporters traveled to Burns to protest the Hammonds' return to prison. On January 2, 2016, they marched through Burns, waving flags, making speeches, and tossing pennies at the courthouse, symbolically "buying back their government."[83] After the demonstration, Ammon Bundy declared that it was time to take a hard stand against the tyrannical federal government. A group led by Bundy drove to the Malheur National Wildlife Refuge an hour away and occupied the headquarters building. This marked the start of an occupation that would last more than a month and result in the death of one person (LaVoy Finicum) while resisting arrest.[84]

From the beginning, Oath Keepers was opposed to using force to prevent the government from returning Dwight and Steven Hammond to prison. The group also opposed the occupation of the refuge. Through the end of 2015, Stewart Rhodes repeatedly urged Ammon Bundy to back down from his heated rhetoric, arguing that the Hammonds had explicitly rejected any offers of armed assistance to keep them out of prison and wanted to serve out their sentences peacefully.[85] By January 6, just four days into the occupation, Rhodes called on Ammon to end the occupation. He said that Bundy and his supporters had no right to take action that local residents did not support.[86]

Despite the opposition from Rhodes and other leaders (like Elias Alias, the Oath Keepers website editor) to the occupation, some members of the group actively participated in the occupation. The most prominent was Jon Ritzheimer. Ritzheimer had gained some notoriety in 2015 for organizing anti-Islam demonstrations in Arizona.[87] In December 2015, he posted a video in which he described plans to confront a Muslim organization in New York State while brandishing a pistol, which prompted the FBI to alert New York law enforcement about Ritzheimer.[88]

Just a few months before this, Ritzheimer announced that he intended to arrest Senator Debbie Stabenow (D-MI) for treason, given her support for the Iran nuclear agreement. Oath Keepers saw this as too drastic. Jason Van Tatenhove, then the group's national media director, told the *Washington Times* that the group did not support this plan and was moving to revoke Ritzheimer's membership.[89]

The winter of 2015–2016 proved to be a busy time for Ritzheimer. After his video threatening a Muslim organization in New York, the FBI tracked him as he drove from his home in Phoenix to the

Northeast. By the end of the month, he was back across the country in rural Oregon for the protests that preceded the Malheur National Wildlife Refuge occupation. Ritzheimer remained in Oregon through the occupation, where he was a prominent figure among the occupiers. Just before law enforcement arrested several of the occupation leaders in late January, Ritzheimer left the refuge and drove back to his home in Arizona. Later that day, he surrendered to the FBI outside of Phoenix. In August, he pleaded guilty to conspiracy charges. In November 2017, he was sentenced to one year in prison plus one year in a residential reentry program.[90]

Throughout the occupation, Rhodes and others in Oath Keepers continued to express their opposition.[91] Despite this, the Pacific Patriots Network (PPN)—an umbrella group that included the Josephine County branch of Oath Keepers, the lead group in the Sugar Pine Mine operation in 2015—was present at the refuge. PPN defined its mission as providing a buffer between law enforcement and the occupiers to prevent any violence, often stationing themselves just outside the refuge.[92] PPN members were heavily armed—even more so than the occupiers—and this raised tensions in the community. Joseph Rice, the leader of the Josephine County Oath Keepers and a cofounder of PPN, was part of this effort. Though the leaders of Oath Keepers opposed the occupation, they supported this operation by PPN.[93] Rhodes, who viewed it "as a buffer to prevent another Waco incident," called it a "righteous mission, if done right, and we stand in full support of it."[94] In the end, PPN took no direct action against either law enforcement or the occupiers.

This early activity in 2016 marked the beginning of what would be a pivotal year for Oath Keepers, just as it was for America at large, and largely for the same reason: Donald Trump's candidacy for president. After he declared his candidacy on June 16, 2015,

Trump gradually gained the support of antiestablishment Americans, particularly those on the political right.[95] Though Oath Keepers as a group never endorsed Trump's candidacy, many members supported him, especially when it became clear that the general election would pit Trump against Hillary Clinton. The Clinton name has long been anathema to the patriot/militia movement, given several events that occurred during Bill Clinton's presidency (including the standoff at Waco in 1993 and the passage of the Assault Weapons Ban in 1994). The movement has also long spread conspiracy theories about the Clintons, and this was true during the 2016 campaign as well.[96]

By early November 2016, Oath Keepers was convinced that Donald Trump would win the popular vote unless there was orchestrated, widespread voter fraud.[97] After Project Veritas (a conservative activist organization) released videos that allegedly captured Democratic Party operatives talking about how they would carry this out, Oath Keepers decided that voter fraud and intimidation was likely and that its members should try to document such activity to prevent Clinton from stealing the election.[98] Stewart Rhodes announced "Operation Sabot," in which he called on the group's members to "form up incognito intelligence gathering and crime spotting teams." The group singled out "our retired police officers, our military intelligence veterans, and our Special Warfare veterans (who are well trained in covert observation and intelligence gathering) to take the lead and apply their considerable training in investigation, intelligence gathering, and fieldcraft to help stop voter fraud."[99] Rhodes and other Oath Keepers held several webinars in the weeks before the election to prepare the group's members to conduct this surveillance operation and to respond to any civil unrest that might occur in the aftermath of the election.[100] For this operation, the group specifically instructed its members to act only as surveillance teams, reporting any voter fraud they witnessed to law enforcement. The call to action for the operation also instructed members to not wear any Oath Keepers clothing or insignia: the group did not want to give "partisan Democrat activists and the media (essentially the same thing)" any ammunition to accuse Oath Keepers of itself engaging in voter intimidation.[101]

In the end, of course, Donald Trump won the election.[102] And, of course, the country did not see the widespread violent uprising led by leftists that Oath Keepers was anticipating after a Trump victory. However, Americans across the country began protesting Trump on November 9—just hours after his victory—and some of the demonstrations saw isolated clashes and vandalism.[103] Petitions urging the Electoral College to choose Clinton received millions of signatures.[104] Some radical groups even pledged that they would prevent Trump from being inaugurated on January 20, 2017.[105]

Oath Keepers viewed the isolated violence in the protests in the days after Election Day as a sign of an orchestrated plan by "the political elite that is determined to subvert the will of the American people."[106] A military veteran writing for the Oath Keepers website under the pseudonym "NavyJack" declared that "Communists Intend to Overthrow the United States before Inauguration Day."[107]

In late November, the group decided to take action again, announcing "Operation HYPO," in which some members were to "burrow deep inside these protest organizations to collect information regarding tactics, motivations, schedules and logistics."[108] In January, the group announced "Operation DefendJ20," encouraging its members to form security teams to prevent violence in Washington, DC, during Trump's inauguration.[109] Stewart Rhodes traveled to Washington for this. He tweeted a picture of himself standing outside the DeploraBall, an inauguration party on January 19 that observers anticipated would have many attendees affiliated with the so-called alt-right.[110] In fact, Oath Keepers claims to have prevented a chemical attack on the DeploraBall by providing the DC police with intelligence about plans for the attack that the group's members had gathered as part of Operation HYPO.[111]

Since Trump's inauguration, Oath Keepers has continued to see anti-Trump activists as the main threat facing America. In response to the appearance of the alt-right's influence in the Trump campaign, a small movement of leftists in the United States known as antifa grew dramatically.[112] Adopting a name, iconography, and tactics rooted in leftist street movements opposed to fascist movements from the early twentieth century, antifa activists began confronting those they identified as fascists, sometimes violently.[113] Those in the movement viewed the rise of the alt-right as a sign that fascism could be growing in size and influence in America, and they believed that fascist groups and movements should be confronted and disrupted—with counter-demonstrations, doxxing (that is, connecting an anonymous online persona to an identifiable person), boycotts, and even violence—before those movements could grow large enough to have a substantial effect on institutional politics, political culture, and public opinion more broadly.[114] Pro-Trump actors framed antifa's actions as attempts by the intolerant left to stifle free speech. Oath Keepers jumped on this framing and began attending far-right rallies featuring the alt-right and the "alt-lite" (allies of the alt-right who are not racist enough to fit in the movement fully), providing security for these groups under the guise of protecting their freedom of speech.[115] Though Oath Keepers condemns racism, the group and others like it have acted as de facto security for racist organizations.[116]

The group has also continued its flirtation with Islamophobia. In June 2017, ACT for America (an anti-Muslim organization founded by Brigitte Gabriel, a notorious Islamophobe) organized "Marches Against Sharia" in cities across the nation. ACT asked groups including Oath Keepers to provide security for the marches after antifa groups announced that they would counterprotest.[117] Oath Keepers encouraged its members to turn out to marches in every city to protect the freedom of speech of those attending the marches, and members were spotted at several of the demonstrations.[118]

Much of what Oath Keepers does walks along the edge of violence in the midst of conflicts with other Americans or with the government, but this is not all they do. The group encourages its supporters to be good members of their community, and they see good neighborly behavior as an opportunity to gain support from the American public. For example, Joseph Rice, formerly the leader of the Josephine County Oath Keepers, organized community service activity in which his chapter built a playground and installed wheelchair ramps for local residents.[119] In 2017, the group encouraged its members to get involved in disaster relief in Texas, Florida, and Puerto Rico, after a series of hurricanes devastated communities in these areas.[120] The group is not consistently active on Twitter, but Stewart Rhodes and other members posted frequently throughout October 2017 as they volunteered in Puerto Rico, delivering supplies to remote locations and helping rebuild homes.[121] Curiously, they also provided security for a hospital, though I could find no reports of violence in Puerto Rico after Hurricane Maria to which Oath Keepers might have been responding.[122]

In November 2017, Oath Keepers' attention returned to a more common focus for the group. A week after a mass shooting at a church in Sutherland Springs, Texas, on November 5, the group called on its members to provide security for the church.[123] In the call to action, the group said that an associate pastor from the church had reached out to Oath Keepers to provide security for the service on November 12 and for funerals of several of those killed in the shooting. Oath Keepers declared that some of its members had been providing security for the church since November 9, and the group requested additional volunteers and donations for the security operation.[124]

Above all else, Oath Keepers is a group animated by the perception of imminent threats: to America, to themselves and their neighbors, and to the ideals of freedom and liberty. These threats come from all over: an international conspiracy of financial and political elites, tyrannical federal and state governments, terrorists, and criminals. Sometimes, the threat is abstract, for example, when American identity is threatened by foreigners flooding across the nation's borders. More often, though, the threat is concrete and dramatic: threats to physical security by terrorists or militarized government officials, threats to economic security by financial and political elites, and threats to liberty and natural rights by the government.

These threats require different responses. Threats to American identity can be combated by reaching, teaching, and inspiring Americans about the founding principles and history of the nation. This approach also serves as an early response to concrete threats by encouraging Americans to prepare for a future armed conflict over physical security, financial security, or natural rights. As these concrete threats become more imminent, increasingly direct responses are required: withdrawing from the normal economy by engaging in hyperlocal barter communities; stockpiling food, medicine, ammunition, and tools; and forming local paramilitary teams that train together regularly. The group responds to critical threats even more directly, traveling across the country to participate in "security operations," using firearms and other overt signs of a willingness to use violence to influence the behavior of the government or other enemies.

These perceptions of threats and responses to threats coexist with an absolute conviction by the group that its members are patriots—model Americans embodying core American values. Oath Keepers describes its members as "guardians of the Republic" and insists that the actions it calls for are honorable and in line with the oath that members of the military and first responders swear to protect the Constitution.

The hostility against these perceived threats sits in tension with this self-perception of honor. Conspiracy theories about nefarious hidden actors and potential violence directed at the government are not typical features of American political activity.

In this book, I explore one strategy that Oath Keepers and other groups in the patriot/militia movement use to resolve this tension: retelling the stories of moments of conflict and crisis to interpret the contemporary political situation and to provide models of the appropriate response.

4

The Ongoing Struggle Over
Natural Rights

We hold these truths to be self-evident, that all men are created equal, that they are endowed by their Creator with certain unalienable Rights, that among these are Life, Liberty and the pursuit of Happiness.

—Declaration of Independence

Rights come first, then government is created to protect them, not the other way around. This is something modern political and legal elites want us to forget. They don't believe in inalienable, natural rights that are ours by virtue of "nature and nature's God."

—Stewart Rhodes

The U.S. Declaration of Independence famously proclaims that individuals have inherent rights, variously described as natural, inalienable, or God-given. Those would-be Americans in favor of independence from Great Britain justified their rebellion by laying out a "long train of abuses and usurpations" that violated their rights. Despite this lengthy list of reasons for independence, this document explicitly provides only a partial list of natural rights: "among these are Life, Liberty and the pursuit of Happiness."[1]

Given Americans' reverence for the Declaration of Independence, it is no surprise that some forms of contemporary American political dissent situate themselves by pointing to inherent rights. If individuals have rights that come from nature or nature's God, then those rights come before any political system and overrule any decisions made by political systems. If threatened, surely natural rights must be defended—and if other means fail, defended by violence.

This line of thought raises several important questions. What are natural rights? How do Americans distinguish between the government doing something that they think is wrong but does not violate their rights from something that does violate their natural rights? And how do they know when they should take up arms to stop government action that they think is wrong?

In this chapter, I argue that Oath Keepers uses this concept of natural rights as a rallying cry without developing a meaningful understanding of it: Oath Keepers insists that natural rights must be defended but says very little about how to know when natural rights are being violated. In using this powerful motivating frame without specifying its contents, Oath Keepers uses a lofty political principle shared widely by Americans as cover for the group's dissenting behavior, which pursues goals not shared widely by Americans.[2] In other words, talking about natural rights serves as a way for Oath Keepers to gain mainstream political legitimacy for their extremist goals and actions.

The analysis in this chapter relies on two key conceptual premises. First, "natural rights" are those that humans have simply because of their being human. Some scholars suggest that there is an alternative understanding of natural rights as those that can be identified by reason alone, with no reliance on political or religious principles that are not universal. Other scholars do not make any distinction between these two understandings. Oath Keepers seems to use the term in the first sense: the usage of "natural rights" as a rallying cry for vigorous dissent derives not from how the rights are identified but from their inherent nature.[3]

This leads to the second conceptual premise: "natural rights," "God-given rights," and "inalienable rights" effectively refer to the same rights, but they emphasize different things about those rights. "Natural rights" conveys the broadest message: these rights belong to individuals simply because they are people. "God-given rights" conveys a similar message but adds a religious component: those inherent rights come from God. "Inalienable rights" conveys a more specific message: these natural rights cannot be legitimately taken from any individual (with possible exceptions made to punish criminals, for example).[4]

As a group, Oath Keepers frequently refers back to America's founding documents (in particular, the Declaration of Independence, the Constitution, and the Bill of Rights). Unsurprisingly, then, the idea of natural rights comes up from time to time—sometimes in texts that explicitly interpret the founding documents, other times in the middle of a discussion of current events. In this second category, "natural rights" and its related terms occur as offhand references: for example, in an assertion that the Bureau of Alcohol, Tobacco, Firearms, and Explosives (ATF, which is the primary federal agency responsible for overseeing the firearms industry) "cares not one whit about your or my unalienable rights or our Constitutional protections as American citizens. Nope. The ATF is hell-bent on tormenting anyone who would dare stand up for the fuller meaning of our Constitution and Bill of Rights."[5]

Much of the time, though, comments about natural rights are more substantial. Two main lines of thought emerge from these more substantial comments. First, natural rights start with life, liberty, and the pursuit of happiness, but they include more than these few that are listed in the Constitution. Second, whatever they are, when threatened, natural rights must be defended—if necessary, with violence.

The starting point for Oath Keepers on natural rights is the Declaration of Independence, which the group says is "fundamentally a *natural law* document." In describing this foundational text this way, Oath Keepers begins to build the case that the political and legal system created by the Founders is based on foundational ideas that were not created by the Founders. Instead, that system is meant to reflect and protect those foundational ideas. In particular, the system is meant to protect preexisting rights. "The 'long train of abuses' that made revolt necessary were not only deprivations of representation . . . but also of natural rights, such as life, liberty, and property."[6]

Following this idea that some rights are natural and preexisting, Oath Keepers echoes an argument from earlier patriot/militia movement actors that the Bill of Rights "does not grant *any* rights."[7] The First Amendment protects "pre-existing natural rights" of free speech, free press, free practice of religion, and free assembly. The Second Amendment "is a prohibition on government action, meant to protect a pre-existing right" to keep and bear arms. The "Fourth Amendment does not grant us a right to be secure in our persons, houses, papers and effects" but "declares that our right to that security '*shall not be violated*' and then it sets forth procedural requirements to protect that preexisting right. Nor does the Fifth Amendment grant us a right to life, liberty, or property. It merely prohibits the government from depriving us of those pre-existing rights without due process of law."[8] Similarly, the group suggests that the Ninth Amendment "speaks of the *enumeration* . . . not the '*creation* by the Constitution of certain rights.'"[9]

Oath Keepers argues, though, that "We the people have natural rights, and those rights go far beyond those explicitly protected by the Bill of Rights."[10] Since the founding documents recognize and protect rights rather than create them, and since those rights extend even beyond what the founding documents mention, those documents are only a partial guide to natural rights. Thus, Stewart Rhodes says, "whenever you find yourself running to look in the Bill of Rights to see whether you have a right to do something, you are making a fundamental error. Your rights are inherently yours by nature and by nature's God."[11]

Ultimately, the group does not elaborate a longer list of natural rights beyond those mentioned in the founding documents. Instead, there is an implicit suggestion that no authoritative list is necessary. Each person can figure out what their natural rights are for themselves. It is self-evident that "all men are created equal" and that "they are endowed by their Creator with certain inalienable rights"; it also is (or should be) self-evident what those inalienable rights are.[12]

At the same time, Oath Keepers insists that the list of natural rights is not up for debate. Nor is it based on what the majority of people think is on that list. Writing before the 2016 presidential election about the possibility of new federal gun control laws if Hillary Clinton were to win on November 8, David Codrea said in an article for the Oath Keepers website that the election—and any legislation or executive orders that might follow—would not affect his behavior or his rights: "Some of us do not consider the 'popularity contest' winner the last word on our unalienable rights."[13] Codrea argued that his natural rights are unaffected by which politician wins an election—and by extension, they are unaffected by the will of the majority of voters. He argued that the right to keep and bear arms is natural and absolute and exists despite any governmental action to the contrary. More importantly, the majority of voters have no say about whether something is a natural right; nor can they put any legitimate limits on natural rights.[14]

By providing only a vague sense of what our natural rights are, this argument results in ambiguity. The founding documents contain only a partial list, guided by the self-evident rights to life, liberty, and the pursuit of happiness and elaborated upon by the Bill of Rights. The full list of natural rights includes more than what these documents contain, but Oath Keepers does not provide any information about how to discover what else is on that list. In other words, the group engages in strategic ambiguity when talking about natural rights, invoking a powerful frame in an abstract way, letting individuals fill in the details for themselves. But the group also definitively argues that natural rights are not up for debate and that they are unaffected by the outcome of collective political decision making.

This argument that all natural rights are self-evident (that is, that each individual can discern what their natural rights are) sits in tension with the assertion that electoral outcomes should not affect interpretations of natural rights (which implies that the list of natural rights is fixed and that some individuals have a complete and correct understanding of that list). This tension implies that natural rights are so self-evident that all people acting in good faith should agree about what they are—and that any disagreement about what natural rights are does not come from good-faith disagreement about natural rights. Instead, such disagreement means that bad-faith, power-hungry, would-be tyrants are trying to violate those rights. In commentary on a speech given by Ron Paul, Stewart Rhodes condemned those who "have no respect for the principles of unalienable, natural rights our Declaration of Independence proclaimed 'to a candid world.'" "Neoconservatives, like their close cousins, the socialist far-left revolutionaries, despise the Constitution of the Founders, with its limited, divided, dual sovereignty structure."[15] These alleged enemies of the Constitution, according to Rhodes, are eager to violate Americans' rights for their own gain.

This combination of ambiguity with a sense that any disagreement results from bad-faith actors leaves open the possibility of violence. Commentary from Oath Keepers recognizes two types of Americans who do not agree with them about natural rights: malevolent elites who are enemies of freedom, and the wider American public that has been misled by these corrupt actors. The group wants to convert the wider American public to its thinking about natural rights, illustrated by its goal to "reach, teach, and inspire." In particular, the group wants to educate military and law enforcement, since those individuals will either be the first line of defense of natural rights or the means with which the elite will steal Americans' rights. But behind this wider misguided public is a nefarious group (variously described as "globalists," "the international elite," "statists," "collectivists," "progressives," or simply "Marxists") who are not well intentioned but misinformed; instead, they are actively plotting to destroy the freedom that the Founders designed the Constitution to protect.[16]

This is an instance of the conspiratorial, us-versus-them reductionism that serves as the bedrock of the group's political beliefs and actions.[17] Those who support policy that Oath Keepers argues would violate personal rights are "loyal only to [political] party, personal ambition, and to the government they are a part of."[18] For Oath Keepers, the contents of natural rights are so self-evident that anyone who disagrees is an enemy (or has been duped by an enemy). And rights must be defended—enemies must be defeated—hopefully with nonviolent resistance but with violence if necessary.

As egregious as these violations of rights described in the Declaration of Independence were, Rhodes said that the colonists did not actively fight back until the British government attempted to remove their last means of defense of their rights: their weapons.[19] This is a core principle for Oath Keepers: one of the proximate causes of the American Revolutionary War was the attempt by the British to disarm the would-be Americans in 1775. Now, as then, when rights are threatened, the first defense is "speech, association, and assembly." But if these rights are denied, "the people will have no recourse but to arms."[20] In its "Declaration of Orders We Will Not Obey," the group described the Revolutionary War: in response to the British attempt to disarm them, "the American people fought back in justified, righteous self-defense of their natural rights."[21]

Oath Keepers argues that defense of natural rights is not just a responsibility of members of the group. Instead, it should be a "personal obligation" for every American patriot, "as the Founders intended."[22] Again, firearms are central here. The Second Amendment protects (but does not grant) an individual right to own firearms, according to this view, and that right is not primarily about hunting or self-defense from criminals. Instead, according to Oath Keepers, the right to keep and bear arms implicitly recognizes that government is the greatest threat to natural rights and that the people should be prepared to defend their rights: the group says that "the purpose of the Second Amendment is to preserve the military power of the people so that they will, in the last resort, have effective final recourse to arms and to the God of Hosts in the face of tyranny."[23]

Given the conspiratorial, us-versus-them reductionism that serves as a foundation for Oath Keepers' ideas about politics, it is no surprise that any violation of natural rights would be interpreted as a malicious plot rather than good-faith disagreement over what rights are or as a limited mistake born out of complicated circumstances (such as gun confiscation during Hurricane Katrina, discussed more in chapter 7).[24] If enemies are working together to steal rights for their benefit, vigorous defense of those rights seems like a duty. If it is true that people have natural rights that are prior to politics (and thus exist despite any political decisions to the contrary), and if it is true that there are bad actors out there trying to deny people those rights, then violent defense of those rights is necessary, justified, and even righteous.

Oath Keepers argues that natural rights are those that people inherently have simply because they are people; the group does not provide a complete list of what these rights are (why provide a complete list when the items on that list are self-evident?), instead providing a partial list that includes those mentioned in the Declaration of Independence (life, liberty, and the pursuit of happiness), adding a few described in the Bill of Rights (such as freedom of speech and the right to keep and bear arms). Oath Keepers then encourages every American to make defense of natural rights a personal obligation.

This argument serves Oath Keepers as a tool for strategic framing. "Natural rights" is a familiar term for those who have even a basic knowledge of early American history. As with all things associated with the Founders, rhetoric about natural rights and the moral argument in favor of rebellion against government that violates those rights is presumed by the American public to be correct, and the dominant story of American identity does not permit dissent on this. In a sense, this is a version of the policing of ideas that the immigration researcher Alex Nowrasteh described as "patriotic correctness."[25] The popular version of American political history ignores the disagreement and compromise at the heart of all of the founding documents, instead portraying early American history as driven by unified patriots with God and an ingenious understanding of politics on their side.[26]

But while natural rights are perhaps uniformly understood as central to America's founding, the very concept is ambiguous. The founding documents refer to natural rights, but always in a way that provides some examples of those rights while leaving the door open for the existence of other unenumerated natural rights. The dominant story of American identity takes it for granted that there are natural rights but says little about them other than that they are inalienable (and perhaps God-given) and that they start with life, liberty, and the pursuit of happiness.

By invoking this open-ended concept that is central to American identity, Oath Keepers is able to leverage American history to make its extremist goals and behavior seem less extreme. It taps into a core part of the American story, but it takes that story in unconventional directions. In pointing to widely accepted American history and providing interpretations that are not implausible on their face, the group (and others like it) may see some success in portraying themselves as American patriots. If this argument is successful, Oath Keepers might be seen as modern-day revolutionaries, the philosophical descendants of George Washington, Thomas Jefferson, and Thomas Paine.

But the group does not only see itself as thinking like the Founders. It also sees itself as acting like them.

5

The American Revolution Redux

J ust as they take it for granted that there are natural rights worth defending, Americans often take it for granted that the War of Independence from Great Britain in the eighteenth century was justified, that the violence of that war was necessary and appropriate. As mentioned in the last chapter, the popular history of that time depicts long-suffering patriots who tolerated a series of violations of natural rights until—finally—they rose up to cast off the shackles of tyranny and proclaim some basic truths.

The eighteenth century was not the last time that some Americans thought that a specific political authority was overbearing. Americans from across the political spectrum have perceived tyranny and violations of basic rights throughout the nation's history. Rural farmers in the 1790s and 1800s mobilized against taxes they saw as unjust in the Whiskey Rebellion and Fries Rebellion.[1] Throughout the twentieth century, economic libertarians railed against redistributive economic policy—or even taxation itself—as theft or slavery.[2] Particularly since 2001, civil libertarians have decried the intrusive surveillance of the national security state.[3] In the political movements that organize around these perceptions, some participants see the history of the nation's birth repeating itself in a very particular way. Once again, these Americans say, patriots are suffering at the hands of tyrants who would deny them natural rights. Once again, these Americans say, there may soon come a day when patriots must rise up and fight these tyrants to reclaim their inalienable, God-given rights.

In this chapter, I examine how Oath Keepers builds on its discussion of natural rights with references to the American Revolutionary War. The group draws direct parallels between contemporary events and the run-up to that war. As with the use of natural rights as a strategic frame, I argue that the group does this in part to garner moral legitimacy and political support for its goals for radical political change and for its preparations to pursue these goals with violence.

As we have already seen, Oath Keepers develops a larger (though still ambiguous) argument about tyranny and rights. Much of this argument is based on American history and American political thought, in which the events around America's struggle for independence from Great Britain hold a prominent place.

The group is deliberate in doing this. In a 2015 essay commemorating Oath Keepers' sixth anniversary, Stewart Rhodes said that he chose the date (April 19) and location (Lexington Common, outside of Boston, Massachusetts) of the first public Oath Keepers event "to remind us all of where we have come from. . . . The blood of patriots was spilled on that Green, and we need to have the same conviction they had, when it comes to carrying out our duty." That battle, he said, was the real "birthday of our Republic—not July 4, 1776." This was where the nation "was born in hot lead, cold steel, and the cries of wounded men. . . . That is when this Republic was born."[4]

Rhodes chose these tangible reminders of the Revolutionary War "because there are obvious parallels to our current situation." "We are in much the same position as the patriots were in that time. We are on the eve of conflict with domestic enemies of liberty who are relentless in their pursuit of power over us."[5] With this essay, Rhodes set the stage for arguments that those with political authority in America abuse that authority, violating individual liberty for their own benefit.

The group takes another step forward in this line of reasoning in the opening of its list of ten "Orders We Will Not Obey." The list opens with a quote from George Washington rallying his troops in 1776, before the Battle of Long Island:

> The time is now near at hand which must probably determine, whether Americans are to be, Freemen, or Slaves; whether they are to have any property they can call their own; whether their Houses, and Farms, are to be pillaged and destroyed, and they consigned to a State of Wretchedness from which no human efforts will probably deliver them. The fate of unborn Millions will now depend, under God, on the Courage and Conduct of this army.[6]

"Such a time is near at hand again," Oath Keepers says. Elsewhere, Rhodes argued that there are obvious parallels between the Revolutionary War and the current political situation. Here, Oath Keepers makes it clear that the parallels are leading toward a crisis that will demand decisive action—violent action—like that of those who resisted the British and won America's independence. Further drawing the parallel, the group says that, yet again, "The fate of unborn millions will now depend, under God, on the Courage and Conduct of this Army—*and* this Marine Corps, This Air Force, This Navy and the National Guard and police units of these sovereign states."[7]

Having set the stage for arguments that depict the contemporary situation as parallel to the situation in the eighteenth century, Oath Keepers uses the remainder of this list of orders its members will not obey to describe specific issues that the group sees as repeating the past. The most important of these is gun control and citizen disarmament. The first of the ten "Orders We Will Not Obey" is any order to disarm the American people. Oath Keepers explains that "the attempt to disarm the people on April 19, 1775, was the spark of open conflict in the American Revolution. . . . Any such order today would also be an act of war against the American people, and thus an act of treason."[8]

Any contemporary attempts by the federal government to implement gun control (especially through executive orders), Oath Keepers argues, should lead Americans to resist, just as the militiamen resisted the British in 1775. As Rhodes explained in his essay marking the sixth anniversary of Oath Keepers, "we need to have the same conviction" as those who fought the British.[9]

The Oath Keepers also circulated an article from the Tenth Amendment Center entitled "How the British Gun Control Program Precipitated the American Revolution." Most of this two-thousand-word essay argues that common understandings about the causes of the Revolutionary War are mistaken: "What finally forced the colonials into a shooting war with the British Army in April 1775 was not taxes or even warrant-less searches of homes and their occupation by soldiers, but one of many attempts by the British to disarm Americans as part of an overall gun control program." The unnamed author of this essay describes at length an alleged relationship between confiscating weapons and enforcing unjust laws. According to this argument, British officials saw the widespread possession of guns and ammunition as a threat to their rule. Therefore, they "were eager to see outright gun confiscation in order to effectively suppress any resistance to their rule." While those other unjust laws may have been egregious violations of rights, it was the attempt to confiscate weapons that pushed the would-be Americans over the edge.[10]

Near its conclusion, the essay turns from a discussion of historical events to an argument about contemporary America: "Many gun control policies in America today follow the British blueprint." Those early Americans resisted and won their freedom. Today, "Americans of the twenty-first century should not squander the heritage of constitutional liberty bequeathed by the Patriots."[11] Many rights might currently be under threat from a tyrannical federal government, but citizen disarmament is still the greatest threat because it could start an avalanche of lost freedoms.[12] "Modern gun control advocates are the spiritual successors of the British government our forefathers opposed," and those who resist gun control are the spiritual successors of those forefathers.[13] This essay argues that Americans know how to respond to the tyranny of gun control: take up those arms that are threatened and fight back.

In total, seven of the ten orders Oath Keepers members will not obey (including the order to disarm Americans) draw explicit parallels between the contemporary political situation and life in the colonies under British rule. The group anticipates orders from the federal government to conduct "sweeping warrantless searches of homes and vehicles"—perhaps in order to find guns to confiscate—and it connects this anticipated violation of rights to another cause of the American Revolution: writs of assistance. Treating American citizens as "unlawful enemy combatants" in the War on Terror is (allegedly) like admiralty courts, the military tribunals that the British used to deny the colonists the right to trial by a jury of their peers.[14] Martial law or a state of emergency would be like the changes in governance that concentrated power in the hands of colonial governors immediately before the Revolutionary War and would likewise result in armed resistance.[15] Blockading cities to turn them into concentration camps would be like the blockade of Boston under martial law during the war.[16] Bringing in foreign troops—perhaps under the command of the United Nations—to serve as peacekeepers in the United States would be like the British bringing in Hessian mercenaries to fight the patriots.[17] Confiscating private property, "including food and other essential supplies, under any emergency pretext whatsoever," would be like the seizure "of American ships, goods, and supplies" before the Revolutionary War—and, of course, confiscating firearms was the spark of open conflict in that war. For Oath Keepers, these are not simply thought experiments or philosophical discussions about potential harms; instead, these are seen as tangible threats, things the group anticipates may happen again soon: "Such a time is near at hand again."[18]

In other documents, Rhodes protests the very notion of a national service draft (whether for military service or civilian service) as a violation of individual rights. In fact, he says that mandatory national service is "institutionalized slavery." He argues that "one of the causes of our rebellion against the Crown had been impressment of Americans into the Royal Navy." Since this was one of the causes of the Revolutionary War, it cannot be the case (Rhodes argues) that the Founders wrote the Constitution to allow compulsory service. In the face of proposals for mandatory national service, Rhodes urges Americans to "resolve ourselves to be as resolute as our forefathers in resisting this new creeping tyranny. . . . Let us do as the Founding generation did when their own government claimed unlimited power over their lives, liberty, and property."[19]

Rhodes also wrote about a resolution proposed in 2009 to the Montana House of Representatives that would have "void[ed] the compact by which Montana became a state" if the federal government took certain actions that some people interpreted as unconstitutional.[20] In arguing in favor of the right for states to assert their sovereignty, Rhodes writes:

This is about self-government, and about being free from oner-
ous, oppressive, and unconstitutional federal laws and actions.
One of the causes of the American Revolution was the claim by
the British Parliament that it could legislate over the colonists in
all cases whatsoever. . . . Our forefathers rejected that absurd
claim. We are now rejecting the same assertion of totalitarian
power by the Mordor on the Potomac [Washington, DC].[21]

Here, Rhodes is arguing that the contemporary federal government is asserting the same kind of tyrannical rule that the British
government tried to assert over the colonies. And states should
respond to the federal government just as the colonies responded
to the British: by asserting their sovereignty in order to protect the
rights of their residents.

When gun rights activists in Washington State disobeyed gun
laws to protest gun control legislation, Rhodes called it "armed
civil disobedience."[22] He argued that

civil disobedience is a much honored American tradition, starting with the Founding Generation which intentionally refused to
comply with multiple edicts, statutes, and rules set by Parliament
and King. They refused to comply and used peaceful civil disobedience for many years leading up to the outset of fighting. . . .
Civil disobedience, nullification, and defiance were the life-blood
of the cause of the Colonists in the years leading up to the out-
break of the actual American Revolution.[23]

With each of these issues, Oath Keepers builds the argument
that the current situation is like the one faced by those who won
America's independence. In the case of the list of ten orders, Oath
Keepers argues that any of these would be a clear sign "that the
time for another American Revolution is nigh."[24] For the group,

this is the present repeating the landmark moments of the past. The group also anticipates imminent events that will parallel the start of that war. This connection does not merely support an argument that the federal government is infringing on the rights of Americans. It provides historical justification for the possibility where members of Oath Keepers and others in the patriot/militia movement take up arms against the federal government: "If you the people decide that you have no recourse, and such a revolution comes . . . we will join [our fellow Americans] in fighting against those who dare attempt to enslave them."[25] The explicit parallels drawn between life under the federal government in the twenty-first century and life under the British government in the eighteenth century are meant to justify the possible use of violence.

Oath Keepers even provides an example of justified violence against tyrannical government with the story of Samuel Whittemore—a lesser-known figure who was also singled out for praise by patriot/militia movement figures from the 1990s.[26] Whittemore was a seventy-eight-year-old farmer on April 19, 1775, living near Boston. On that day, he was working outside when he saw British troops marching after the battles at Lexington and Concord. Upon seeing the troops, he grabbed his weapons, hid until they were close, then opened fire. Whittemore killed three soldiers. He was then shot and stabbed multiple times before the British soldiers "left him for dead." Despite his wounds, Whittemore lived for another eighteen years.[27] After telling this story during Oath Keepers' first event on April 19, 2009, Rhodes declared that Whittemore "was an Oath Keeper." He

> understood the big picture. When he was asked later why he fought that day, he said he fought because he did not want to see his

children and grandchildren to be subjects of a distant king. He wanted them to be free. . . . Now there's a man who understood the big picture. . . . And that is that none of us gets out of here alive. What counts is whether or not our children are free. That's all that counts.[28]

Even his grammar and physical gestures reveal that Rhodes was telling a story of a historical figure in order to derive lessons for himself and those in his audience. As he talked about Whittemore, Rhodes used past tense verbs ("he *said*," "he *wanted*," "he *understood*"); at the end of the story, he switched to present-tense verbs and used first-person pronouns ("none of *us gets* out of here alive," "what *counts* is whether *our* children are free"). At the point in the video when Rhodes switched from talking about *him* to talking about *us*, he also switched from gesturing with his arm extended slightly away from his body to gesturing with his hand pointed back toward his chest.

Despite the details of grammar and body language here, most of these examples are somewhat abstract. Even if gun-control measures in the twenty-first century were similar to firearms confiscation in the eighteenth century, contemporary gun control mostly consists of proposals rather than explicit measures backed by legislation, much less attempts to enforce such legislation. Even if a draft for national service were similar to impressment in the Royal Navy, such a draft has been no more than a discussion point since military conscription ended in 1973.[29] Even if contemporary martial law were similar to the state of martial law imposed by the British, the government has not declared martial law. Even if Americans have an example of justified violence against tyranny, there are no hostile troops marching down American roads for Americans to fight. Most of the group's discussions of these parallels lay the groundwork for future possibilities—not current events.

However, one argument the group has made about parallels between the current situation and the eighteenth century is more concrete and immediate: the occupation of the Malheur National Wildlife Refuge in Harney County, Oregon, in January and February 2016.

In late 2015, supporters of the patriot/militia movement traveled to rural Burns, Oregon, to protest the federal government's treatment of Dwight and Steven Hammond, father and son ranchers who were convicted of arson after burning brush on public land. Dwight was sentenced to three months in jail, and Steven was sentenced to one year in prison—substantially less than the statutory mandatory minimum of five years for the federal crimes for which they were convicted. The Department of Justice filed an appeal over the sentencing; after the Hammonds finished serving their original sentences, a federal court resentenced them to the mandatory minimums. Some in the patriot/militia movement saw this as an example of the tyranny of the federal government.[30] A group led by Ammon Bundy (one of Cliven Bundy's sons) asked the sheriff of Harney County to prevent federal law enforcement from enforcing the new sentence, and his group offered armed protection to the Hammonds if Dwight and Steven decided to refuse to comply with the court order to return to prison.

The Hammonds instead decided to return to prison voluntarily.[31] As their primary cause for gathering in Harney County dissipated, Bundy and some of the others who had traveled to Burns to demonstrate on behalf of the Hammonds decided to switch gears. Bundy led a convoy of several vehicles to the Malheur National Wildlife Refuge, beginning an occupation that Ammon described as a "hard stand" to fight the injustice of the federal government.[32] The occupiers framed their actions as a protest against the federal government controlling public land (like his father, Ammon Bundy believes that the Constitution only allows the federal government to control land for Washington, DC, and for military bases), with the occupiers stating that they would remain—for years if necessary—until the federal government relinquished control of the refuge to Harney County.[33] The occupation was also an attempt to repeat the movement's success at the Bundy Ranch in 2014: using inflammatory rhetoric and a visible arsenal to prevent the federal government from doing things with which the movement disagreed.

Unsurprisingly, the patriot/militia movement viewed the occupation of the refuge through the lens of the Revolutionary War. Those involved in the occupation intentionally cultivated this comparison. For example, Ammon Bundy and his supporters encouraged the residents of Harney County to form a "Committee of Safety," adopting the name used by groups to organize resistance to the British before the Revolutionary War.[34]

Oath Keepers also saw the occupation through the lens of specific events in the lead-up to the War of Independence. In three separate articles, different prominent members of the group condemned the occupation for not following the example set by those who fought the British. Elias Alias, then editor in chief of the Oath Keepers website, argued that "at Lexington and Concord, the Minute Men were defending, not aggressing," unlike Bundy and his allies, who had traveled from across the country to occupy the refuge proactively. Alias suggested that, if the occupation has a historical precedent, that precedent was the federal response to the Branch Davidians in Waco, which ended with several federal law enforcement agents and approximately eighty Branch Davidians dead. If the government killed the occupiers, that might be the only way that the occupation would lead Americans to fight the tyrannical federal government.[35]

Brandon Smith, a member of the group who has written numerous articles that appear on its website, made a slightly different argument: "To compare events [around the occupation] to the first American Revolution, I do not see the standoff and the shooting of [LaVoy] Finicum as a Lexington Green moment. . . . Rather, I see it as a Boston Massacre moment."[36] Even 250 years later, many details of the Boston Massacre remain unknown, except that a group of British soldiers fired their guns into a crowd of Bostonians who were armed with nothing more than sticks and snowballs, killing several people.[37] For advocates of independence from Britain, this event demonstrated the brutality of British rule and later catalyzed support for an armed revolution against the crown.[38]

During the Malheur Refuge occupation, law enforcement attempted to wait out the occupation to avoid violence, and this effort was largely successful. After almost a month, when leaders of the occupation left the refuge for a meeting with the supportive sheriff of a neighboring county on January 26, law enforcement took the opportunity to arrest these central figures. Ammon Bundy, his brother Ryan, Ryan Payne, and Brian "Booda" Cavalier all surrendered and were peacefully arrested, along with several other less prominent members of the occupation. LaVoy Finicum, however, was shot and killed by Oregon state police when he reached into a pocket where he was known to carry a firearm.[39]

Oath Keepers saw Finicum's death as a tragedy; the patriot/militia movement more broadly has viewed Finicum as a martyr murdered by the government.[40] But Oath Keepers also anticipates that the American people are not yet ready to resist the federal government openly.[41] This "martyrdom" may be one of the grievances that those who fight the government might later point to as a catalyzing moment, but the group did not believe that Finicum's death would lead to an immediate start of open hostility.

Rhodes agreed with Alias and Smith: the occupation was not like Lexington and Concord. "Those who intend to try to force this into some form of modern 'Lexington Green' or 'Concord Bridge' against the wishes of the Hammonds and their neighbors need to take a hard look at the Founders' example and their wisdom," he wrote.[42] He urged the patriot/militia movement to wait for a better opportunity to start the Second American Revolution:

> Get organized, get trained, get equipped, and help your neighbors unite in mutual defense and help to train them. Form minuteman companies and Quick Reaction Forces (QRF) in your town and county. Then let "them" come and try to take your guns. Make THAT the modern Lexington and Concord, and we will have the greatest number of Americans on our side, and the greatest number of the current serving military on our side, as possible.[43]

As in so many other documents, Rhodes here anticipated a true parallel to the start of the Revolutionary War. But he argues that the model of that war must be followed carefully and that the circumstances are yet not right for an open conflict.

Time and time again, Oath Keepers perceives or anticipates tyrannical abuses of its natural rights. Members of the group look to American history—especially the Revolutionary War—to understand these violations better. This history also provides them with a model for responses to their grievances that are widely considered justified and righteous. By looking to the past, they make sense of the present and plan for the future. Just as importantly, this precedent might provide them with moral and political support for their understanding of the problems of contemporary America.

Oath Keepers' many attempts to draw parallels between recent or imminent events and early American history are not merely examples of thinking about the nation's history or trying to learn from that history. They serve a larger purpose. Generally speaking, Americans' reverence for the Founders does not leave open the possibility of questioning whether their revolution was just. Those types of questions are out of bounds.[44] Most Americans understand that eighteenth-century movement for independence as being an excellent example of the reasons that justify rebellion against a government and of the best methods to carry out that rebellion.

Thus, if a group can convincingly connect its action with the actions that founded the nation, that group will benefit from American reverence for the Founders. It gains some degree of their moral legitimacy for its own political goals and the steps it takes to pursue them.[45] This is one of the ways in which Oath Keepers engages in strategic framing. As scholars of social movements have long observed, political actors talk about the political issues that are important to them in ways that are meant to build support for their cause.[46] Here, it is likely that the members of Oath Keepers who are making political arguments recognize that they have a difficult task in front of them: gaining support from larger groups of Americans, especially those who are not actively worried about tyranny on a daily basis.[47] The widespread reverence for the Founders and the default assumption that America's independence from Britain was just and provides an excellent template for contemporary political movements mean that this may be a successful strategy, to the extent that the parallels that Oath Keepers identifies are convincing to the Americans that the group wants to reach.

Of course, Oath Keepers is not the first group to do this.[48] The historian David Sehat has convincingly argued that even the Founders themselves fought over the legacy of the Revolutionary

War for their later political activity.[49] Women's suffrage advocates wrote a document modeled on the Declaration of Independence in 1848.[50] Explaining its reasons for secession just before the Civil War, the General Assembly of South Carolina argued that the behavior of the United States government and various state governments violated the Constitution and the principles of the Declaration of Independence, using the language of the Declaration to assert its sovereignty after seceding. A similar declaration from Mississippi declared that its grievances against the federal government were greater than those that led to the War of Independence.[51] More recently, the Tea Party has wrapped itself in symbols that evoke the movement for independence and the founding generation, from its very name to its fondness for the Gadsden Flag, whose coiled snake above the words "Don't Tread on Me" was first used by American marines during the Revolutionary War.[52] And, as the historian D. J. Mulloy argues, many members of the patriot/militia movement in the 1990s pointed back to the Declaration of Independence to justify their goals and behavior.[53]

In invoking the Founders and the struggle for independence from Britain, Oath Keepers attempts to claim the Founders' legitimacy for itself. Oath Keepers explicitly argues that its members are the spiritual successors of the Founders and that the federal government is the spiritual successor of the British government. For those Americans who find this compelling, it means that Oath Keepers (and the larger patriot/militia movement) is in the right and that the federal government must be resisted—with violence if necessary.

If anything will convince Americans to prepare to take up arms against their government, it is invoking the Founders and the creation of the nation. But for this invocation to be compelling—for it to motivate Americans to take direct action against the government—Americans need to be convinced that that the government does in fact pose threats to Americans. Americans need to be convinced that tyranny is not just something to read about in history books but is something that they may well experience for themselves.

6

"No More Free Wacos"

As the previous chapters have shown, Oath Keepers often discusses (relatively) distant history. The group talks about old, core political values that it sees as foundational for America; it also talks about old historical moments from the birth of the nation. These references to the nation's early history help the group make sense of twenty-first-century America. They also send an implicit (sometimes even explicit) message that history repeats itself in concrete ways and that there are timeless political values that are just as important today as they were 250 years ago.

But Oath Keepers is not only focused on history long removed from the lived experiences of Americans today. More recent events—events that many Americans alive today remember—also help the group make sense of ongoing political events. In this chapter, I explore two moments of crisis from recent American history that are important for Oath Keepers: the Waco siege of 1993 and the government's response to Hurricane Katrina, the storm that devastated New Orleans in 2005. I argue that, for Oath Keepers, these two episodes demonstrate that the federal government today is willing—even eager—to violate the rights of Americans and to use violence in the process. Through the group's references to Waco and Katrina, its supporters hear stories of the calamities that can result if Americans today are not constantly ready to resist a tyrannical government.

The Waco Siege: 1993

As many scholars have noted, two moments loom large for the patriot/militia movement.[1] First, in August 1992, an attempt to arrest Randy Weaver—an antigovernment extremist associated with the antisemitic Christian Identity movement who sold an illegally modified shotgun to an informant for the Bureau of Alcohol, Tobacco, and Firearms (ATF, now called the Bureau of Alcohol, Tobacco, Firearms, and Explosives)—led to an armed standoff between the Weaver family and law enforcement (including the FBI and the U.S. Marshals Service). Before Weaver surrendered, his wife, Vicki, and fourteen-year-old son, Samuel, were killed along with a deputy marshal. This conflict, which took place on a remote hilltop in northern Idaho called Ruby Ridge, received substantial media coverage and drew the public's attention to the tactics used by law enforcement when confronting armed Americans accused of crimes.[2]

Just a few months later, in early 1993, the ATF attempted to execute a search warrant on the compound of the Branch Davidian group outside of Waco, Texas. The Branch Davidians, led by David Koresh, were an apocalyptic offshoot of the Seventh-day Adventist Church. The ATF had received information suggesting that the group was illegally manufacturing firearms and explosives; the agency also believed that the group was manufacturing illegal drugs and abusing children. In response to these allegations, the ATF partnered with other law enforcement agencies to raid the Branch Davidians' compound; because of the alleged drug activity and the ongoing War on Drugs, the ATF was able to borrow equipment from military units. When planning the raid, the agency also invited media, which allowed the early moments of the ATF's action and the Branch Davidians' response to be recorded and broadcast.[3]

Shortly before the raid began, a local journalist asked a mail carrier for directions to the compound; the mail carrier, who was Koresh's brother-in-law, warned the Branch Davidians about the ATF's plan. Though they had lost the element of surprise, the ATF decided to go forward with the raid.[4]

From the beginning, the raid had a paramilitary posture: ATF agents were heavily armed, and several military helicopters were used to monitor the raid and to distract the Branch Davidians. Before they had a chance to execute their search warrant, ATF agents responded to the sound of gunfire by shooting at the compound, though it is unclear which side fired their weapons first. The Branch Davidians also began to fire, resulting in a shootout that lasted several hours, during which several members of law enforcement and several of the Branch Davidians were killed.

After this, the FBI took over the operation. As at Ruby Ridge the previous year, the FBI's elite Hostage Response Team (HRT) came to Waco. For the next fifty-one days, law enforcement camped out around the Branch Davidian compound, negotiating with Koresh and pressuring the group to surrender. Government officials felt pressure to end the siege, and on April 19 the FBI took action to do just that. Using military-style vehicles to punch holes in the walls of the compound, law enforcement filled the Branch Davidian buildings with tear gas, attempting to drive the group's members out. Few people left the compound despite the gas. After several hours of this, fires broke out throughout the compound. Investigators later concluded that the Branch Davidians started the fires, but some people believe that the FBI was to blame for the conflagration.[5] Even after the fire began, few people attempted to surrender. In the end more than seventy Branch Davidians—including around twenty children—died on April 19.

For some Americans, both Ruby Ridge and Waco have become metonyms for violent government abuse: the names of these places where Americans and law enforcement exchanged gunfire in 1992 and 1993 are now shorthand among large parts the far right for the evils of government.[6] These events went on to inspire the largest act of terrorism in America before 9/11: Timothy McVeigh's bombing of the Murrah Federal Building in Oklahoma City on April 19, 1995, two years to the day after the end of the Waco siege. McVeigh claimed that the government's actions in Waco were one of the motivations for his attack.[7] Ruby Ridge and Waco are often mentioned in the same breath, frequently in the context of arguments by antigovernment extremists that the government regularly violates First Amendment rights to religious freedom and Second Amendment rights to possess firearms. For some groups, though, Waco is more important and is mentioned more often (perhaps because of the associations of Ruby Ridge with overt white supremacy, or perhaps because of the larger scale of the violence at Waco).

At the same time, both of these events are widely understood as debacles, and not just by the patriot/militia movement. Waco in particular demonstrates the potential negative consequences of police militarization and of law enforcement not taking into account the worldview of those they interact with.[8] But while many observers see Waco and Ruby Ridge as disastrous law enforcement activity born of hubris—mistakes that law enforcement has learned from—the patriot/militia movement understands these events as examples of government's worst inclinations toward violence and tyranny. In other words, the movement is not surprised by how the FBI acted in Idaho and Texas; these events fit perfectly with the movement's understanding of how the federal government acts.

Oath Keepers is certainly among the groups that hold this interpretation of Waco (and, to a much lesser extent, Ruby Ridge).[9] This interpretation conforms to its belief that the government is ready, willing, and able to use violence against Americans who are simply exercising their rights, rights granted by God and protected by the Constitution.

In part, the story of Waco helps Oath Keepers illustrate this understanding of government: as the group says, that moment of conflict is "an undying testament to the inherent abusive nature of government."[10] The group argues that it also exemplifies the self-fulfilling prophecy of the militarization of police. Agencies like the ATF conduct militarized law enforcement action—sometimes with the explicit help of the military—in part to demonstrate that these agencies need to increase their militarized capabilities, which they hope will lead to increased appropriations to support increased militarization, which in turn allows them to conduct more militarized operations, which further demonstrate the need for increased capabilities, in an unending cycle that leads to more abuse of Americans by their government.[11]

Oath Keepers (along with others in the patriot/militia movement) anticipates that the events of Waco are likely to repeat themselves. But the group does not intend to allow the ATF and the FBI to repeat their actions unchallenged. In 2009, Mike Vanderboegh, the founder of the Three Percenter movement, wrote an open letter to Eric Holder (who was then the U.S. attorney general) titled "No More Free Wacos," warning him that gun owners would not sit by and allow the ATF to disarm them, given the ATF's involvement in violence.[12]

Since then, as the phrase has been picked up by others in the patriot/militia movement including Oath Keepers, it has come to mean something more specific: actors like Oath Keepers will not allow the federal government to engage in violence against

Americans without facing vigorous resistance. For Oath Keepers and other like-minded Americans, "Waco" is now synonymous with murder by government agents, and Oath Keepers pledges to do everything it can to prevent the government from "murdering" more Americans.[13] In fact, "Waco" has become a verb for the group. For example, Oath Keepers urged its members to travel to the Bundy Ranch standoff in 2014 "specifically to prevent them [the Bundy Family] from being 'Waco'd' after we saw clear preparation and intent by the Feds to use military trained snipers and Special Forces veteran mercenaries against cowboys and their families."[14]

As this statement shows, Oath Keepers makes sense of new threats that it perceives through its understanding of the government's actions in Waco. In the days after the Bureau of Land Management stopped its operation to round up Cliven Bundy's cattle, the group described the events at the Bundy Ranch as "part of a land grab dispute that threatened to escalate into a Waco-style confrontation."[15] The group alleged that the government "brought in special forces veterans, they hired mercenaries, they brought in snipers." Stewart Rhodes said that the response by Oath Keepers and others to step up and defend the Bundy family in response to this threat made that operation "very righteous."[16]

Waco would also help Oath Keepers think about the 2016 Malheur National Wildlife Refuge Occupation and the protests that led up to that occupation. Near the end of 2015, Ammon Bundy began urging those who had supported his family in 2014 to support the Hammond family in rural southeastern Oregon. As discussed in the previous chapter, Bundy argued that Dwight and Steven Hammond were the victims of a tyrannical government who deserved to be defended just as his family had been. Bundy said that supporters of the Hammonds were taking steps to peacefully stop the government from harming the family but were prepared to take "a physical stand" if necessary.[17]

Though the group supported Cliven Bundy and the security operation at the Bundy ranch in 2014, Oath Keepers argued that this operation in Oregon was inappropriate. The group argued that the Malheur Refuge occupation didn't follow the model of the Revolutionary War, but it also had other objections. First, the Hammond family explicitly stated that they did not want armed supporters to prevent Dwight and Steven from returning to jail; no one had any right to put the family in a more serious situation without the family's buy-in. Second, there was no evidence that the Hammonds faced a threat of violence similar to that faced by the Bundys in 2014. Oath Keepers explained that, in 2014, "All indicators were that the Bundy's [sic] were at risk of being killed in a Ruby Ridge or Waco type incident. And that is why we went." But "in the Hammond case, there is no clear and present danger of the family being mass murdered."[18] In several responses to this situation, Oath Keepers indicated that it did not see a reason to believe that the events of Waco would be repeated in Oregon (perhaps because the Hammonds had already agreed to surrender to the government). For this reason, the group did not support any type of armed intervention in support of the family.

The situation in Oregon changed within days. Despite Oath Keepers having made its position clear, Ammon Bundy led a group of armed individuals to occupy the Malheur Refuge on January 2, 2016. Though the group did not support the occupation and urged Bundy and the other occupiers to reconsider their action, Oath Keepers also clearly stated that it would try to prevent any violence between the government and the occupiers. In several articles on its website, the group even noted with some frustration that it might be forced to respond to government violence "with equal f*cking measure" because the conscience of members of the group "simply will not allow the rationalization of the deaths of liberty minded people even if their stupidity brought about the circumstances."[19]

It did not take long for Oath Keepers to believe that this concern had become more concrete. On January 5, the group issued an "urgent warning" that "Military Special OP Assets" were being sent to the occupation.[20] Fearing that violence was imminent, Oath Keepers quickly endorsed a plan by the Pacific Patriots Network (PPN) to act as a "neutral buffer" to separate those occupying the refuge from law enforcement.[21] The PPN claimed its intention was to mediate discussions between the occupiers and law enforcement and to prevent violence; nevertheless, the group came heavily armed.

By January 15, Oath Keepers was warning the military and law enforcement: don't Waco the occupiers or "you risk pushing this nation over the edge into a civil war, because there are 'no more free Wacos.'"[22] The same day, retired Sergeant Major Joseph Santoro, a member of the Oath Keepers board of directors and the group's national operations noncommissioned officer, told media near the refuge that Oath Keepers' "concern is that the federal government 'Wacos' the people right down that hill. It is our opinion, that, as men and women, as free Americans—patriots—that if they do that, they will start a conflagration so great—nobody wants it, nobody needs it, but I think it will grow out of hand exactly like the American Revolution."[23]

Clearly, Waco serves as an important event from recent American history that helps Oath Keepers understand things that happen in America today. It also guides the group's responses to the crises it perceives: Oath Keepers members have committed themselves to preventing that tragedy from unfolding again in another context. Oath Keepers argues repeatedly that it wants to prevent violence between Americans and the government, but the group also makes it clear that, if the government does engage in violence against Americans, violating their rights, Oath Keepers will respond in kind. The government will not be able to get away with murdering Americans again; there will be no more free Wacos. The government should know that any such action will lead to another American Revolution, and Americans should recognize that they may be forced to take up arms against the government.

Hurricane Katrina: 2005

Waco was a conflict that (according to the interpretation put forward by Oath Keepers) was clearly caused by an overzealous, violent government hell-bent on violating the rights of Americans. Not all the crises that help Oath Keepers make sense of contemporary America are seen as being so explicitly manufactured by the government, though. Some of these crises develop out of the government's response to events initially beyond its control.

In August 2005, a massive storm approached the Gulf Coast of Louisiana and Mississippi. Though it weakened shortly before making landfall on August 29, Hurricane Katrina devastated New Orleans and the surrounding area with winds topping 120 miles per hour, a storm surge as high as twelve feet, and rainfall of as much as twelve inches.[24] The damage increased when levees meant to protect New Orleans from floods failed. An enormous number of people evacuated the city—around four hundred thousand out of five hundred thousand residents—and the surrounding areas, but many people remained trapped in the city, forced to ride out the storm.[25] More than ten thousand people eventually sought shelter in the Superdome, the New Orleans Saints' large indoor football stadium. Thousands more attempted to stay in their homes; many of these were later forced to sit on their roofs and await rescue. In total, more than 1,800 people died in the storm, which also caused more than $100 billion in damage.

After the storm, the city was plagued by flooding, shortages of basic necessities, and crime and rumors of crime. The Federal Emergency Management Agency's response to the disaster was woefully inadequate. FEMA's slow response contributed to widespread looting, which led to rumors of widespread lawlessness. In fact, some members of the New Orleans Police Department report being given orders to shoot looters on sight.[26] Later, journalists found that reports of crime were overblown: most looters took food, clothing, and other necessities, a far cry from the media focus on the few individuals stealing DVDs, TVs, and other high-price goods. Rumors of rampant murder at the Superdome were also shown to be false. Authorities who were expecting to recover hundreds of bodies at the makeshift shelter only found six: four who died of natural causes, one a drug overdose, and one an apparent suicide.[27]

In the confusion of the storm and its aftermath, reports also began to emerge alleging that not only was the government failing to respond adequately to the disaster but that some governmental agencies were actually making things worse. Police officers from Gretna, a suburb of New Orleans, refused to let evacuees cross the bridge leading from New Orleans into their town, with Gretna officials later arguing that the city had to take care of its own residents rather than care for others.[28] There were reports of blanket firearms bans and widespread gun confiscation in the city, as some city officials declared that "only law enforcement are allowed to have weapons."[29] Four New Orleans police officers shot and killed two unarmed civilians, wounding four more; the officers later falsely claimed that they shot these individuals after being shot at themselves.[30] These actions by government officials compounded the crisis caused by the storm itself.

In the following years, the government's response to Hurricane Katrina has become notorious for its shortcomings. FEMA in particular has been widely criticized for poor preparation and inadequate action. Generally, this criticism depicts the government's response as resulting from mismanagement, incompetence, and inattention.[31]

For some people, however, the response to Hurricane Katrina demonstrates the government's readiness to use any justification to violate the rights of Americans. The journalist Adam Weinstein has argued that the NRA pushed a narrative about disarmament after the storm that exaggerated the problem.[32] Groups like Oath Keepers have taken this narrative further, arguing that the gun confiscation that took place prevented residents of the city and surrounding areas from defending themselves and their property from organized crime; further, it amounted to an orchestrated attempt by the government to disarm a large group of Americans. For the NRA, this was not an isolated incident born out of the panicked response to a natural disaster that overwhelmed authorities but a widespread practice that law-abiding gun owners needed to be prepared for and ready to resist. For Oath Keepers, this was not a spontaneous, bungled response to an emergency but yet another episode in a long line of examples of the government eagerly working to disarm Americans and see them suffer.

As we have seen, Oath Keepers is quick to identify instances of government acting badly, often asserting evil motives that drove the government action the group opposes. For example, one of the early videos that the group uploaded to its YouTube channel was about its "Declaration of Orders We Will NOT Obey." The text version of this document begins with an invocation of the Revolutionary War. In this video version, though, Oath Keepers prefaces the list of orders with a reference to Hurricane Katrina. After telling viewers that "Oath Keepers is an association of active-duty military, veterans and peace officers who will honor the oath we swore . . . to support and defend the Constitution against all enemies, foreign and domestic so help us God!" the video cuts to a clip of a Marines public affairs officer. The officer says, "Would we take away people's guns? Frankly, I don't see that happening." The video then cuts to a clip of a New Orleans Police Department official saying, "No one will be able to be armed. We're gonna take all weapons." The public affairs officer returns to the screen, saying that "Marines obey orders." A caption appears, asking, "And if that order is an 'unlawful order?'" The public affairs officer then says, "Marines have the right to refuse an unlawful order." Then Stewart Rhodes says that service members have an obligation, not a right, to refuse an unlawful order.[33]

As in the text version of the list of orders Oath Keepers urges its members not to obey, the video version sets the stage for why this sort of list is appropriate—even important—by describing a moment of crisis from American history. In this case, that moment is more recent, and it provides an example of a situation where, according to Oath Keepers, had all the members of the military and first responders involved in the situation honored their oaths to the Constitution, the crisis would have been substantially mitigated.

For the most part, this video contains a brief version of the list of orders Oath Keepers will not obey. Unlike the text version, the video does not explain why each order is included. The first five orders pass fairly quickly, listed as captions over an image of a waving flag with martial music in the background:

1. We will NOT obey orders to disarm the American people. 2. We will NOT obey orders to conduct warrantless searches of the American people. 3. We will NOT obey orders to detain American citizens as "unlawful enemy combatants." 4. We will

NOT obey orders to impose martial law or a "state of emergency" on any state. 5. We will NOT obey orders to invade or subjugate any state that asserts its sovereignty.

Then, order number 6: "We will NOT obey orders to blockade American cities, thus turning them into giant concentration camps." This is the only order in the video that is followed by commentary. After stating this order, the video cuts to a clip of Fox News's Geraldo Rivera reporting in New Orleans after the storm, asking why people are still taking shelter in a convention center rather than walking down a highway away from the devastation.

The video then switches to a clip of Shepard Smith, another reporter for Fox News, who says that the government has "locked" people in the convention center and the Superdome, promising locals that they would receive help at these locations but not fulfilling that promise. Smith, becoming more animated, says that the government set up a checkpoint at the bridge connecting New Orleans to Gretna: "It's the only way out. . . . They set up a checkpoint, and anyone who walks up out of that city now is turned around, you are not allowed to go to Gretna. . . . Over there [in Gretna], there's hope. Over there, there's electricity. Over there, there's food and water. But you cannot go from [New Orleans] to [Gretna]. The government will not allow you to do it."

With these clips, this Oath Keepers video conjures a scene where "government" (implicitly depicted as a unitary actor) was actively hurting Americans by refusing to let them leave the devastation of New Orleans. At this point in the video, government has been described as a bad actor that has made the situation after Hurricane Katrina worse.

The video then provides more detail about how the government made the situation worse. The next clip shows Aaron Broussard, president of Jefferson Parish (the county-level jurisdiction that neighbors New Orleans), describing specific things FEMA did to make the situation in his parish worse:

> We had Wal-Mart deliver three trucks of water, trailer trucks of water. FEMA turned them back. They said we didn't need them. This was a week ago. FEMA—we had 1,000 gallons of diesel fuel on a Coast Guard vessel docked in my parish. The Coast Guard said, "Come get the fuel right away." When we got there with our trucks, they got a word. "FEMA says don't give you the fuel." Yesterday—yesterday—FEMA comes in and cuts all of our emergency communication lines. They cut them without notice. Our sheriff, Harry Lee, goes back in, he reconnects the line. He posts armed guards on our line and says, "No one is getting near these lines."[34]

With this clip, Oath Keepers depicts FEMA as an agency plainly taking actions that prevent Americans from receiving help. This organization tasked with helping Americans prepare for and recover from emergencies seems malicious, as if it intentionally wants to harm Americans rather than help them.

At this point, this relatively short video (nine minutes and eleven seconds long) has spent two minutes describing the federal government's response to Hurricane Katrina, just after declaring that the group will not obey orders to blockade cities. With the clips from Rivera, Smith, and Broussard, Oath Keepers makes the argument that New Orleans and the surrounding region effectively had been blockaded by the federal government: it had been turned into a concentration camp from which the residents of New Orleans could not leave and where they suffered and died because of action undertaken by the government.[35]

But Oath Keepers is not done describing the government's response to the hurricane in this video. It next pivots to discuss the issue that is the primary focus for Oath Keepers when it talks about Hurricane Katrina: gun control. Immediately after the clip of Aaron Broussard, the video cuts to news footage of heavily armed individuals in military and police uniforms banging on doors and entering homes. Next, a clip from Fox News shows a woman standing in her kitchen with a small revolver in her hand. Rather than holding the butt of the gun in her palm, she has her fingers wrapped around the cylinder and the barrel—she is clearly not preparing to use the weapon. The video cuts again, showing a police officer tackling this woman. While these images appear, Stewart Rhodes says, "That's why we issued our declaration of ten orders that we will not obey. What those are designed to do is to get the troops thinking ahead of time about where their line in the sand is in advance." After this, the video quickly moves through the remaining four orders, which, without explanation, Oath Keepers urges people to not obey.[36] In this presentation of this core document for the group, Oath Keepers chose to focus on Hurricane Katrina rather than the Revolutionary War.

In other documents, when Oath Keepers discusses Hurricane Katrina, it is typically in the context of gun confiscation. For example, in 2009 the group posted two speeches on its blog that it encouraged individuals to use at Tea Party events held on July 4. One of the speeches spends time talking about ongoing events "that aren't receiving coverage . . . things we the people need to be aware of." The first of these is a discussion of the illegal and unconstitutional actions taken by the government in the response to Katrina. First, the group describes the use of the U.S. military and "armed government contractors" as "a direct violation" of the Posse Comitatus Act of 1878, which severely restricts the ability of the federal government to use "Big Army" (as opposed to the Army National Guard and state guard units) and the other branches of the military for domestic law enforcement purposes.[37] Oath

Keepers objected to the military in particular taking part in "mass gun confiscations, including door to door searches for weapons in parts of the city that were not flooded. A natural disaster is NOT a legal reason to deny citizens of their 2nd Amendment Rights."[38]

In 2010, Bill O'Reilly interviewed Stewart Rhodes on his show on Fox News. O'Reilly quickly demonstrated his lack of respect for Oath Keepers, derisively asking Rhodes, "Who's gonna try to disarm people and place them under martial law? Why would that even be something you would be discussing?" Rhodes responded that

> it happened as recently as Katrina. You've probably seen the videos there of an old lady being tackled in her kitchen and disarmed of her revolver. And there were house-to-house searches for firearms. You had the police chief declare that no one would be allowed to have weapons, we're gonna take all the guns. And they did. So they disarmed Americans over bad weather, as though the bad weather suspended the Second Amendment.

When O'Reilly countered that it was a state of emergency that demanded a response, Rhodes retorted, "Where does it say in the Constitution that bad weather suspends the Constitution?"[39] Here, the group's leader argued that the government had unjustly, unconstitutionally confiscated weapons in the aftermath of Hurricane Katrina; that action demonstrates that the government might again carry out a systematic attempt to disarm the American people.

The government's response to Hurricane Katrina was also a theme during the group's first public event on Lexington Common, on April 19, 2009. In one of the speeches delivered there, Stewart Rhodes provided yet another perspective on the orders the group will not obey. After declaring that its members "will not obey orders to conduct warrantless searches of the American people," Rhodes offered the same explanation provided in the text version of the declaration of orders found on the group's website: one of the causes of the American Revolution was the use of writs of assistance by the British, "which were essentially warrantless searches because there was no requirement of a showing of probable cause to a judge."[40] Then Rhodes said that contemporary Americans have experienced similar things, "whether it's the NSA or whether it's through national security letters or whatever other mechanism is used." He pointed to one primary example of this:

> In Katrina, we saw house-to-house searches without warrant, and we saw disarmament of people. And the two go together. How do you think they're going to do it if they want to take your guns away from you? They're gonna go get a warrant for your house in particular with probable cause? No! It will be by general sweeps through your homes or roadblocks and sweeps through your cars.[41]

Here, Rhodes invoked the government's response to Hurricane Katrina to provide an example of how the government violates certain rights (in this case, the right to be free from unreasonable searches and seizures) in the process of violating other rights (in this case, the right to keep and bear arms). And in this speech, Rhodes implicitly argued that Hurricane Katrina and the Revolutionary War share common features: government violating privacy rights in order to confiscate weapons.

Repeatedly, Oath Keepers has invoked the government's response to Hurricane Katrina as an example of government hurting Americans, particularly through the widespread confiscation of firearms. In this way, talking about the storm can remind Americans of the dangers posed by their government—not an abstract danger or one experienced centuries ago but one that happened within recent memory.

But the group also finds hope in the aftermath of the storm. In May 2010, Oath Keepers posted a series of videos in which the group "PROVE[D] SOME TROOPS REFUSED TO CONFISCATE GUNS DURING KATRINA."[42] In these videos, Stewart Rhodes talked with Joshua May, a sergeant in the Utah National Guard who was deployed to New Orleans after the storm. May told the story of his unit hearing rumors that other units were being ordered to confiscate firearms. Some of the members of his unit got together and "came to the consensus that no, we will not be taking firearms." May proactively explained to their commander that "there's a group of us who won't do that."[43] Across the five videos in this series, Rhodes and May spoke for nearly an hour about May's experiences in New Orleans: when his unit proactively declared their intention not to engage in gun confiscation, when they interacted with locals who worried that May and his unit would confiscate their guns, and when they witnessed armed locals forming security teams to protect their neighborhoods more effectively than the government could. For Oath Keepers, Sgt. May's actions when deployed in response to Hurricane Katrina provide a model for how Americans in the military and law enforcement should act: if faced with a situation where they might be ordered to violate Americans' rights, they should proactively affirm their commitment to protect those rights and to refuse to comply with orders to violate them.

Hurricane Katrina serves two purposes for Oath Keepers. It provides an example of a recent event during which the government acted to harm Americans, violating their rights and causing them to suffer by not providing aid and even by interfering with other efforts to help Americans in need. It also provides an example of how Americans can resist tyranny by refusing to comply with unconstitutional government action.

The most important moment of conflict and crisis that Oath Keepers uses to make sense of contemporary America while also gaining support from the American public at large is the Revolutionary War. That event holds more tacit moral authority and political legitimacy than any other event in American history. But the group can also use other moments of crisis to make sense of ongoing events, provide models of appropriate (or even righteous) behavior, and gain support. Using more recent events can illustrate that the threats Oath Keepers is concerned about are not remote, abstract, or hypothetical; the group can point to events like the Waco siege or the response to Hurricane Katrina to illustrate that, even today, Americans should be wary of the government, which is always on the verge of harming Americans and violating their rights.

These three different events also serve different purposes. Talking about the Revolutionary War can provide support for Oath Keepers' argument that sometimes revolution is warranted and that Americans have examples for how to respond to tyranny effectively. Talking about Waco can provide support for Oath Keepers' argument that the government is willing—or perhaps even eager—to use violence against Americans, especially Americans who hold beliefs the government deems unacceptable. Talking about Hurricane Katrina can provide support for the group's argument that the government will use any excuse it can to violate Americans' core rights, especially their Second Amendment rights.

More importantly, Oath Keepers might talk about these different events to communicate to different audiences. The group may talk about the American Revolution to speak to the American public at large, given widespread (if shallow) familiarity with and approval of that event. Talking about Katrina might help the group speak to a subset of the American public who might be receptive to the ideas of Oath Keepers if they can be convinced that the threats are real. And invocations of Waco may be more narrowly targeted at the far right and at federal law enforcement, two groups for whom the Waco siege is a familiar event.

CONCLUSION
The Importance of Oath Keepers

I n this book, I have argued that Oath Keepers—a group that exemplifies many of the characteristics of the patriot/militia movement and of antigovernment extremism more broadly— talks about core American political ideas and pivotal moments from American history for three purposes. First, these rhetorical frames help the group make sense of the contemporary political situation in which it finds itself. In particular, talking about historical threats that Americans have faced can help its members make sense of the ongoing threats they perceive. Second, retelling the stories of how Americans whom the group describes as heroes have responded to the threats they faced provides the group's members with models for how they should respond to ongoing threats. Third, to the extent that the group is able to draw convincing parallels between the contemporary situation in America and historical situations—between Oath Keepers and American heroes from historical conflicts—these frames might help the group gain support from Americans who do not already support the patriot/militia movement.

Core political ideas like natural rights are important rhetorical devices in American politics. They function as ideographs: abstract ideas that carry stable moral value but are only vaguely defined.[1] For example, "natural rights" (or the related idea of human rights) has consistent—perhaps universal—moral weight in America. No one is against natural rights; no one favors their restriction or violation. But this consensus hides the fact that the *contents* of natural rights are unclear. In other words, Americans might agree that natural rights should be protected, but they do not agree on what constitutes natural rights and thus deserve protection. Is the right to keep and bear arms truly a right that belongs to all people simply because they are people, or is it a right that exists within a particular political context and is contingent on how people understand it in a particular moment? Is the right to privacy truly a natural right, and if it is, what does it mean?

Oath Keepers benefits from the abstract nature of natural rights (and other ideographs it references, like "republic," "tyranny," and "fascism"). Americans will respond to "natural rights" in a consistent manner, as long as the concept is left abstract or ambiguous. Americans will only object if they are confronted with an example of a natural right that they think is *not* a natural right. Oath Keepers engages in strategic ambiguity in its discussion of these core political values, providing minimal specifics and thus potentially gaining more support from individuals with whom this rhetorical frame resonates but who might disagree with Oath Keepers about what these values mean in a more concrete way.

Some events from U.S. history function similarly. For example, few Americans question the legitimacy of the Revolutionary War, but this is less often a carefully thought-out position than one reached by default, perhaps with little knowledge of the actual details of the conditions that led to the war or the circumstances of how the war was carried out. Americans "know" that Thomas Jefferson, Samuel Adams, and Thomas Paine were right when these men identified conditions that justified rebellion against the British crown, even if Americans *don't* know anything about life under the Crown or haven't thought carefully about whether the conditions of that life justified violence. This is not to suggest that the American Revolution was not justified; rather, I am suggesting that the conflict out of which the nation was born holds moral and political authority in spite of (or perhaps because of) Americans' lack of detailed engagement with the history of that event. To the extent that Oath Keepers can convincingly tie itself to the Patriots in the Revolution, the group gains some of the tacit moral and political authority attached to these actors and this event.

Other events from American history serve different purposes for Oath Keepers. As I argued in chapter 7, Waco and Hurricane Katrina are recent moments of crisis that demonstrate that Americans still face threats from their government. The American Revolution demonstrates that government can be tyrannical and that armed resistance can be righteous and justified. Waco demonstrates that government is eager to use violence against Americans, especially when it thinks it can get away with that violence by targeting fringe groups. Hurricane Katrina demonstrates that government will use natural disasters and other emergencies as cover to put into motion long-standing plans to violate Americans' rights. The American Revolution might contain the best example of tyranny (in the form of the British) and the appropriate responses to tyranny (in the form of the resistance to the British), but Oath Keepers benefits from having more recent events that it can point to as well, sending the message that tyranny isn't something confined to the eighteenth century—tyranny still exists, and it still threatens America.

Oath Keepers uses these different rhetorical strategies to target different audiences. Ideographs like natural rights and events like the Revolutionary War are widely familiar (in a general way) and held in esteem by Americans. The group talks about these ideas and events in part to convince the wider American public that Oath Keepers' cause is legitimate and its resistance is justified.

Events like Hurricane Katrina are widely familiar as well, but the group talks about them in uncommon ways. Those who might be led to support the group based on its invocation of Hurricane Katrina are those who already worry about government infringing rights in a general sense but who may have previously thought that those threats posed by government are remote or unlikely. The way that Oath Keepers talks about the storm might convince these individuals that the threat is still very real, even in twenty-first-century America.

Events like Waco are much less widely known—many people have heard of Waco, and those who watched television news at the time were inundated with coverage while the standoff was happening, but few Americans today likely have a detailed knowledge of that event. Oath Keepers talks about Waco with two potential audiences in mind: far-right extremists who are familiar with the event and government officials who are (or should be) familiar with the event. For potential supporters, Waco demonstrates the worst-case scenario of government action if Americans aren't vigilant in resisting it. For the government, Waco is used as a warning that Americans won't allow government to harm its citizens again without repercussions.

Each of these rhetorical strategies simultaneously serves three purposes. First, they help Oath Keepers make sense of the contemporary political situation. Members of the group perceive threats in a general sense, but they may have difficulty identifying these threats. By looking to historical moments of conflict and crisis (or the ideas that motivate those moments), the group can find examples of political threats that the nation has experienced before. These examples can help the group argue that contemporary Americans still face these threats. The clearest example of Oath Keepers doing this is in its list of ten orders their members will not obey.[2]

Second, these rhetorical strategies help members of the group identify models of the appropriate responses to the ongoing threats they perceive. If the contemporary situation is like the Revolutionary War, then patriotic Americans should be ready to fight the strongest military in the world (the U.S. military), just like the patriots who fought the eighteenth century's strongest military (the British military). If ongoing interactions between Americans and the government threaten to turn into situations like the Waco siege, with militarized law enforcement murdering Americans, then patriotic Americans must not allow that event to repeat itself without grave cost to the government. If the government is going to use disasters like Hurricane Katrina to violate Americans' rights, then patriotic Americans should proactively refuse to take part in those plans, just like the patriots who proactively refused to disarm Americans in and around New Orleans in 2005.

Third, these rhetorical strategies help Oath Keepers gain support for its cause. Some of these strategies help the group depict its cause as part of a long history of Americans standing up for core political values, even to the point of using weapons to protect those values: if the threats that contemporary Americans face really are like those that the colonists faced under British rule, then surely resistance today is just as warranted as resistance 250 years ago. Some of them remind other extremists of events they care about (like Waco) and send the message that Oath Keepers will not allow those catastrophes to repeat themselves. And other strategies encourage Americans to reinterpret crises they may have lived through (like Hurricane Katrina) as being exacerbated by a tyrannical government.

It is worth mentioning another feature of the often ambiguous ways that Oath Keepers talks about these important political ideas and events: the group rarely (if ever) addresses race or gender except to deny that its members are bigots. "Natural rights," the

Revolutionary War, Waco, and Katrina: Oath Keepers talks about all of these to point to threats that *Americans* face—not just white Americans or male Americans but all Americans. Because it sees itself as definitively nonracist, Oath Keepers does not even address how the Revolutionary War might not hold the same default veneration by African Americans. Gender is not a prominent a frame for the group, so it does not even address how firearms in America are often bound up with constructions of masculinity and traditional gender roles. As the sociologist Amy Cooter has pointed out in her excellent ethnography of militia members in Michigan from 2008 to 2011, members of the patriot/militia movement believe they promote a politics that opposes racism and other forms of bigotry, but they overlook issues of race and gender in their ideas, goals, and actions.[3]

Of course, the examples I have discussed in this book are not the only ways that Oath Keepers builds a political identity for its supporters and pursues these three purposes. Place and space also help Oath Keepers accomplish these things, both in terms of the places that the group goes and the spaces that the group talks about.[4] This can be seen in several of the events that were the focus of previous chapters.

For example, the group's first event demonstrated that the group would (at least occasionally) take into account the importance of physical places for the task of building identity: during his speech on April 19, 2009, Stewart Rhodes explicitly said that he chose to have that first event on Lexington Common to commemorate the first battle of the Revolutionary War and to build a connection between Oath Keepers gathered on that day and those who fought the British at the same place 234 years earlier. In this case, the symbolic connotations of the physical place—how activists perceive and understand the physical geographies where they act—supported Rhodes's goal of building a new identity around this new group.[5]

Sometimes, invocations of geography are more abstract. For example, one of Oath Keepers' objections to the United Nations comes in the form of criticisms of Agenda 21. The group interprets this nonbinding plan for sustainable development as an attempt to "depopulate the rural areas of America"—particularly areas of the West like Montana and Wyoming.[6] Oath Keepers depicts the West as a space where "liberty-minded" Americans can live independently, free from government overreach.[7] It views the West as a space that fosters independent life, an understanding that conjures the idea of the frontier as a quintessential American space where hardworking men (and occasionally women) with few resources can tame nature and make something of themselves. This view of the West also harks back to the Jeffersonian valorization of "yeoman farmers"—farmers with modest means who worked hard to provide a life for their families.[8]

In some cases, abstract ideas about space become reinforced by concrete actions in particular places. For example, ideas about the West as a space where gritty Americans can build successful lives were reinforced when Oath Keepers traveled to the Bundy Ranch in Nevada to protect Cliven Bundy's rights and property and when Oath Keepers traveled to the Sugar Pine Mine in rural Oregon to defend the rights of two men who operated a small mine to continue their work of extracting resources from the land.

There are still more ways that the group engages in ideational work to help its supporters understand the political context in which they find themselves, provide its supporters with models of how they should act in that context, and gain additional support from other Americans: through affiliations with the Tea Party movement,[9] by talking about issues of broader concern like terrorism and organized crime, and by explicitly mirroring the model of federal programs (like FEMA's Community Emergency Response Teams program).[10] A full inventory of the rhetorical strategies that the group uses would reveal many ways that the group attempts to motivate and justify its political goals and the actions it takes to pursue those goals; my focus here has been on those rhetorical strategies that attempt to draw parallels between Oath Keepers and venerated ideas, actors, and events in American political history.

It is also worth emphasizing that many of these rhetorical strategies were not newly invented by Oath Keepers. The ways that the group interprets foundational documents and looks to events from early American history to guide its actions today continue trends from earlier patriot/militia movement figures.[11] In fact, some of these figures wrote lengthy essays—Samuel Sherwood even wrote entire books[12]—about those documents and events, relating them to twentieth- and twenty-first-century America. In a sense, then, Oath Keepers is just another in a long line of political actors in America who use the past to make sense of the present and to plan for the future.

Who Cares About Oath Keepers?

Why should anyone care that Oath Keepers uses these rhetorical strategies to make sense of the contemporary political situation in America, to guide its behavior in that situation, and to gain support for its cause and behavior? In short, Oath Keepers (and the patriot/militia movement more generally) poses two threats to contemporary America, both of which are directly shaped by the group's understanding of America and feed off its ability to gain supporters.

First, the group poses a physical security threat. Though Oath Keepers does not explicitly encourage the proactive use of violence, it does encourage conflict. Every time the group talks about violence in its conflicts with the government, that violence is depicted as defensive and as the last resort, when all other means of resistance fail. Yet Oath Keepers' rhetorical strategies clearly make violence more likely: if natural rights are currently being threatened, if twenty-first-century America faces a crisis like the American Revolution, if the government is eager to murder Americans and use emergencies as cover to violate Americans' rights, then clearly patriotic Americans must be ready to fight the government. More concretely, the group repeatedly describes the armed standoff at Bundy Ranch in 2014 as a justified, righteous response to government.[13] It praised its members who, as part of the Pacific Patriots Network, acted as a heavily armed "security buffer" outside of the Malheur Refuge occupation in 2016. It has been involved in other so-called security operations, for example at the Sugar Pine Mine in Oregon and the White Hope Mine in Montana, where its members brought military-style weapons in preparation for a shooting war with the government.

Situations in which heavily armed members of Oath Keepers put themselves in situations where they might shoot at law enforcement have not been one-offs; the group has a pattern of engaging in them. And the group's understanding of American history and the threats posed by the American government means that its members are always looking for potential violations of rights and uses of violence by the government. They anticipate that the nation might soon face a second American revolution; they anticipate that the events of Waco might repeat any time law enforcement engages in a protracted enforcement action.

The government should (and does) respond to these security operations. Sometimes, its response should be like the response to the Sugar Pine Mine security operation: Oath Keepers declared that it would continue the operation until the miners were able to appeal a decision by the Bureau of Land Management, and the government declared it had no intention of taking any action until the legal process was finished. But some of these situations (like the Bundy Ranch standoff and the Malheur Refuge occupation) involve criminal behavior and require a more active law enforcement response. And given that Oath Keepers' members and others in the patriot/militia movement are often heavily armed, it is entirely appropriate that law enforcement should also be armed in these situations.

But a heavily militarized police response to situations involving armed members of the group makes violence more likely. Oath Keepers understands government to be an inherently violent actor willing to use force to violate basic rights; when law enforcement shows up dressed in uniforms that look like military fatigues, sporting beards that conform to stereotypes about Special Forces operators, with long guns, body armor, and armored vehicles, this response reinforces Oath Keepers' understanding of government.

By better understanding how the group makes sense of contemporary America through reference to these core political ideas and historical moments, law enforcement and policy makers can make better, more informed decisions about how to respond when members of Oath Keepers engage in armed criminal behavior. The general principle of using the least violence necessary is appropriate, but law enforcement can further help themselves achieve their mission if they specifically adopt tactics that do not resemble the tactics used by the ATF and FBI in Waco and Ruby Ridge, for example. Again, it is not always possible for law enforcement to carry out enforcement activity through everyday police action; sometimes the FBI's Hostage Rescue Team or SWAT teams are appropriate responders. But law enforcement should be aware of how Oath Keepers will perceive the police response and should design that response so it will not feed into the group's understandings of government and violence. A better understanding of Oath Keepers can help the FBI not repeat the mistakes it made in Waco, where a lack of understanding about the Branch Davidians' worldview led the FBI to fill the apocalyptic role the Branch Davidians expected of it.[14]

This physical threat that Oath Keepers poses is not where the group's biggest influence lies, however. The group periodically organizes security operations, but there are substantial gaps between them. All the time, though, Oath Keepers contributes to a broader discourse in American politics that pits the people against the government and that views violence as a legitimate form of resistance to government—this is the group's RTI (reach, teach, and inspire) mission. The group may discourage proactive, aggressive acts of violence, but it still shifts political culture in a way that makes attacks like that of Jerad and Amanda Miller (who killed two police officers and a civilian in Nevada in June 2014, weeks after spending time at the Bundy Ranch standoff) more likely.[15]

In this way, Oath Keepers shifts the Overton Window, or the limits of acceptable political discourse.[16] Often the Overton Window is a concept used in reference to particular issues (for example, education policy and school choice or, more recently, race), but it can also apply to broader political discourse around values, norms, and behavior.[17] Whether Oath Keepers actually intends to do this, its attacks on the government—wrapped in the mantle of patriotism, drawing from the legitimacy of the Revolution—shift the normal range of Americans' understanding of government. As the sociologist Ruth Braunstein found, Tea Party–affiliated actors tend to have a conflictual understanding of the relationship between citizens and politicians (which Braunstein contrasts with actors affiliated with Interfaith, an umbrella organization of progressive faith-based groups, who tend to have a cooperative understanding of that relationship).[18] Oath Keepers promotes a more extreme version of the Tea Party's conflictual understanding, arguing that government is a nefarious actor hell-bent on violating Americans' rights.

Similarly, Oath Keepers shifts the normal understandings of appropriate political behavior. The group argues that electoral politics are broken, that voting might not even be a worthwhile form of political engagement.[19] It suggests that Americans should act as vigilantes—whether by monitoring polling places for voter fraud or by volunteering with civilian paramilitary groups on the U.S.-Mexico border.[20] The group also takes the implications of the conflictual understanding of the Tea Party and makes them more extreme, suggesting that not only do politicians (and by extension, the government writ large) need to be watched to make sure they don't abuse their power but that Americans must actually be ready to use violence in their role as government watchdogs—for example, by offering Kim Davis armed protection to keep federal law enforcement from returning her to jail, had she continued to prevent LGBT couples in a county in Kentucky from receiving marriage licenses.[21]

For those who view violence as an unacceptable form of political behavior, for those who value norms of peaceful deliberative democracy, for those who do not see government as an existential threat, Oath Keepers is a worrisome force in American politics. It is certainly true that dissent is protected by the First Amendment. It is also true that vigorous dissent has sometimes been a positive thing in American history (for example, with the civil rights movement). The type of dissent that Oath Keepers advocates for is not inherently criminal, but the group's values represent a shift of American political culture that would make conflict more vociferous—perhaps even more violent. For this reason above all, the group should be understood so that we can minimize its harmful impacts.

The Future of Oath Keepers

This book has focused on the activity of Oath Keepers from its founding in 2009 through February 2016. Since then, the group has undergone some important changes, which are tied to Donald Trump's victory in the 2016 presidential election. When Trump (whom the members of Oath Keepers overwhelmingly supported, along with others in the patriot/militia movement) won, the group quickly changed its understanding of the most critical threat that Americans face. Until November 9, 2016, Oath Keepers consistently viewed the federal government as the source of the gravest threats facing Americans. Certainly, the group also worried about the threats posed by progressives, Islam, and immigrants, but these threats were secondary to that of a tyrannical government.

This changed with Trump's election. On November 9, Oath Keepers rapidly pivoted its focus, asserting instead that the greatest threat facing Americans was no longer the government but other Americans who opposed Donald Trump. The group's leaders anticipated large-scale violence, orchestrated by leftists, in response to Trump's victory. They organized an informal security force to attend Trump's inauguration, anticipating more violence from Trump protestors. The group's members became regular participants in clashes with antifa activists opposing the Trump administration. No longer, it seems, does Oath Keepers believe that dissent is the appropriate political attitude in America; now, dissent (at least in some forms) is seen as treason, as an attempt to overthrow the government and replace it with collectivist authoritarianism—for example, in 2019 Stewart Rhodes described the potential impeachment of President Trump as an illegitimate attempt "to simply undo the 2016 election results that they [the left] don't like."[22] In many ways, Oath Keepers has become the mirror image of what it was before the 2016 election.

But not in every way. The group still worries about progressives, Muslims, and immigrants. It still advocates for the possible use of violence (now targeted against these newly elevated threats rather than the government). It still vehemently opposes any efforts at gun control.

Only time will tell whether these changes will last. This new focus on threats outside of government is likely to continue as long as Donald Trump or other similar figures in the Republican Party retain political power. If the Democrats gain control of both houses of Congress or win the presidency in the future, if Trump is forced to resign or is impeached by the House and convicted by the Senate, or if the moderate or neoconservative segments of the GOP reclaim leading roles in the party, the group may well pivot back, once again focusing on government as the primary threat.

As long as Trump remains in power, Oath Keepers faces a challenge of retaining supporters. For now, potential supporters have their man in the Oval Office. The threats long described by the group are less salient than they had been under an Obama presidency. As long as this remains true, Oath Keepers will likely continue to identify new threats outside of government, like antifa and the gun-control movement that emerged after the Parkland, Florida, school shooting in 2018.

If Oath Keepers is able to survive as a group, it will likely find better conditions for recruitment if American politics swings away from the values epitomized by Trump. If the Democrats retake political power, the group is likely to have more grievances to talk about that will resonate with a larger audience.

Even if the group does not survive the next few years, though, the patriot/militia movement is unlikely to go anywhere. If movements like the Three Percenters are able to take root in Canada (which doesn't have the national history to support the Three Percenters' ideology), then Oath Keepers is likely to be able to weather the quiet seas of Republican power.[23]

Acknowledgments

The list of people who have inspired this project or helped it to take shape is long indeed. I am incredibly grateful to Michael Barkun, David Bennett, Mark Rupert, Jennifer Stromer-Galley, and Edwin Ackerman for support, advice, and encouragement. Thanks especially to Michael, David, and Mark, who encouraged me to take up this project in its earliest days.

Early on, I realized that I wanted to do computational things that I did not have the skill set to do. Sincere thanks to the numerous people who helped me find tools, suggested new skill sets that would be helpful, reviewed code, and helped me develop new tools and ways of thinking about data: J. M. Berger, Mahboobeh Harandi, Yatish Hegde, Jeff Hemsley, Nancy McCracken, Todd Metcalfe, Justin Seitz, and Shan Zhang.

A number of people provided invaluable conversations and feedback on drafts and related projects—in seminars, over email, and at conferences. Thanks to Brandon Behlendorf, J. M. Berger, Olga Boichak, Jeff Broxmeyer, John Burdick, Joel Busher, Robert Churchill, Elizabeth Cohen, Lindsay Cohn, Francesca Grandi, Alex Greer, Matt Lacombe, J. J. MacNab, Alex Meleagrou-Hitchens, Cynthia Miller-Idriss, Mark Pitcavage, Victoria Reyes, Amber Silver, Fabian Virchow, and Liz Yates. Special thanks to

Stephen Wesley at Columbia University Press for very helpful editorial guidance.

A number of other scholars served as inspiration for this project from a distance. Ruth Braunstein, Mark Juergensmeyer, and Rogers Smith led me to new ways of thinking about the relationship between political identity and various forms of political behavior. James Aho pointed my attention at understudied forms of American political extremism. Saul Cornell, Jill Lepore, David Sehat, and Garry Wills helped me think about the enduring legacy of the nation's founding—in particular, the ways that remembering the American Revolution shapes contemporary political thought and behavior.

More directly, this book owes much to D. J. Mulloy's *American Extremism*, Robert Churchill's *To Shake Their Guns in the Tyrant's Face*, and Amy Cooter's "Americanness, Masculinity, and Whiteness: How Michigan Militia Men Navigate Evolving Social Norms." These scholars have all conducted excellent studies of militia groups, ideas, and precedents. Those studies directly inspired this work and deserve substantial credit for helping me form the argument presented here.

All of these folks helped shape this project. I hope they all find something to appreciate in this.

APPENDIX 1
Data and Methods

n this project, I investigated the ways that Oath Keepers makes sense of its political context. In particular, I focused on how the group talks about American history to help its members understand the threats they face and to help them decide how to confront those threats; this same rhetoric may also attempt to convince the wider public that Oath Keepers isn't the bad actor it is sometimes made out to be. This kind of research fits into the branch of social movement research focused on strategic framing, and the methods I use here are a form of framing analysis.[1] In short, framing analysis examines the language used by social movement actors in order to discover the ideas these actors use to make sense of themselves, their context, and their behavior.

Perhaps the dominant trend in social movement research focuses on developing broad explanations for social movement outcomes (such as social movement size and activity, changes in public opinion, or even policy change). This follows a common motivation to understand why and how some social movements succeed in achieving their goals while others do not. This is true of research on strategic framing, as well, where researchers look to uncover general patterns (for example, by classifying the type of content of different frames—with diagnostic, prognostic, or

motivational framing—or by classifying the purposes that different frames serve—with frame bridging, frame extension, and
frame amplification) that explain why certain frames work while
others don't.[2]

Rather than looking to contribute to general explanations of how
social movements work, my goal in this project is to explore how
Oath Keepers engages in meaning making: what the group does to
make sense of the world around it, a world it perceives as so hostile.
Put more formally, this research project follows the logic of interpre-
tivism.[3] Instead of looking for consistent patterns that might indicate a causal relationship, this project aims to present a rich, detailed
investigation of a group that is a prominent actor in the antigovernment extremism space, a form of extremism too rarely studied.

In this appendix, I present the methods I used for this project.
I describe the sources of the data and how I collected and pro-
cessed that data. I elaborate briefly on the analytic methods I
employ. Finally, I present a brief summary of the data.

Data

Data for this project consist of textual, audio, and video material
posted by Oath Keepers online. The internet provides a means
for the group to spread its message to a wide public, recruiting new
members, portraying itself as mainstream or legitimate, and organizing on-the-ground activity. The group receives coverage in
mainstream media outlets from time to time.[4] It sees this coverage as collectivist propaganda meant to slander the group and
depict its members as racists and terrorists.

The internet allows Oath Keepers to present its own side of the
story. Unlike older forms of communication used by right-wing
extremists (like pamphlets, telephone hotlines, and video

cassettes), having a website means that even those with a casual interest in the group might easily come across an essay or video produced by Oath Keepers.[5] Oath Keepers is able to tell its own version of its involvement in the Bundy Ranch standoff or the Ferguson, Missouri, protests after Michael Brown's death. This is not to say that the internet levels the information playing field for Oath Keepers—the group still does not have as much control over its reputation as national media outlets. But the internet makes it possible for the group to present itself to a wider public than was previously possible.

The data used in this project is all publicly available: none of it requires membership in Oath Keepers or special permission to view. This project investigates the public story that the group tells about what it means to be an American. This story helps its supporters make sense of the threat they perceive, and the group may hope that it will justify Oath Keepers' vigorous dissent and possible use of violence.

Since this project focuses on the ways that Oath Keepers makes sense of the contemporary political situation facing America, my data consist exclusively of material posted by Oath Keepers or by Stewart Rhodes, the group's founder and president. While there is much more material featuring Oath Keepers or members of the group but disseminated by others (for example, some speeches given by Stewart Rhodes are only shared by social media accounts and websites not controlled by the group), this data-collection strategy allows me to focus on the material the group wants to share widely. This strategy assumes that the material shared on various platforms by accounts belonging to the group is material that the group most wants a large audience to see. Oath Keepers curates certain information for the public, selecting what it wants the public to see coming from the group, and in doing so shapes the public's perception of the group.[6]

Any project that studies ongoing activity threatens to never be finished. For this project, I examine material posted to the web on or before February 23, 2016. This date includes material produced during and immediately after the occupation of the Malheur National Wildlife Refuge in Harney County, Oregon. With this cutoff date, I miss the reaction of Oath Keepers to the shooting at the Pulse nightclub in Orlando, Florida, in June 2016, but I include the group's reaction to the shooting in San Bernardino, California, in December 2015. In any event, the group's reactions to terrorist attacks do not contribute to the themes that are the focus of this book.

Since forming in 2009, Oath Keepers has maintained an active presence on the internet. Initially, it utilized the Blogspot platform to host its content. Later, it created a free-standing website. This change is reflected in the bibliography, which indicates whether articles were posted to *"Oath Keepers* (blog)" or "OathKeepers .org." The group conducted a major renovation of this website in December 2014, just before my first round of collecting data from this site; more recent renovations mean that some of the pages present in my dataset are no longer on the group's website. Most do remain. Before starting the group, Stewart Rhodes also had a personal blog (http://stewart-rhodes.blogspot.com). His activity on this blog decreased dramatically after he started Oath Keepers. In total, his personal blog contains 113 posts, ranging from October 28, 2006, to November 6, 2012, with no posts appearing in 2010 or 2011. I collected data from Rhodes's blog on May 8, 2015. As of February 2020, the most recent post on this blog was dated November 6, 2012.

The Oath Keepers Blogspot site (http://oath-keepers.blogspot .com) contains 334 posts, posted between March 2, 2009, and April 6, 2015. There were no posts to the Blogspot site between November 2009 and April 2014, and there were no posts between

May and November 2014. The site was briefly used in December 2014 and January 2015 while the main Oath Keepers website
was being updated. I collected data from this blog on May 20, 2015.
As of February 2020, the most recent post on this blog is dated
April 6, 2015.

The primary Oath Keepers website (http://oathkeepers.org) first
came online shortly before July 13, 2009. Initially, I had planned
to create a local archive of the website on January 1, 2016, and I
had intended to use that date for my cutoff point for data collec-
tion. Given certain technical hurdles, I was unable to collect data
from the group's website until February 23, 2016.[7] (This happy acci-
dent meant that the group's discussion of the Malheur Refuge
occupation appeared in the original dataset created for this project.) The local archive I created on this date contains more than
9,000 pages; after filtering out duplicate pages, the archive contains more than 1,600 pages.[8]

The group has also been active on YouTube since March 2009.
For this project, I examined videos uploaded to three YouTube
channels. "OathKeepersOK" was the group's primary channel,
with 132 videos uploaded as of February 23, 2016, totaling 34 hours
and 35 minutes. Videos posted by "OathKeepersOK" range from
March 2009 to January 2016, with a gap from June 2015 to late
October 2015. Videos posted to/by "OathKeepersOK" are now
listed on YouTube as being posted by "Oath Keepers," and the bibliography reflects this change. Links to YouTube from the group's
website and blog point to this channel. The national group also
uses a channel called "Oath Keepers National," which contains
six videos totaling two hours and thirty minutes. All videos posted
by "Oath Keepers National" were posted between September 4,
2015, and October 23, 2015. The group also used a channel called
"Oath Keepers," which contains nine videos totaling twenty-five
minutes. All of the videos on this channel relate to the security

operation at the Sugar Pine Mine in Josephine County, Oregon, in late spring 2015, with each video uploaded between April 18 and May 3.

In total, this project examines approximately 2,000 webpages across the primary Oath Keepers website, the Oath Keepers blog, and Stewart Rhodes's personal blog, along with 147 videos totaling 37.5 hours.

Though it is all publicly available online, I archived all of the material used as data for this project, creating digital copies on my local computer that can be accessed without the internet. There is a growing recognition that qualitative researchers need to think carefully about long-term data preservation and access.[9] While there are legitimate reasons for qualitative researchers to avoid creating durable and accessible versions of their data (for example, when conducting sensitive interviews that, if made publicly available, could lead to harm for research participants), those concerns do not exist for this project: Oath Keepers has already made the decision to make this material publicly available.

Several reasons motivated my decision to create local copies for all data. First, it is possible that Oath Keepers could decide to take down individual pages of its website or individual YouTube videos—perhaps no longer devoting financial resources to keeping this information available online, or perhaps deciding that it no longer wants certain information to be available to the public. It is also possible that the group could face a cyber attack that closes off access to its web presence. In an otherwise excellent study, the historian Robert Churchill did not make durable and accessible versions of important internet-based data for his study of the militia movement, and some of this data is now inaccessible (notably, the website of J. J. Johnson, a black militia member from Ohio).[10] For this project, I have developed strategies to ensure the long-term durability and accessibility of all internet-based data, both to increase transparency for this study and to preserve data for future scholarship on Oath Keepers. This type of archive is permissible under fair use doctrine.[11]

I used two primary tools for collecting data for this project. For websites and blogs, I used wget (https://www.gnu.org/software /wget/). This tool allows users to download all items and information necessary for pages to display without an internet connection, which includes images, embedded video, and other non-textual items. This results in a fully functional local copy of each website, which can be browsed without an internet connection. This tool does not result in a perfect copy: for example, page layout looks different and some page dependencies (such as some pictures) are not included.

I collected videos hosted on YouTube using youtube-dl (https://rg3.github.io/youtube-dl/). I used this tool to download three files for each video: the video file, usually in the highest available resolution; a file containing the description of the video, which appears immediately below the video on YouTube; and a metadata file containing a wide range of information about the video, such as the name of the account that uploaded the video, the length of the video, the number of views at the time of downloading, and tags specified by the user who uploaded the video (such as "politics," "Oath Keepers," "2nd Amendment," etc.). YouTube generates automatic captions for many videos uploaded to the site, including many of the videos in my archive. These captions are included in the metadata file for each video. I do not use these automatic captions for my analysis, though, because they are often not very accurate even on videos with high-quality audio. Many of these videos do not have high-quality audio, leading to unreliable automatic captions.

Data Processing and Analysis

After creating local archives of the website and blogs, I used software to extract the text from each page.[12] This tool allowed me to set aside information like page headers, banners, and other items that appear on each page. For example, each page on the Oath Keepers website contains a sidebar with links to external sites and brief descriptions of important Oath Keepers documents and individuals (such as their "Declaration of Orders We Will Not Obey" and their board of directors). Using this tool, I ignored this text and only extracted the body of the content on each page. In addition, I excluded comments left on each page, most of which are written by visitors to the site. Social movement scholars have argued that both elites and nonelites participate in discourse that helps social movements make sense of their world; importantly, the results of framing analysis may differ dramatically depending on which group is the focus of analysis.[13] For this study, I focus on content produced or shared by Oath Keepers rather than content produced or shared by individual supporters (or opponents) of the group. After excluding repeated content and comments from readers, I am able to get a more accurate sense of the amount of textual data that I have. This process also allows me to use automated text analysis to get an overview of my data.

Video data poses a greater challenge for analysis. My analysis in this project focuses on text. For videos, that means analyzing what those who appear in the video say, setting aside characteristics of the audio (for example, voice pitch or speaking speed).[14] I mostly set aside images that appear in videos as well, though I include some particular images that serve an important function for Oath Keepers.

To facilitate analysis, I created transcriptions of each of the 136 videos collected for this project. Most videos (99, totaling nearly

29.5 hours) I transcribed by hand. Thirty-seven videos I transcribed with Trint (http://www.trint.com), an automated audio-to-text service, totaling just over eight hours of content. For each video automatically transcribed by Trint, I watched the video and corrected the transcript where necessary.

In total, the data used for this project (website pages, blog posts, and video transcripts) contain approximately 1.4 million words, or more than 2,500 single-spaced pages. Given this large amount of data, I used automatic text analysis to create an overview of the data. I created a list of more than 400 keywords that signify the presence of certain topics and actors; several keywords also identify types of documents (for example, testimonials and documents originally published on a different website).[15] I use this list of keywords to identify eight topics (American history, people, political issues, P/M movement, gear and tactics, political system, conspiracies, and miscellaneous) in the documents; many of these topics also contain subtopics (see figure A.1). Each document may contain more than one topic and subtopic.

Table A.1 shows a breakdown of how many documents mention each of the main seven topics (excluding the miscellaneous category). In this project, I am particularly interested in how Oath Keepers uses American national history to make sense of its political context and to gain mainstream support. Thus, table A.2 shows a breakdown of how many documents mention each of the subtopics in American history.

It is important to note that this method of automated text analysis does not reveal anything other than the number of documents that mention a certain topic. It does not say how much that document talks about a certain topic or how important that topic is for the document. It does not say anything about what the author says about a topic. For example, documents about civil rights might praise civil rights activists for their bravery in opposing violent

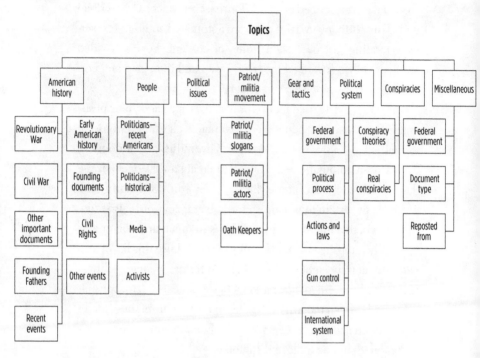

Figure A.1 Topics and subtopics in Oath Keepers documents

systemic racism, or they might attack civil rights activists for alleged connections to communists. In other words, this automated topic identification work provides insight into the distribution of important themes and topics across documents but it does not reveal anything about what those themes and topics mean. To understand *how* Oath Keepers talks about these topics, rather than just *whether* they talk about them, requires carefully reading each document.

As mentioned above, this project focuses on how Oath Keepers talks about American history to help its members understand

Table A.1

Topics	Number of documents
American history	777
Conspiracy theories	130
Gear and tactics	506
Patriot/militia movement	1073
Public figures (contemporary and historical)	582
Political ideas	737
Political system and policies	560

Table A.2

American history subtopics	Number of documents
Civil rights	15
Civil War	99
Early American history	10
Founding Fathers	158
Founding documents	558
Recent events	206
Revolutionary War	80
Other events	67
Other important documents	7

the threats they face and decide how to confront those threats; this same rhetoric may also convince the wider public that members of Oath Keepers aren't the bad actors they are sometimes made out to be. This analysis is a form of framing analysis, which investigates the rhetorical strategies that actors use to help themselves and others make sense of their identity, the issues they care about, and the proper way to get involved in those issues.

To do this, I analyzed the texts that form the data for this project using an inductive coding strategy. Rather than defining codes beforehand and looking for instances of those codes, I closely read each text and assigned codes based on what those texts say or do. Important codes include "2nd Amendment," "Founding Fathers," "nullification," "crisis," and "Waco." Some codes are short quotes from the text; others are summaries of what the text discusses or are analytical codes that summarize conclusions I draw from the text. Given the large amount of textual data involved in this project, I used ATLAS.ti, a computer-assisted qualitative data analysis program, to manage and assign these inductive codes to the texts as I read them. These codes helped me identify (and relocate) discussions of themes and events that were important for the argument presented in this book.

Ongoing Data Access

To ensure transparency and allow other researchers to access the data, I have placed the data in an online repository (https://github .com/sjacks26/OK-archive-2020). Along with the data, this repository contains descriptions of the data, Python code that I used to collect and process the data, and the list of keywords used for computational topic identification as it existed at that stage of the project.

As a practical matter, the easiest way for researchers to gain access to the primary data used in this project is to use the hyperlinks provided in the endnotes and the bibliography. If no hyperlink is provided or the provided hyperlink no longer works, the second strategy should be to use standard internet searches to see if the desired data still exists on the open web. If the data does not exist on the open web, the Wayback Machine (https://archive.org /web/) may provide access to a version of the data. The archived data for this project is primarily intended for one of two cases: if the desired data cannot be found in one of the previously described ways, or if researchers specifically want the version of data as I have captured it (for example, if a live page does not contain text as described in this book). Looking for data on the open web is likely to yield results much more quickly than looking for specific pages or videos in the data archive.

APPENDIX 2

Oath Keepers' "Declaration of Orders We Will Not Obey"

The time is now near at hand which must probably determine, whether Americans are to be, Freemen, or Slaves; whether they are to have any property they can call their own; whether their Houses, and Farms, are to be pillaged and destroyed, and they consigned to a State of Wretchedness from which no human efforts will probably deliver them. The fate of unborn Millions will now depend, under God, on the Courage and Conduct of this army.

Gen. George Washington, to his troops before the battle of Long Island

Such a time is near at hand again. The fate of unborn millions will now depend, under God, on the Courage and Conduct of this Army—and this Marine Corps, This Air Force, This Navy and the National Guard and police units of these sovereign states.

Oath Keepers is a non-partisan association of currently serving military, reserves, National Guard, peace officers, fire-fighters, and veterans who swore an oath to support and defend the Constitution against all enemies, foreign and domestic . . . and meant it. We won't "just follow orders."

Below is our declaration of orders we will NOT obey because we will consider them unconstitutional (and thus unlawful) and immoral violations of the natural rights of the people. Such orders would be acts of war against the American people by their own government, and thus acts of treason. We will not make war against our own people. We will not commit treason. We will defend the Republic.

Declaration of Orders We Will Not Obey

Recognizing that we each swore an oath to support and defend the Constitution against all enemies, foreign and domestic, and affirming that we are guardians of the Republic, of the principles in our Declaration of Independence, and of the rights of our people, we affirm and declare the following:

1. We will NOT obey any order to disarm the American people.

The attempt to disarm the people on April 19, 1775 was the spark of open conflict in the American Revolution. That vile attempt was an act of war, and the American people fought back in justified, righteous self-defense of their natural rights. Any such order today would also be an act of war against the American people, and thus an act of treason. We will not make war on our own people, and we will not commit treason by obeying any such treasonous order. Nor will we assist, or support any such attempt to disarm the people by other government entities, either state or federal.

In addition, we affirm that the purpose of the Second Amendment is to preserve the military power of the people so that they will, in the last resort, have effective final recourse to arms and to the God of Hosts in the face of tyranny. Accordingly, we oppose any and all further infringements on the right of the people to keep and bear arms. In particular we oppose a renewal of the misnamed "assault-weapons" ban or the enactment of H.R. 45 (which would register and track gun owners like convicted pedophiles).

2. We will NOT obey any order to conduct warrantless searches of the American people, their homes, vehicles, papers, or effects—such as warrantless house-to house searches for weapons or persons.

One of the causes of the American Revolution was the use of "writs of assistance," which were essentially warrantless searches because there was no requirement of a showing of probable cause to a judge, and the first fiery embers of American resistance were born in opposition to those infamous writs. The Founders considered all warrantless searches to be unreasonable and egregious. It was to prevent a repeat of such violations of the right of the people to be secure in their persons, houses, papers, and effects that the Fourth Amendment was written.

We expect that sweeping warrantless searches of homes and vehicles, under some pretext, will be the means used to attempt to disarm the people.

3. We will NOT obey any order to detain American citizens as "unlawful enemy combatants" or to subject them to trial by military tribunal.

One of the causes of the American Revolution was the denial of the right to jury trial, the use of admiralty courts (military tribunals) instead, and the application of the laws of war to the colonists. After that experience, and being well aware of the infamous Star Chamber in English history, the Founders ensured that the international laws of war would apply only to foreign enemies, not to the American people. Thus, the Article III Treason Clause establishes the only constitutional form of trial for an American, not serving in the military, who is accused of making war on his own nation. Such a trial for treason must be before a civilian jury, not a tribunal.

The international laws of war do not trump our Bill of Rights. We reject as illegitimate any such claimed power, as did the Supreme Court in Ex Parte Milligan (1865). Any attempt to apply the laws of war to American civilians, under any pretext, such as against domestic "militia" groups the government brands "domestic terrorists," is an act of war and an act of treason.

4. We will NOT obey orders to impose martial law or a "state of emergency" on a state, or to enter with force into a state, without the express consent and invitation of that state's legislature and governor.

One of the causes of the American Revolution was the attempt "to render the Military independent of and superior to the Civil Power" by disbanding the Massachusetts legislature and appointing General Gage as "military governor." The attempt to disarm the people of Massachusetts during that martial law sparked our Revolution. Accordingly, the power to impose martial law—the absolute rule over the people by a military officer with his will alone being law—is nowhere enumerated in our Constitution.

Further, it is the militia of a state and of the several states that the Constitution contemplates being used in any context, during any emergency within a state, not the standing army.

The imposition of martial law by the national government over a state and its people, treating them as an occupied enemy nation, is an act of war. Such an attempted suspension of the Constitution and Bill of Rights voids the compact with the states and with the people.

5. We will NOT obey orders to invade and subjugate any state that asserts its sovereignty and declares the national government to be in violation of the compact by which that state entered the Union.

In response to the obscene growth of federal power and to the absurdly totalitarian claimed powers of the Executive, upwards of 20 states are considering, have considered, or have passed courageous resolutions affirming states rights and sovereignty.

Those resolutions follow in the honored and revered footsteps of Jefferson and Madison in their Kentucky and Virginia Resolutions, and likewise seek to enforce the Constitution by affirming the very same principles of our Declaration, Constitution, and Bill of Rights that we Oath Keepers recognize and affirm.

Chief among those principles is that ours is a dual sovereignty system, with the people of each state retaining all powers not granted to the national government they created, and thus the people of each state reserved to themselves the right to judge when the national government they created has voided the compact between the states by asserting powers never granted.

Upon the declaration by a state that such a breach has occurred, we will not obey orders to force that state to submit to the national government.

6. We will NOT obey any order to blockade American cities, thus turning them into giant concentration camps.

One of the causes of the American Revolution was the blockade of Boston, and the occupying of that city by the British military, under martial law. Once hostilities began, the people of Boston were tricked into turning in their arms in exchange for safe passage, but were then forbidden to leave. That confinement of the residents of an entire city was an act of war.

Such tactics were repeated by the Nazis in the Warsaw Ghetto, and by the Imperial Japanese in Nanking, turning entire cities into death camps. Any such order to disarm and confine the people of an American city will be an act of war and thus an act of treason.

7. We will NOT obey any order to force American citizens into any form of detention camps under any pretext.

Mass, forced internment into concentration camps was a hallmark of every fascist and communist dictatorship in the 20th Century. Such internment was unfortunately even used against American citizens of Japanese descent during World War II. Whenever a government interns its own people, it treats them like an occupied enemy population. Oppressive governments often use the internment of women and children to break the will of the men fighting for their liberty—as was done to the Boers, to the Jewish resisters in the Warsaw Ghetto, and to the Chechens, for example.

Such a vile order to forcibly intern Americans without charges or trial would be an act of war against the American people, and thus an act of treason, regardless of the pretext used. We will not commit treason, nor will we facilitate or support it. "NOT on Our Watch!"

8. We will NOT obey orders to assist or support the use of any foreign troops on U.S. soil against the American people to "keep the peace" or to "maintain control" during any emergency, or under any other pretext. We will consider such use of foreign troops against our people to be an invasion and an act of war.

During the American Revolution, the British government enlisted the aid of Hessian mercenaries in an attempt to subjugate the rebellious American people. Throughout history, repressive regimes have enlisted the aid of foreign troops and mercenaries who have no bonds with the people.

Accordingly, as the militia of the several states are the only military force contemplated by the Constitution, in Article I, Section 8, for domestic keeping of the peace, and as the use of even our own standing army for such purposes is without such constitutional support, the use of foreign troops and mercenaries against the people is wildly unconstitutional, egregious, and an act of war.

We will oppose such troops as enemies of the people and we will treat all who request, invite, and aid those foreign troops as the traitors they are.

9. We will NOT obey any orders to confiscate the property of the American people, including food and other essential supplies, under any emergency pretext whatsoever.

One of the causes of the American Revolution was the seizure and forfeiture of American ships, goods, and supplies, along with the seizure of American timber for the Royal Navy, all in violation of the people's natural right to their property and to the fruits of their labor. The final spark of the Revolution was the attempt by the government to seize powder and cannon stores at Concord.

Deprivation of food has long been a weapon of war and oppression, with millions intentionally starved to death by fascist and communist governments in the 20th Century alone.

Accordingly, we will not obey or facilitate orders to confiscate food and other essential supplies from the people, and we will consider all those who issue or carry out such orders to be the enemies of the people.

10. We will NOT obey any orders which infringe on the right of the people to free speech, to peaceably assemble, and to petition their government for a redress of grievances.

There would have been no American Revolution without fiery speakers and writers such as James Otis, Patrick Henry, Thomas Paine, and Sam Adams "setting brushfires of freedom in the minds of men."

Notes

Introduction

1. This book is a case study of Oath Keepers, a right-wing antigovernment extremist group in the patriot/militia movement in the United States. As will become clear, the group is the unit of study, rather than prominent individuals or the rank-and-file membership. That leads to a strange grammatical situation. "Oath Keepers" sounds like a plural noun, which may lead readers to expect plural verbs. But as the group is the unified unit of study for this project, I deliberately use "Oath Keepers" as a singular noun, and I accompany it with singular verbs. Unless otherwise indicated, "Oath Keepers" refers to the group, not to multiple members of the group.

   To reduce the confusion that this may cause, I frequently refer to Oath Keepers as "the group," which seems a better match for the singular verbs that follow it.

2. Oath Keepers, "Hundreds of Volunteers Needed at the Sugar Pine Mine Security Operation in Oregon," OathKeepers.org, May 1, 2015, https://www.oathkeepers.org/hundreds-of-volunteers-needed-at-the-sugar-pine-mine-security-operation-in-oregon/.

3. Tay Wiles, "Sugar Pine Mine, the Other Standoff," *High Country News*, February 2, 2016, http://www.hcn.org/issues/48.2/showdown-at-sugar-pine-mine; Oath Keepers, "Stewart Rhodes and Oath Keepers of Josephine County, Oregon—Sugar Pine Mine," 2015, YouTube video, https://www.youtube.com/watch?v=XYmVure11FA.

4. James Pogue, "The Oath Keepers Are Ready for War with the Federal Government," *Vice*, September 14, 2015, http://www.vice.com/read/miner-threat-0000747-v22n9.

5. Pogue, "The Oath Keepers Are Ready for War."

6. Pogue, "The Oath Keepers Are Ready for War."

7. Wiles, "Sugar Pine Mine, the Other Standoff."

8. Pogue, "The Oath Keepers Are Ready for War."

9. Some scholars would refer to this as discourse analysis. I choose not to use that term because it means different things to different scholarly communities.

10. David A. Snow et al., "Frame Alignment Processes, Micromobilization, and Movement Participation," *American Sociological Review* 51, no. 4 (1986): 464–81; David A. Snow and Robert D. Benford, "Ideology, Frame Resonance, and Participant Mobilization," in *From Structure to Action: Comparing Social Movement Research Across Cultures*, ed. Bert Klandermans, Hanspeter Kriesi, and Sidney G. Tarrow (Greenwich: JAI, 1988), 197–217; Robert D. Benford and David A. Snow, "Framing Processes and Social Movements: An Overview and Assessment," *Annual Review of Sociology* 26 (January 2000): 611–39, https://doi.org/10.2307/223459; David A. Snow, Rens Vliegenthart, and Pauline Ketelaars, "The Framing Perspective on Social Movements: Its Conceptual Roots and Architecture," in *The Wiley Blackwell Companion to Social Movements*, 2nd ed., ed. David A. Snow et al. (Hoboken, NJ: Wiley, 2019), 393.

11. Snow and Benford, "Ideology, Frame Resonance, and Participant Mobilization"; Snow et al., "Frame Alignment Processes, Micromobilization, and Movement Participation."

12. Jennifer Williams, "The Oath Keepers, the Far-Right Group Answering Trump's Call to Watch the Polls, Explained," *Vox*, November 7, 2016, http://www.vox.com/policy-and-politics/2016/11/7/13489640/oath-keepers-donald-trump-voter-fraud-intimidation-rigged.

1. Understanding Right-Wing Extremism in the United States

Portions of this chapter are derived in part from two other articles: Sam Jackson, "Non-Normative Political Extremism: Reclaiming a Concept's Analytical Utility," *Terrorism and Political Violence* 31, no. 2 (2019): 244–59, https://doi.org/10.1080/09546553.2016.1212599; Sam Jackson, "A Schema of Right-Wing Extremism in the United States," Policy Briefs, International Centre for Counter-Terrorism—The Hague (November 4, 2019), https://icct.nl/publication/a-schema-of-right-wing-extremism-in-the-united-states/.

1. "Right wing" and "conservative" can be thought of synonymous so long as "right wing" does not exclusively mean the far right (or radical right or right-wing extremism) but also includes mainstream right-leaning politics. For relevant discussions, see, among many others, Martin Durham, *The*

Christian Right, the Far Right, and the Boundaries of American Conserva-
tism (New York: Manchester University Press, 2000), chap. 1; Corey
Robin, *The Reactionary Mind: Conservatism from Edmund Burke to Sarah*
Palin (New York: Oxford University Press, 2011), chap. 1; Tore Bjørgo,
"Introduction: Terror from the Extreme Right," *Terrorism and Political*
Violence 7, no. 1 (March 1995): 1–16, https://doi.org/10.1080/0954655
9508427283; David H. Bennett, *The Party of Fear: From Nativist Move-*
ments to the New Right in American History, 2nd ed. (New York: Vintage,
1995), 3; Kathleen M. Blee and Kimberly A. Creasap, "Conservative and
Right-Wing Movements," *Annual Review of Sociology* 36, no. 1 (2010):
269–86, https://doi.org/10.1146/annurev.soc.012809.102602; George Hawley,
Making Sense of the Alt-Right (New York: Columbia University Press,
2017), chap. 1; Rory McVeigh, "What's New About the Tea Party Movement?," in *Understanding the Tea Party Movement*, ed. Nella Van Dyke and
David S. Meyer (Burlington, VT: Ashgate, 2014), 15–34.

2. George Washington, "Farewell Address," September 19, 1796, http://www
   .presidency.ucsb.edu/ws/index.php?pid=65539.

3. Uwe Backes, "Meaning and Forms of Political Extremism in Past and Present," *Středo Evropské Politické Studie* (2007): 244.

4. Barry Goldwater, "1964 Republican Party Nomination Acceptance
   Speech," https://www.washingtonpost.com/wp-srv/politics/daily/may98
   /goldwaterspeech.htm.

5. Albert Breton et al., eds., *Political Extremism and Rationality* (New York:
   Cambridge University Press, 2002); Ronald Wintrobe, *Rational Extremism:*
   The Political Economy of Radicalism (New York: Cambridge University
   Press, 2006); Manus I. Midlarsky, *Origins of Political Extremism: Mass Vio-*
   lence in the Twentieth Century and Beyond (New York: Cambridge Uni-
   versity Press, 2011).

6. Backes, "Meaning and Forms of Political Extremism"; Cas Mudde, "Introduction: Political Extremism—Concepts, Theories, and Democratic
   Responses," in *Political Extremism*, ed. Cas Mudde (Los Angeles: SAGE,
   2014), 1:xxiii–xxix.

7. Jackson, "Non-Normative Political Extremism," 245; Jackson, "A Schema
   of Right-Wing Extremism," 4.

8. Richard Mack, who will be discussed briefly later in this book, is a former
   Arizona county sheriff who advocates for the idea that county sheriffs are
   the ultimate law enforcement authority within their jurisdictions, with the
   right and responsibility to prevent any other law enforcement agents
   (including federal authorities like the FBI) from undertaking law enforcement activity that the sheriff considers to be beyond those agents' authority. Mack, who is the main figure associated with the Constitutional

Sheriffs and Peace Officers Association, has argued that true "constitutional sheriffs" would have refused to arrest Rosa Parks for sitting in the whites-only section of the bus in Montgomery, Alabama; Mack says that a true constitutional sheriff would have driven Parks home instead of to jail and would have made sure that Parks and her husband had armed protection. Similarly, Mike Vanderboegh long tried to draw connections between his antigovernment extremism and the Civil Rights Movement. Jackson, "Non-Normative Political Extremism," 251–52; Sam Jackson, "'Nullification Through Armed Civil Disobedience': A Case Study of Strategic Framing in the Patriot/Militia Movement," *Dynamics of Asymmetric Conflict* 12, no. 1 (2019): 90–109, https://doi.org/10.1080/17467586.2018.1563904.

9. J. M. Berger, *Extremism* (Cambridge, MA: MIT Press, 2018), 44. Berger's objection to my definition based on Nazis comes from personal correspondence. He provides more general critique of definitions of extremism that he argues misclassify Nazis in J. M. Berger, "TASM 2019: J.M. Berger Keynote," 2019, YouTube video, https://www.youtube.com/watch?v=VfYuJ R2z24U&feature=youtu.be&list=PLA9DF592615F3FCAD&t=756.

10. In Corey Robin's language, right-wing extremism is "reactionary." Robin uses that label for the right more broadly, not just for right-wing extremism. Robin, *The Reactionary Mind*.

11. Andrew R. Murphy, "Longing, Nostalgia, and Golden Age Politics: The American Jeremiad and the Power of the Past," *Perspectives on Politics* 7, no. 1 (2009): 125–41, https://doi.org/10.1017/S1537592709090148; Andrew R. Murphy, "Two American Jeremiads: Traditionalist and Progressive Stories of American Nationhood," *Politics and Religion* 1, no. 1 (2008): 85–112, https://doi.org/10.1017/S1755048308000059.

12. For examples of other definitions, see Blee and Creasap, "Conservative and Right-Wing Movements"; Durham, *The Christian Right*, xii–xiii.

13. Stephanie Russell-Kraft, "The Rise of Male Supremacist Groups," *New Republic*, April 4, 2018, https://newrepublic.com/article/147744/rise-male-supremacist-groups.

14. Helen Lewis, "To Learn About the Far Right, Start With the 'Manosphere,'" *The Atlantic*, August 7, 2019, https://www.theatlantic.com/international/archive/2019/08/anti-feminism-gateway-far-right/595642/; Anti-Defamation League, "When Women Are the Enemy: The Intersection of Misogyny and White Supremacy," Anti-Defamation League Center on Extremism, 2018, https://www.adl.org/resources/reports/when-women-are-the-enemy-the-intersection-of-misogyny-and-white-supremacy; Simon Purdue, "Toxic Masculinity and Lone Wolf Radicalization," *Centre for Analysis of the Radical Right* (blog), November 21, 2019,

https://www.radicalrightanalysis.com/2019/11/21/toxic-masculinity-and-lone -wolf-radicalization/; Ashley Mattheis, "Understanding Digital Hate Culture," *Centre for Analysis of the Radical Right* (blog), August 19, 2019, https:// www.radicalrightanalysis.com/2019/08/19/understanding-digital-hate -culture/.

15. Stephanie Lamy, personal correspondence.

16. Mark Juergensmeyer, *Terror in the Mind of God: The Global Rise of Religious Violence* (Berkeley: University of California Press, 2003), 19–31; Jessica Stern, *Terror in the Name of God: Why Religious Militants Kill*, 1st ed. (New York: Ecco, 2003), 147–71; David Neiwert, *Alt-America: The Rise of the Radical Right in the Age of Trump* (New York: Verso, 2017), 62–65; Robin Abcarian and Nicholas Riccardi, "Abortion Doctor George Tiller Is Killed; Suspect in Custody," *Los Angeles Times*, June 1, 2009, https://www.latimes .com/archives/la-xpm-2009-jun-01-na-tiller1-story.html.

17. Juergensmeyer, *Terror in the Mind of God*, 30–31; Neiwert, *Alt-America*, 64–65.

18. James Aho, *The Politics of Righteousness: Idaho Christian Patriotism* (Seattle: University of Washington Press, 1990); Michael Barkun, *Religion and the Racist Right: The Origins of the Christian Identity Movement*, rev. ed. (Chapel Hill: University of North Carolina Press, 1997); Kathleen M. Blee, *Inside Organized Racism: Women in the Hate Movement* (Berkeley: University of California Press, 2002); Martin Durham, *White Rage: The Extreme Right and American Politics* (New York: Routledge, 2007); Hawley, *Making Sense of the Alt-Right*; Leonard Zeskind, *Blood and Politics: The History of the White Nationalist Movement from the Margins to the Mainstream* (New York: Farrar Straus Giroux, 2009); Arie Perliger, "Identifying Three Trends in Far Right Violence in the United States," *CTC Sentinel* 5, no. 9 (September 2012): 5–7; Durham, *The Christian Right*, xii.

19. The "alt-right" has come to refer to a new racist movement that has endeavored to clean up the reputation of white supremacy in the United States. Most famously, self-described members of the alt-right movement gathered in Charlottesville, Virginia, on August 11 and 12, 2017, where they marched through the streets, chanted racist slogans, and brawled with counterdemonstrators. Hawley, *Making Sense of the Alt-Right*; Dara Lind, "Unite the Right, the Violent White Supremacist Rally in Charlottesville, Explained," *Vox*, August 12, 2017, https://www.vox.com/2017/8 /12/16138246/charlottesville-nazi-rally-right-uva; John Daniszewski, "Writing About the 'Alt-Right,'" *Definitive Source* (blog), Associated Press, November 28, 2016, https://blog.ap.org/behind-the-news/writing-about -the-alt-right.

20. Aho, *The Politics of Righteousness*; Barkun, *Religion and the Racist Right*; Blee, *Inside Organized Racism*; Durham, *White Rage*; Hawley, *Making Sense of the Alt-Right*; Zeskind, *Blood and Politics*; Perliger, "Identifying Three Trends in Far Right Violence."

21. Kathleen M. Blee and Elizabeth A. Yates, "The Place of Race in Conservative and Far-Right Movements," *Sociology of Race and Ethnicity* 1, no. 1 (2015): 131, https://doi.org/10.1177/2332649214555031.

22. Bennett, *The Party of Fear*, is the definitive work on nativism in the United States.

23. Bennett, *The Party of Fear*, 315–21; Jackson, "Non-Normative Political Extremism," 9–10; Bill Morlin, "ACT's Anti-Muslim Message Fertile Ground for Oath Keepers," Southern Poverty Law Center, June 12, 2017, https://www.splcenter.org/hatewatch/2017/06/12/act%E2%80%99s-anti-muslim-message-fertile-ground-oath-keepers; Harel Shapira, *Waiting for José: The Minutemen's Pursuit of America* (Princeton, NJ: Princeton University Press, 2013).

24. Southern Poverty Law Center, "Antigovernment Movement," n.d., https://www.splcenter.org/fighting-hate/extremist-files/ideology/antigovernment; Anti-Defamation League, "Defining Extremism: A Glossary of Anti-Government Extremist Terms, Movements and Philosophies," n.d., https://www.adl.org/education/resources/glossary-terms/defining-extremism-anti-government.

25. Antigovernment extremism comes in a range of perspectives, from those that anticipate that the government (perhaps the federal government, perhaps a state government) might one day descend into tyranny to those that view the government now as tyrannical to an extent that demands violent resistance. Michael Barkun, "Violence in the Name of Democracy: Justifications for Separatism on the Radical Right," *Terrorism and Political Violence* 12, no. 3–4 (2000): 193–208; Mark Pitcavage, "Camouflage and Conspiracy: The Militia Movement from Ruby Ridge to Y2K," *American Behavioral Scientist* 44, no. 6 (February 2001): 957–81, https://doi.org/10.1177/00027640121956610; Michael Barkun, "Purifying the Law: The Legal World of 'Christian Patriots,'" *Journal for the Study of Radicalism* 1, no. 1 (April 2007): 57–70; Michael Barkun, "Appropriated Martyrs: The Branch Davidians and the Radical Right," *Terrorism and Political Violence* 19, no. 1 (January 2007): 117–24, https://doi.org/10.1080/09546550601054956; D. J. Mulloy, *American Extremism: History, Politics, and the Militia Movement* (New York: Routledge, 2004); Jackson, "'Nullification Through Armed Civil Disobedience.'"

26. Matthew Sweeney, "What Is the Sovereign Citizen Movement, What Do They Believe, and How Are They Spreading?," Radicalisation Research,

June 19, 2018, https://www.radicalisationresearch.org/guides/sweeney-sovereign-citizen-movement/; J. M. Berger, "Without Prejudice: What Sovereign Citizens Believe," GW Program on Extremism (June 2016), https://extremism.gwu.edu/sites/extremism.gwu.edu/files/downloads/JMB%20Sovereign%20Citizens.pdf.

27. Anti-Defamation League, "The Sovereign Citizen Movement," 2016, https://www.adl.org/education/resources/reports/the-sovereign-citizen-movement; Barkun, "Purifying the Law"; Berger, "Without Prejudice."

28. Jessica Rivinius, "Sovereign Citizen Movement Perceived as Top Terrorist Threat," START, July 30, 2014, https://www.start.umd.edu/news/sovereign-citizen-movement-perceived-top-terrorist-threat; David Carter et al., "Understanding Law Enforcement Intelligence Processes," Report to the Office of University Programs, Science and Technology Directorate, U.S. Department of Homeland Security, START, 2014, 7, https://www.start.umd.edu/pubs/START_UnderstandingLawEnforcementIntelligenceProcesses_July2014.pdf.

29. Nella Van Dyke and Sarah A. Soule, "Structural Social Change and the Mobilizing Effect of Threat: Explaining Levels of Patriot and Militia Organizing in the United States," *Social Problems* 49, no. 4 (2002): 497–520, https://doi.org/10.1525/sp.2002.49.4.497; J. M. Berger, "PATCON: The FBI's Secret War Against the 'Patriot' Movement, and How Infiltration Tactics Relate to Radicalizing Influences," New America Foundation (May 2012); Steven M. Chermak, *Searching for a Demon: The Media Construction of the Militia Movement* (Boston, MA: Northeastern University Press, 2002); Robert H. Churchill, *To Shake Their Guns in the Tyrant's Face: Libertarian Political Violence and the Origins of the Militia Movement* (Ann Arbor: University of Michigan Press, 2009); Department of Homeland Security, "Domestic Extremism Lexicon," March 26, 2009; Mulloy, *American Extremism*; Mark Potok, "The Year in Hate and Extremism," Southern Poverty Law Center, February 15, 2017, https://www.splcenter.org/fighting-hate/intelligence-report/2017/year-hate-and-extremism.

30. Sam Jackson, "'We Are Patriots:' Uses of National History in Legitimizing Extremism," *Europe Now*, October 2, 2018, https://www.europenowjournal.org/2018/10/01/we-are-patriots-uses-of-national-history-in-legitimizing-extremism/.

31. Berger, *Extremism*, 30–33.

32. For a longer discussion of the ideas in this paragraph, see the introduction of Fernando Bravo López, "Towards a Definition of Islamophobia: Approximations of the Early Twentieth Century," *Ethnic and Racial Studies* 34, no. 4 (April 2011): 556–73, https://doi.org/10.1080/01419870.2010.528440.

33. Roxana Hegeman, "Militia Member Sentenced to 25 Years in Kansas Bomb Plot," *US News & World Report*, January 25, 2019, https://www.usnews.com /news/us/articles/2019-01-25/3-militia-members-face-sentencing-in-kansas -bomb-plot.

34. On dehumanizing language, see, for example, Susan Benesch et al., "Dangerous Speech: A Practical Guide," Dangerous Speech Project, December 31, 2018, https://dangerousspeech.org/guide/.

35. Mitch Smith, "Kansas Trio Convicted in Plot to Bomb Somali Immigrants," *New York Times*, September 10, 2018, https://www.nytimes.com /2018/04/18/us/kansas-militia-somali-trial-verdict.html.

36. Sam Jackson, "Don't Assume the Militias at the Charlottesville Rally Were White Supremacists. This Is What They Believe Now," *Washington Post*, September 8, 2017, https://www.washingtonpost.com/news /monkey-cage/wp/2017/09/08/remember-those-militias-at-the-charlottesville -unite-the-right-rally-heres-what-they-believe/; Mulloy, *American Extremism*, 6–9.

37. Eric V. Larson and John E. Peters, "Appendix D: Overview of the Posse Comitatus Act," in *Preparing the U.S. Army for Homeland Security: Concepts, Issues, and Options* (Santa Monica, CA: Rand, 2001), https://www .rand.org/pubs/monograph_reports/MR1251.html.

38. Barkun, "Purifying the Law," 62; Barkun, "Violence in the Name of Democracy." I discuss this set of ideas that Barkun calls "radical localism" in Jackson, "Non-Normative Political Extremism," 251–52.

39. Barkun, *Religion and the Racist Right*, 69, 207; Churchill, *To Shake Their Guns in the Tyrant's Face*, 178–80.

40. Barkun, *Religion and the Racist Right*, 66–68, 180–82; Barkun, "Purifying the Law," 65.

41. Bennett, *The Party of Fear*, 353–54.

42. Pitcavage, "Camouflage and Conspiracy," 959–60; Robert L. Tsai, "The Troubling Sheriffs' Movement That Joe Arpaio Supports," *Politico*, September 1, 2017, http://politi.co/2er3E3M; Churchill, *To Shake Their Guns in the Tyrant's Face*, 178–80.

43. CSPOA, "About," Constitutional Sheriffs and Peace Officers Association, accessed July 28, 2015, http://cspoa.org/about/; CSPOA, "Our Leadership," Constitutional Sheriffs and Peace Officers Association, accessed November 22, 2017, http://cspoa.org/about/our-leadership/.

44. Capitalization in original. CSPOA, "The Sheriff," Constitutional Sheriffs and Peace Officers Association, accessed July 28, 2015, http://cspoa.org /about/sheriff-mack/.

45. Tom Jackman, "National Sheriffs' Group, Opposed to Federal Laws on Guns and Taxes, Calls for Defiance," *Washington Post*, April 28, 2016,

https://www.washingtonpost.com/news/true-crime/wp/2016/04/28/national-group-of-sheriffs-opposed-to-federal-government-overreach-gains-size-momentum/; Oath Keepers National, "Oath Keepers Offer of Protection for Embattled Clerk Kim Davis," 2015, YouTube video, https://www.youtube.com/watch?v=x2Z5e13hZzw; Ashley Powers, "The Renegade Sheriffs," New Yorker, April 23, 2018, https://www.newyorker.com/magazine/2018/04/30/the-renegade-sheriffs; Tsai, "The Troubling Sheriffs' Movement."

46. The arcane legal theorizing of Posse Comitatus also has a direct descendant in the sovereign citizen movement, as described earlier in this chapter. Jackson, "Non-Normative Political Extremism"; Michael Barkun, A Culture of Conspiracy: Apocalyptic Visions in Contemporary America, 2nd ed. (Berkeley: University of California Press, 2013), 196–98; Berger, "Without Prejudice"; Sweeney, "What Is the Sovereign Citizen Movement?"

47. Casey Michel, "How Militias Became the Private Police for White Supremacists," Politico, August 17, 2017, https://www.politico.com/magazine/story/2017/08/17/white-supremacists-militias-private-police-215498; Jackson, "Don't Assume the Militias at the Charlottesville Rally Were White Supremacists."

48. Jackson, "Don't Assume the Militias at the Charlottesville Rally Were White Supremacists"; Jennifer Williams, "The Oath Keepers, the Far-Right Group Answering Trump's Call to Watch the Polls, Explained," Vox, November 7, 2016, http://www.vox.com/policy-and-politics/2016/11/7/13489640/oath-keepers-donald-trump-voter-fraud-intimidation-rigged; Shapira, Waiting for José.

49. Oath Keepers, "Oath Keepers Call to Action: Border Operation," OathKeepers.org, December 4, 2018, https://oathkeepers.org/2018/12/oath-keepers-call-to-action-border-operation/.

50. Anti-Defamation League, "ACT for America," n.d., https://www.adl.org/resources/profiles/act-for-america.

51. Anti-Defamation League, "ACT for America"; Morlin, "ACT's Anti-Muslim Message Fertile Ground for Oath Keepers."

52. The Three Percenters movement is the other major faction with the patriot/militia movement. This movement (also called III% and Threepers) was founded by Mike Vanderboegh, whose blog contains a wealth of information about ideas prevalent within the movement. Though many groups have incorporated some version of "III%" in their names, there is no official Three Percenter organization. For more on the Three Percenters movement, see Jackson, "'Nullification Through Armed Civil Disobedience,'" 97–98; Southern Poverty Law Center, "Michael Brian Vanderboegh," n.d.,

https://www.splcenter.org/fighting-hate/extremist-files/individual/michael-brian-vanderboegh-o.

53. Amy B. Cooter, "Americanness, Masculinity, and Whiteness: How Michigan Militia Men Navigate Evolving Social Norms," PhD diss., University of Michigan, 2013, 47, https://deepblue.lib.umich.edu/bitstream/handle/2027.42/98077/cooterab_1.pdf; Churchill, *To Shake Their Guns in the Tyrant's Face*, 3; Mulloy, *American Extremism*, x.

54. Mulloy, *American Extremism*, 2.

55. Churchill, *To Shake Their Guns in the Tyrant's Face*, 7, 188.

56. Cooter, "Americanness, Masculinity, and Whiteness," 71–72.

57. Mulloy, *American Extremism*, 4.

58. Mulloy, *American Extremism*, 5.

59. Mulloy, *American Extremism*, 1.

60. J. M. Berger, "The Hate List," *Foreign Policy*, March 12, 2013, http://www.foreignpolicy.com/articles/2013/03/12/the_hate_list.

61. McVeigh is another illustration of the overlap between different categories of right-wing extremism. He responded to events that were important for the patriot/militia movement, and in the wake of the attack, much attention was given to militia groups that were believed to be affiliated with McVeigh in some way. McVeigh was more closely affiliated with racist right-wing extremism: he had speculated ties to Christian Identity groups, and *The Turner Diaries*, a 1978 novel written by William Pierce—described as "white nationalism's deadly Bible"—served as inspiration for his attack on the Murrah Building. Barkun, *Religion and the Racist Right*, 255–90; J. M. Berger, "The Turner Legacy: The Storied Origins and Enduring Impact of White Nationalism's Deadly Bible," International Centre for Counter-Terrorism—The Hague (2016), https://icct.nl/publication/the-turner-legacy-the-storied-origins-and-enduring-impact-of-white-nationalisms-deadly-bible/.

62. Stuart A. Wright, *Patriots, Politics, and the Oklahoma City Bombing*, Cambridge Studies in Contentious Politics (New York: Cambridge University Press, 2007), 164.

63. See the discussion in Mulloy, *American Extremism*, 4–5; Pitcavage, "Camouflage and Conspiracy."

64. Pitcavage, "Camouflage and Conspiracy."

65. Michael Vanderboegh, "What Is a 'Three Percenter'?," *Sipsey Street Irregulars* (blog), February 17, 2009, http://sipseystreetirregulars.blogspot.com/2009/02/what-is-three-percenter.html; Michael Vanderboegh, "A Brief Three Percent Catechism—a Discipline Not for the Faint-Hearted," *Sipsey Street Irregulars* (blog), June 29, 2014, http://sipseystreetirregulars.blogspot.com/2014/06/a-brief-three-percent-catechism.html.

66. Southern Poverty Law Center, "The Second Wave: Return of the Militias,"
    August 2009, https://www.splcenter.org/20090731/second-wave-return
    -militias. Cooter, "Americanness, Masculinity, and Whiteness," 54–59,
    describes important differences between militia groups of the 1990s and
    those that emerged starting in 2008, including dramatically smaller num-
    bers and less hierarchical structure.

67. Sam Jackson, "Conspiracy Theories in the Patriot/Militia Movement," GW
    Program on Extremism (May 2017), https://cchs.gwu.edu/sites/cchs.gwu
    .edu/files/downloads/Jackson%2C%20Conspiracy%20Theories%20Final
    .pdf; Barkun, A *Culture of Conspiracy*.

68. For example, see Casey Michel, "Opinion: How the Russians Pretended
    to Be Texans—and Texans Believed Them," *Washington Post*, Octo-
    ber 17, 2017, https://www.washingtonpost.com/news/democracy-post/wp
    /2017/10/17/how-the-russians-pretended-to-be-texans-and-texans-believed
    -them/; Casey Michel, "Former CIA Director Says Russian Bots Ampli-
    fied Jade Helm Conspiracies," *ThinkProgress* (blog), May 3, 2018, https://
    thinkprogress.org/russian-bots-amplified-jade-helm-conspiracies
    -6caa41073c08/.

69. Williams, "The Oath Keepers."

2. Introducing Oath Keepers

1. Oath Keepers, "Welcome to Oath Keepers," *Oath Keepers* (blog), March 2,
   2009, http://oath-keepers.blogspot.com/2009/03/welcome-to-oath-keepers
   _02.html.

2. Oath Keepers, "Welcome to Oath Keepers."

3. It is not clear how often state chapters lack local leadership or exist only on
   paper. Oath Keepers, "Board of Directors," OathKeepers.org, https://www
   .oathkeepers.org/board-of-directors/, accessed November 22, 2017; Oath
   Keepers, "Find a Chapter Near You," OathKeepers.org, https://www
   .oathkeepers.org/find-a-chapter-near-you/, accessed December 8, 2017. In
   the past, the group has provided information about state chapter leadership (for example, the name of the president of some state chapters); as of
   April 2019, the only information provided about chapters is a generic state
   email address and links to state chapter Facebook pages and websites, if
   any exist. Oath Keepers, "State Chapters," OathKeepers.org, July 15, 2018,
   https://oathkeepers.org/state-chapters/.

4. Oath Keepers, "Oath Keepers Muster on Lexington Green 4/19/2009 3 of
   10," 2009, YouTube video, https://www.youtube.com/watch?v=NED1UJ
   vXSRQ.

5. Oath Keepers, "Bylaws of Oath Keepers," OathKeepers.org, https://www
.oathkeepers.org/bylaws/.

6. Oath Keepers, "Board of Directors."

7. IN THE MATTER OF: ELMER S. RHODES, An Attorney at Law,
Respondent, No. PR 14-0698 (Montana Supreme Court December 8,
2015).

8. Ryan Lenz, "Montana Moves to Strip Oath Keepers' Founder of License
to Practice Law," Southern Poverty Law Center, November 4, 2015, https://
www.splcenter.org/hatewatch/2015/11/04/montana-moves-strip-oath
-keepers%E2%80%99-founder-license-practice-law.

9. Jesse Bogan, "Police Shut Down Mysterious 'Oath Keepers' Guarding
Rooftops in Downtown Ferguson," St. Louis Post-Dispatch, November 30,
2014, http://www.stltoday.com/news/local/crime-and-courts/police-shut
-down-mysterious-oath-keepers-guarding-rooftops-in-downtown/article
_f90b6edd-acf8-52e3-a020-3a78db286194.html; Anti-Defamation League,
"The Oath Keepers: Anti-Government Extremists Recruiting Military and
Police," September 16, 2015, http://www.adl.org/combating-hate/domestic
-extremism-terrorism/c/the-oath-keepers.html.

10. Oath Keepers, "Bylaws of Oath Keepers."

11. Oath Keepers, "Oath Keepers Update and SITREP," Oath Keepers (blog),
March 11, 2009, http://oath-keepers.blogspot.com/2009/03/oath-keepers
-update.html.

12. Oath Keepers, "About," OathKeepers.org, https://www.oathkeepers.org
/about/.

13. Alan Feuer, "The Oath Keeper Who Wants to Arm Black Lives Matter,"
Rolling Stone, January 3, 2016, http://www.rollingstone.com/politics/news
/the-oath-keeper-who-wants-to-arm-black-lives-matter-20160103;   Oath
Keepers, "4-16-09 Oath Keepers Stewart Rhodes on Alex Jones 1 of 2," 2009,
YouTube video, https://www.youtube.com/watch?v=PdiXbSV21mk.

14. Oath Keepers, "Principles of Our Republic Oath Keepers Are Sworn to
Defend," Oath Keepers (blog), March 5, 2009, http://oath-keepers.blogspot
.com/2009/03/principles-of-our-republic-oath-keepers.html.

15. Oath Keepers, "Stewart Rhodes on the 'Baldy & the Blonde Radio Show'
Discussing Senate Bill 1867: Audio," 2011, YouTube video, https://www
.youtube.com/watch?v=4IQnObVjLOo.

16. Oath Keepers, "Stewart Rhodes Interview—Senate Detention Bill Is Pure
Treason—Declares War on American People," 2011, YouTube video, https://
www.youtube.com/watch?v=stFsg-LQGlM.

17. Oath Keepers, "OK4TROOPS Constitutional Care Package Drive Promo
Video," 2009, YouTube video, https://www.youtube.com/watch?v=Spq1
N8ELHj8.

18. The organization says this in many places, including Oath Keepers, "About."

19. Oath Keepers, "4-16-09 Oath Keepers Stewart Rhodes on Alex Jones 1 of 2."

20. Oath Keepers, "Oath Keepers Muster on Lexington Green 4/19/2009 2 of 10," 2009, YouTube video, https://www.youtube.com/watch?v=osP45wNR D1w&list=PL5AE72FAE3DE00667&index=2; Catherine Thompson, "Oath Keepers Founder: Traitor McCain Should Be 'Hung by the Neck Until Dead,'" *Talking Points Memo* (blog), May 13, 2015, http:// talkingpointsmemo.com/livewire/stewart-rhodes-hang-john-mccain.

21. George Hawley, *Making Sense of the Alt-Right* (New York: Columbia University Press, 2017).

22. Oath Keepers, "Bylaws of Oath Keepers," sec. 8.02(b).

23. Brian Heffernan, "In Ferguson, Oath Keepers Draw Both Suspicion and Gratitude," *Al Jazeera America*, December 14, 2014, http://america.aljazeera .com/articles/2014/12/14/oath-keepers-fergusonprotests.html.

24. Casey Michel, "How Militias Became the Private Police for White Supremacists," *Politico*, August 17, 2017, https://www.politico.com/magazine/story /2017/08/17/white-supremacists-militias-private-police-215498.

25. Sam Jackson, "Don't Assume the Militias at the Charlottesville Rally Were White Supremacists. This Is What They Believe Now," *Washington Post*, September 8, 2017, https://www.washingtonpost.com/news/monkey-cage /wp/2017/09/08/remember-those-militias-at-the-charlottesville-unite-the -right-rally-heres-what-they-believe/; Amy B. Cooter, "Americanness, Masculinity, and Whiteness: How Michigan Militia Men Navigate Evolving Social Norms," PhD diss., University of Michigan, 2013, https://deepblue .lib.umich.edu/bitstream/handle/2027.42/98077/cooterab_1.pdf.

26. Oath Keepers, "True Grit—An Interview with Tim 'Nailer' Foley of AZBR," 2015, YouTube video, https://www.youtube.com/watch?v=3pobe4ZPLzY; Oath Keepers, "Oath Keepers Call to Action," December 4, 2018; Oath Keepers, "Urge President Trump to Deploy U.S. Military to Secure ENTIRE Border and Build the Wall!," OathKeepers.org, January 8, 2019, https://oathkeepers.org/2019/01/urge-president-trump-to-deploy-u-s -military-to-secure-entire-border-and-build-the-wall/; Oath Keepers, "Critical Updates! Call to Action: March 2—Human Wall of Patriots on Border to Support Trump's Emergency Declaration," OathKeepers.org, February 20, 2019, https://oathkeepers.org/2019/02/call-to-action-march-2 -human-wall-of-patriots-on-border-to-support-trumps-emergency -declaration/.

27. Oath Keepers, "Border Rancher Warns of Cartel Border Takeover on U.S. Soil," 2014, YouTube video, https://www.youtube.com/watch?v=eE_Ix6O

EaMI; Oath Keepers, "Border Rancher Overrun by Men with Gang Tattoos, Not 'Children,'" 2014, YouTube video, https://www.youtube.com/watch?v=sxnwYg7dMZI.

28. Jennifer Williams, "The Oath Keepers, the Far-Right Group Answering Trump's Call to Watch the Polls, Explained," *Vox*, November 7, 2016, http://www.vox.com/policy-and-politics/2016/11/7/13489640/oath-keepers-donald-trump-voter-fraud-intimidation-rigged; Oath Keepers, "Oath Keepers Pledges to Fight ISIS in U.S.," OathKeepers.org, June 13, 2016, https://www.oathkeepers.org/oath-keepers-pledges-to-fight-isis/. J. M. Berger argues that Matt Bracken has a complicated relationship with issues of race and bigotry, writing a series of novels that feature protagonists who are people of color but also featuring plot points that suggest that Bracken perceives large-scale cultural conflict between different racial and ethnic groups. J. M. Berger, "The Patriot Movement's New Bestseller Tests Their Anti-Racism," *Daily Beast*, June 8, 2012, http://www.thedailybeast.com/articles/2012/06/08/the-patriot-movement-s-new-bestseller-tests-their-anti-racism.html.

29. Bill Morlin, "ACT's Anti-Muslim Message Fertile Ground for Oath Keepers," Southern Poverty Law Center, June 12, 2017, https://www.splcenter.org/hatewatch/2017/06/12/act%E2%80%99s-anti-muslim-message-fertile-ground-oath-keepers.

30. Michael Barkun, *A Culture of Conspiracy: Apocalyptic Visions in Contemporary America*, 2nd ed. (Berkeley: University of California Press, 2013); David H. Bennett, *The Party of Fear: From Nativist Movements to the New Right in American History*, 2nd ed. (New York: Vintage, 1995); James Aho, *Far-Right Fantasy: A Sociology of American Religion and Politics* (New York: Routledge, 2016).

31. For example, Oath Keepers, "A Snowball Named Reuters," OathKeepers.org, August 12, 2015, https://www.oathkeepers.org/a-snowball-named-reuters/; Oath Keepers, "A Century of American Figurehead Presidents Marching to the Beat of Wall Street and the New World Order," OathKeepers.org, February 23, 2015, https://www.oathkeepers.org/a-century-of-american-figurehead-presidents-marching-to-the-beat-of-wall-street-and-the-new-world-order/.

32. Anti-Defamation League, "Jewish 'Control' of the Federal Reserve: A Classic Anti-Semitic Myth," Anti-Defamation League, https://www.adl.org/education/resources/backgrounders/jewish-control-of-the-federal-reserve-a-classic-anti-semitic-myth.

33. Sam Jackson, "Conspiracy Theories in the Patriot/Militia Movement," GW Program on Extremism (May 2017), https://cchs.gwu.edu/sites/cchs.gwu

.edu/files/downloads/Jackson%2C%20Conspiracy%20Theories%20Final
.pdf.

34. Oath Keepers, "Stewart Rhodes on the 'Baldy & the Blonde Radio Show' Discussing Senate Bill 1867."

35. Oath Keepers, "Declaration of Orders We Will Not Obey," OathKeepers .org, https://www.oathkeepers.org/declaration-of-orders-we-will-not-obey/.

36. Oath Keepers, "U.S.-EU Statement Calls for Enforcement of UN Arms Treaty," OathKeepers.org, March 30, 2014, https://www.oathkeepers.org/u -s-eu-statement-calls-for-enforcement-of-un-arms-treaty/.

37. Jackson, "Conspiracy Theories in the Patriot/Militia Movement"; Oath Keepers, "Wilderness Corridors: Agenda 21 Under a New Name," Oath-Keepers.org, July 7, 2015, https://www.oathkeepers.org/wilderness-corridors -agenda-21-under-a-new-name/; Oath Keepers, "Agenda 21 Primer," OathKeepers.org, January 14, 2016, https://www.oathkeepers.org/agenda-21 -for-dummies/.

38. Jackson, "Conspiracy Theories in the Patriot/Militia Movement."

3. An Operational History of Oath Keepers

1. Oath Keepers, "Oath Keepers Muster on Lexington Green 4/19/2009 4 of 10," 2009, YouTube video, https://www.youtube.com/watch?v=t7sCHPU7 30w&list=PL5AE72FAE3DE00667&index=4.

2. Oath Keepers, "Oath Keepers Muster on Lexington Green 4/19/2009 7 of 10," 2009, YouTube video, https://www.youtube.com/watch?v=Fcsousr6BR0.

3. Ilya Somin, "Federalism, the Constitution, and Sanctuary Cities," *Washington Post*, November 26, 2016, https://www.washingtonpost.com/news /volokh-conspiracy/wp/2016/11/26/federalism-the-constitution-and -sanctuary-cities/; Printz v. United States, https://www.oyez.org/cases/1996 /95-1478; Steven D. Schwinn, "It's Time to Abandon Anti-Commandeering (but Don't Count on This Supreme Court to Do It)," *SCOTUSblog*, August 17, 2017, https://www.scotusblog.com/2017/08/symposium-time -abandon-anti-commandeering-dont-count-supreme-court/.

4. "National Instant Criminal Background Check System (NICS)," Federal Bureau of Investigation, https://www.fbi.gov/services/cjis/nics; Oath Keepers, "Oath Keepers Muster on Lexington Green 4/19/2009 7 of 10."

5. Ernest Guy Cunningham, "The 29 Palms Survey," https://www .29palmssurvey.com/survey.html.

6. Oath Keepers, "Ernest Guy Cunningham Lexington Green April 19 2009," 2009, YouTube video, https://www.youtube.com/watch?v=5bSdtWfkiz4.

7. John F. McManus, "Twenty-Nine Palms Survey: What Really Motivated Its Author?," October 2, 1995, http://jpfo.org/articles-assd/29palms-mcmanus.htm.

8. Oath Keepers, "Knoxville Tea Party: How's This for an April 19 Warm Up?," *Oath Keepers* (blog), April 15, 2009, http://oath-keepers.blogspot.com/2009/04/knoxville-tea-party.html; Anti-Defamation League, "The Oath Keepers: Anti-Government Extremists Recruiting Military and Police," September 16, 2015, http://www.adl.org/combating-hate/domestic-extremism-terrorism/c/the-oath-keepers.html.

9. Anti-Defamation League, "The Oath Keepers: Anti-Government Extremists Recruiting Military and Police."

10. David Neiwert, "After Dyer's Rape Arrest, 'Oath Keepers' Disavow Any Association With Onetime Key Figure," *Crooks and Liars*, January 21, 2010, https://crooksandliars.com/david-neiwert/after-dyers-rape-arrest-oath-keepers.

11. Neiwert, "After Dyer's Rape Arrest"; Bill Morlin, "Ex-Marine and Fugitive Tied to Oath Keepers Arrested," Southern Poverty Law Center, August 25, 2011, https://www.splcenter.org/hatewatch/2011/08/25/ex-marine-and-fugitive-tied-oath-keepers-arrested.

12. Oath Keepers, "Oath Keepers Tucson Memorial Day to Honor Jose Guerena and Our War Dead," 2011, YouTube video, https://www.youtube.com/watch?v=dKrSQY_w34M; Oath Keepers, "Oath Keepers Rally to Honor Jose Guerena and Oppose SWAT Searches," 2011, YouTube video, https://www.youtube.com/watch?v=S6NOx5Cx8Ws.

13. Ellen Tumposky, "Arizona SWAT Team Defends Shooting Iraq Vet 60 Times," *ABC News*, May 20, 2011, https://abcnews.go.com/US/tucson-swat-team-defends-shooting-iraq-marine-veteran/story?id=13640112.

14. Oath Keepers, "Oath Keepers Tucson Memorial Day to Honor Jose Guerena and Our War Dead"; Oath Keepers, "Oath Keepers Rally to Honor Jose Guerena and Oppose SWAT Searches."

15. Ryan Lenz, "Oath Keepers Group Takes on 'Pivot Point' Arizona Town," Southern Poverty Law Center, August 29, 2011, https://www.splcenter.org/hatewatch/2011/08/29/oath-keepers-group-takes-%E2%80%98pivot-point%E2%80%99-arizona-town.

16. Lenz, "Oath Keepers Group Takes on 'Pivot Point' Arizona Town"; Jennifer Medina, "Arizona Town's Mayor at Center of Dispute," *New York Times*, July 15, 2011, https://www.nytimes.com/2011/07/16/us/16quartzsite.html.

17. Medina, "Arizona Town's Mayor at Center of Dispute."

18. Jillian Rayfield, "Oath Keeper–Backed AZ Mayor Says His Recall Election Was Rigged Thanks to 'Nazi' Police Force," *Talking Points Memo,*

September 2, 2011, https://talkingpointsmemo.com/muckraker/oath-keeper
-backed-az-mayor-says-his-recall-election-was-rigged-thanks-to-nazi
-police-force.

19. Medina, "Arizona Town's Mayor at Center of Dispute."
20. Oath Keepers, "Two Arizona State Legislators Will March with Oath Keep-
    ers and Speak in Quartzsite This Saturday, August 27, 2011!," August 24,
    2011, https://myemail.constantcontact.com/Two-Arizona-State-Legislators
    -Will-March-With-Oath-Keepers-and-Speak-In-Quartzsite-this-Saturday
    -August-27-2011-.html?soid=1102755758632&aid=FHVHi3BHDuw.
21. Oath Keepers, "Oath Keepers Quartzsite Muster 8–27–2011," 2011, YouTube
    video, https://www.youtube.com/watch?v=hpBCFgKRvdk&list=PLE6FEC
    C4A590A3771&index=48&t=0s.
22. Oath Keepers, "Oath Keepers Is Going 'Operational' by Forming Special
    'Civilization Preservation' Teams," Infowars, October 1, 2013, http://www
    .infowars.com/oath-keepers-is-going operational-by-forming-special
    -civilization-preservation-teams/.
23. Oath Keepers, "CPT—Community Preparedness Teams," OathKeepers
    .org, https://www.oathkeepers.org/cpt-community-preparedness-teams/.
24. Oath Keepers, Webinar, March 4, 2016, not available online, locally
    archived copy in possession of author.
25. Dylan Matthews, "All 20 Previous Government Shutdowns, Explained,"
    Vox, January 19, 2018, https://www.vox.com/policy-and-politics/2018/1/19
    /16905584/government-shutdown-history-clinton-obama-explained.
26. Kirsten Appleton and Veronica Stracqualursi, "Here's What Happened the
    Last Time the Government Shut Down," ABC News, November 18, 2014,
    https://abcnews.go.com/Politics/heres-happened-time-government-shut
    /story?id=26997023.
27. Jose Delreal, "Memorial Circus Outrages Visitors," Politico, October 5,
    2013, https://www.politico.com/story/2013/10/government-shutdown-wwii
    -memorial-97875.html.
28. "Honor Flight Network," https://www.honorflight.org/.
29. Oath Keepers, "Removed Barricades from WW2 Memorial and Oath
    Keepers Talk to Police," 2013, YouTube video, https://www.youtube.com
    /watch?v=ypTD8RIydmI; Oath Keepers, "Barricades Removed," 2013, You-
    Tube video, https://www.youtube.com/watch?v=EorCtwFjXmQ; Oath
    Keepers, "Oath Keepers Remove Barricades from WW2 Memorial in DC,"
    2013, YouTube video, https://www.youtube.com/watch?v=85FGRpg_5VE.
30. Oath Keepers, "Removed Barricades from WW2 Memorial and Oath
    Keepers Talk to Police."
31. Adam Nagourney, "A Defiant Rancher Savors the Audience That Rallied
    to His Side," New York Times, April 23, 2014, https://www.nytimes.com/2014

/04/24/us/politics/rancher-proudly-breaks-the-law-becoming-a-hero-in
-the-west.html; Jaime Fuller, "The Long Fight Between the Bundys and
the Federal Government, from 1989 to Today," *Washington Post*, January 4,
2016,   https://www.washingtonpost.com/news/the-fix/wp/2014/04/15
/everything-you-need-to-know-about-the-long-fight-between-cliven
-bundy-and-the-federal-government/; Niraj Chokshi, "The Federal Government Moved Some Cattle and Nevada's Governor Isn't Happy About
It," *Washington Post*, April 9, 2014, https://www.washingtonpost.com/blogs
/govbeat/wp/2014/04/09/the-federal-government-moved-some-cows-and
-nevadas-governor-isnt-happy-about-it/.

32. Fuller, "The Long Fight Between the Bundys and the Federal
Government."

33. Bundy Ranch, "DONATE," *Bundy Ranch* (blog), April 6, 2014, http://
bundyranch.blogspot.com/2014/04/you-have-been-asking-what-you-can
-do_6.html.

34. Grace Wyler, "The Bundy Ranch Standoff Was Only the Beginning for
America's Right-Wing Militias," *Vice*, April 16, 2014, https://www.vice.com
/en_us/article/dpwykw/an-armed-standoff-in-nevada-is-only-the
-beginning-for-americas-right-wing-militias; Oath Keepers, "Untitled Post,"
Oath Keepers (blog), April 16, 2014, http://oath-keepers.blogspot.com/2014
/04/note-first-at-moment-things-are-quiet.html.

35. Fuller, "The Long Fight Between the Bundys and the Federal
Government."

36. Oath Keepers, "Bundys Cowboy Up and Get Cattle Back," 2014, YouTube
video, https://www.youtube.com/watch?v=WQ_5b1z-HW4.

37. Fuller, "The Long Fight Between the Bundys and the Federal
Government."

38. Oath Keepers, "Untitled Post."

39. Oath Keepers, "Oath Keepers Bundy Ranch Debrief," 2014, YouTube
video, https://www.youtube.com/watch?v=4HkSAewoESg.

40. David Neiwert, "Back at the Bundy Ranch, It's Oath Keepers vs. Militiamen as Wild Rumors Fly," Southern Poverty Law Center, April 30, 2014,
https://www.splcenter.org/hatewatch/2014/04/30/back-bundy-ranch-its
-oath-keepers-vs-militiamen-wild-rumors-fly.

41. Oath Keepers, "Oath Keepers Bundy Ranch Debrief."

42. This perception of the standoff is promoted by other leading figures in the
patriot/militia movement as well. Sam Jackson, "'Nullification Through
Armed Civil Disobedience': A Case Study of Strategic Framing in the
Patriot/Militia Movement," *Dynamics of Asymmetric Conflict* 12, no. 1
(2019): 90–109, https://doi.org/10.1080/17467586.2018.1563904.

43. Wesley Lowery, "Black Lives Matter: Birth of a Movement," *Guardian*, January 17, 2017, http://www.theguardian.com/us-news/2017/jan/17/black -lives-matter-birth-of-a-movement; Shannon Luibrand, "How a Death in Ferguson Sparked a Movement in America," *CBS News*, August 7, 2015, https://www.cbsnews.com/news/how-the-black-lives-matter-movement -changed-america-one-year-later/.

44. Oath Keepers, "Open Letter of Warning to Governor Nixon from Missouri Oath Keepers," OathKeepers.org, August 22, 2014, https://www.oathkeepers .org/open-letter-of-warning-to-governor-nixon-from-missouri-oath -keepers-2/.

45. Jesse Bogan, "Police Shut Down Mysterious 'Oath Keepers' Guarding Rooftops in Downtown Ferguson," *St. Louis Post-Dispatch*, November 30, 2014, http://www.stltoday.com/news/local/crime-and-courts/police-shut -down-mysterious-oath-keepers-guarding-rooftops-in-downtown/article _f9ub6edd-acf8-52c3 a020 3a78db286194.html; Andy Cush, "Whose Side Are the Oath Keepers in Ferguson On?," *Gawker*, August 18, 2015, http:// gawker.com/whose-side-are-the-oath-keepers-in-ferguson-on-17239 17237.

46. Oath Keepers, "Oath Keepers Guarding Businesses in Ferguson, Missouri: Calling on Volunteers to Assist," OathKeepers.org, November 25, 2014, https://www.oathkeepers.org/oath-keepers-guarding-businesses-in -ferguson-missouri-calling-on-volunteers-to-assist/.

47. Bogan, "Police Shut Down Mysterious 'Oath Keepers' Guarding Rooftops"; Brian Heffernan, "In Ferguson, Oath Keepers Draw Both Suspicion and Gratitude," *Al Jazeera America*, December 14, 2014, http://america.aljazeera .com/articles/2014/12/14/oath-keepers-fergusonprotests.html.

48. Heffernan, "In Ferguson, Oath Keepers Draw Both Suspicion and Gratitude."

49. Oath Keepers, "Oath Keepers Guarding Businesses in Ferguson"; Heffernan, "In Ferguson, Oath Keepers Draw Both Suspicion and Gratitude." Ellipsis in the original article.

50. James Pogue, "The Oath Keepers Are Ready for War with the Federal Government," *Vice*, September 14, 2015, http://www.vice.com/read/miner -threat-0000747-v22n9; David Neiwert, "Oath Keepers Descend Upon Oregon with Dreams of Armed Confrontation Over Mining Dispute," Southern Poverty Law Center, April 22, 2015, https://www.splcenter.org /hatewatch/2015/04/23/oath-keepers-descend-upon-oregon-dreams-armed -confrontation-over-mining-dispute.

51. Pogue, "The Oath Keepers Are Ready for War with the Federal Government."

52. Tay Wiles, "Sugar Pine Mine, the Other Standoff," *High Country News*, February 2, 2016, http://www.hcn.org/issues/48.2/showdown-at-sugar-pine-mine.

53. Sam Jackson, "Conspiracy Theories in the Patriot/Militia Movement," GW Program on Extremism (May 2017), https://cchs.gwu.edu/sites/cchs.gwu.edu/files/downloads/Jackson%2C%20Conspiracy%20Theories%20Final.pdf; Christian Belanger, "What Is Jade Helm 15," *PolitiFact*, July 14, 2015, http://www.politifact.com/truth-o-meter/article/2015/jul/14/what-jade-helm-15/; Manny Fernandez, "Conspiracy Theories Over Jade Helm Training Exercise Get Some Traction in Texas," *New York Times*, May 6, 2015, https://www.nytimes.com/2015/05/07/us/conspiracy-theories-over-jade-helm-get-some-traction-in-texas.html.

54. Belanger, "What Is Jade Helm 15."

55. Oath Keepers, "Jade Helm 15—to 'Operate Undetected Amongst Civilian Populations,'" OathKeepers.org, March 30, 2015, https://www.oathkeepers.org/jade-helm-15-to-operate-undetected-amongst-civilian-populations/.

56. Liberty Brothers Radio Show, "If We Do Not Stop Jade Helm 15 There May Be No Future for Our Children!," 2015, YouTube video, https://www.youtube.com/watch?v=P_uLoGwpQEc.

57. Oath Keepers, "JADE HELM 2015: Questions and Reflections," OathKeepers.org, May 5, 2015, https://www.oathkeepers.org/jade-helm-2015-questions-and-reflections/.

58. Liberty Brothers Radio Show, "Stewart Rhodes on Jade Helm 15 on the Liberty Brothers," 2015, YouTube video, https://www.youtube.com/watch?v=8CC7c9aoKT8.

59. Doug Stanglin and Kyle Jahner, "Controversial Jade Helm Military Exercise Opens in Texas," *USA Today*, July 15, 2015, http://www.usatoday.com/story/news/nation/2015/07/15/operation-jade-helm-texas/30191795/; Kim LaCapria, "Jade Helm Concludes," *Snopes*, September 15, 2015, http://www.snopes.com/2015/09/15/jade-helm-over/.

60. Richard Fausset, Alan Blinder, and Michael S. Schmidt, "Gunman Kills 4 Marines at Military Site in Chattanooga," *New York Times*, July 16, 2015, https://www.nytimes.com/2015/07/17/us/chattanooga-tennessee-shooting.html.

61. Tamerra Griffin et al., "New Details in Chattanooga Shooting Reveal How Unarmed Marines Fled from Shooter," *BuzzFeed*, July 23, 2015, https://www.buzzfeed.com/tamerragriffin/officer-involved-shooting-at-a-military-center-in-tennessee.

62. Oath Keepers, "Oath Keepers National Call to Action: Help Us 'Protect the Protectors' by Guarding Recruiting and Reserve Centers," OathKeepers.org, July 21, 2015, https://www.oathkeepers.org/oath-keepers-national

-call-to-action-help-us-protect-the-protectors-by-guarding-recruiting-and
-reserve-centers/.

63. Oath Keepers, "Oath Keepers National Call to Action."

64. Oath Keepers, "Protect the Protectors—Update," OathKeepers.org, July 22, 2015, https://www.oathkeepers.org/protect-the-protectors-update/.

65. Victoria Bekiempis, "Oath Keepers Want to Arm Ferguson Protesters," *Newsweek*, August 19, 2015, https://www.newsweek.com/oath-keepers -ferguson-blacklivesmatter-michael-brown-black-lives-matter-second -363994; Alan Feuer, "The Oath Keeper Who Wants to Arm Black Lives Matter," *Rolling Stone*, January 3, 2016, http://www.rollingstone.com /politics/news/the-oath-keeper-who-wants-to-arm-black-lives-matter -20160103.

66. Michael Sainato, "Ferguson Oath Keepers Leader Sam Andrews Forms Splinter Group," *Observer*, August 30, 2015, http://observer.com/2015/08 /ferguson-oath-keepers-leader-sam-andrews-forms-splinter-group/.

67. Jesse Walker, "Oath Keeper Who Called for #BlackOpenCarry March in Ferguson Leaves the Group, Plans His Own March; Oath Keepers Say the Original March Will Proceed—Hit & Run," *Reason.com*, August 27, 2015, http://reason.com/blog/2015/08/27/oath-keeper-who-called-for -blackopencarr.

68. Feuer, "The Oath Keeper Who Wants to Arm Black Lives Matter"; Oath Keepers National, "Urgent Message About Sam Andrews," 2015, YouTube video, https://www.youtube.com/watch?v=4tR-QoeoHxA.

69. Feuer, "The Oath Keeper Who Wants to Arm Black Lives Matter."

70. Oath Keepers, "Operation Big Sky: Protecting Rights of Miners in Montana," OathKeepers.org, August 6, 2015, https://www.oathkeepers.org /operation-big-sky-protecting-rights-of-miners-in-montana/; Sanjay Talwani, " 'Patriot' Groups Protecting White Hope Mine near Lincoln in 'Operation Big Sky,' " *KRTV*, August 15, 2015, http://www.krtv.com/story /29731505/patriot-groups-protecting-white-hope-mine-near-lincoln-in -operation-big-sky.

71. Sanjay Talwani, "Lincoln Remains Quiet as Oath Keepers Continue 'Operation Big Sky,' " *KRTV*, August 21, 2015, http://www.krtv.com/story /29762011/lincoln-remains-quiet-as-oath-keepers-continue-operation-big -sky.

72. Oath Keepers, "After Action Report—Operation Big Sky—Lincoln Montana," OathKeepers.org, September 18, 2015, https://www.oathkeepers.org /after-action-report-operation-big-sky-lincoln-montana/. In fact, this operation faded from attention to such a degree that Oath Keepers does not provide information about its resolution, either more narrowly in terms of their involvement or more broadly in terms of the miners' situation.

73. Alan Blinder and Richard Pérez-Peña, "Kentucky Clerk Denies Same-Sex Marriage Licenses, Defying Court," *New York Times*, September 1, 2015, https://www.nytimes.com/2015/09/02/us/same-sex-marriage-kentucky-kim -davis.html.

74. Erik Ortiz, Gabe Gutierrez, and Daniella Silva, "Kim Davis, Kentucky Clerk Blocking Gay Marriages, Held in Contempt," *NBC News*, September 3, 2015, https://www.nbcnews.com/news/us-news/kentucky-clerk-kim -davis-held-contempt-court-n421126.

75. Oath Keepers, "Oath Keepers Offers Kim Davis Protection from Further Imprisonment by Judge," OathKeepers.org, September 9, 2015, https://www .oathkeepers.org/oath-keepers-offer-of-protection-for-embattled-clerk -kim-davis/.

76. Oath Keepers National, "Oath Keepers Offer of Protection for Embattled Clerk Kim Davis," 2015, YouTube video, https://www.youtube.com/watch ?v=x2Z5e13hZzw.

77. For example, Bethania Palma Markus, "Oath Keepers Put 'Boots on the Ground' to Guard Oath-Breaking Kim Davis from 'Dictator' Judge," *Raw Story*, September 10, 2015, https://www.rawstory.com/2015/09/oath-keepers -vow-to-defend-oath-breaking-kim-davis-with-guns-from-dictator-judge/; Wilson Dizard, "Oath Keepers Armed Group Offers to Protect Kim Davis from Arrest," *Al Jazeera America*, September 11, 2015, http://america .aljazeera.com/articles/2015/9/11/oath-keeper-davis-rowan-county-clerk .html; Tierney Sneed, "Oath Keepers on Their Way to 'Protect' KY Clerk Kim Davis from US Marshals," *Talking Points Memo*, September 10, 2015, http://talkingpointsmemo.com/livewire/kim-davis-oath-keepers.

78. Scott Masters Pierce, "Kim Davis Turned Down the Oath Keepers' Offer of Armed Security," *Vice*, September 15, 2015, https://www.vice.com/en_au /article/nn93g8/kim-davis-turned-down-the-oath-keepers-offer-of-armed -security-vgtrn-915; "Kim Davis Declines Offer from Oath Keepers to Protect Her from the Feds," *Talking Points Memo*, September 14, 2015, http:// talkingpointsmemo.com/livewire/kim-davis-declines-oath-keepers.

79. Oath Keepers, "Kim Davis' Legal Team Declines Oath Keepers' Offer to Protect Her Against Unlawful Arrrest [*sic*]," OathKeepers.org, September 11, 2015, https://www.oathkeepers.org/kim-davis-legal-team-declines -oath-keepers-offer-to-protect-her-against-unlawul-arrrest/.

80. Claudia Koerner, "Here's the Story of the Ranchers Whose Case Sparked a Militia Standoff in Oregon," *BuzzFeed*, January 5, 2016, https://www .buzzfeed.com/claudiakoerner/heres-the-story-of-the-ranchers-whose -case-sparked-a-militia.

81. See, for example, Sam Levin, "'I Still Don't Believe It': Hammond Family Feels Forgotten in Oregon Standoff," *Guardian*, January 17, 2016,

http://www.theguardian.com/us-news/2016/jan/17/oregon-militia-standoff -occupation-dwight-steven-hammond; Tré Goins-Phillips, "Glenn Beck: Re-Sentencing Oregon Ranchers Is 'Double Jeopardy,'" *TheBlaze*, January 4, 2016, http://www.theblaze.com/news/2016/01/04/glenn-beck-re-senten cing-oregon-ranchers-is-double-jeopardy/; Andre' Gabriel Esparza, "Civil Unrest, Militia on Alert as Government Attempts Double Jeopardy by Imprisoning Ranchers," *DontComply.Com* (blog), January 1, 2016, https:// www.dontcomply.com/civil-unrest-militia-alert-government-attempts -double-jeopardy-imprisoning-ranchers/.

82. Bundy Ranch, "Facts & Events in the Hammond Case," *Bundy Ranch* (blog), November 12, 2015, http://bundyranch.blogspot.com/2015/11/facts -events-in-hammond-case.html.

83. "Protesters Led by Cliven Bundy's Son Occupy a Building at Oregon Wildlife Refuge," *Los Angeles Times*, January 2, 2016, http://www.latimes.com /nation/nationnow/la-na-nn-oregon-ranchers-protest-20160102-story.html.

84. Rebecca Hersher, "'It Was Time to Make a Hard Stand'; Closing Arguments Completed in Malheur Trial," NPR.org, October 19, 2016, http:// www.npr.org/sections/thetwo-way/2016/10/19/498526768/it-was-time-to -make-a-hard-stand-closing-arguments-underway-in-malheur-trial; "LaVoy Finicum's Death, One Year Later," *KOIN 6* (blog), January 25, 2017, http:// koin.com/2017/01/25/lavoy-finicums-death-one-year-later/.

85. Oath Keepers, "The Hammond Family Does NOT Want an Armed Stand Off, and Nobody Has a Right to Force One on Them," OathKeepers.org, January 1, 2016, https://www.oathkeepers.org/the-hammond-family-does/.

86. Oath Keepers, "A Recommended Honorable Exit Strategy for Ammon Bundy," OathKeepers.org, January 6, 2016, https://www.oathkeepers.org/a -recommended-honorable-exit-strategy-for-ammon-bundy/.

87. Vivian Padilla, "Jon Ritzheimer, Organizer of Various Anti-Islam Rallies, Appears in Oregon Protest Videos," *ABC News*, January 4, 2016, http://www .abc15.com/news/national/jon-ritzheimer-organizer-of-various-anti-islam -rallies-appears-in-oregon-protest-videos; Evan Wyloge, "Hundreds Gather in Arizona for Armed Anti-Muslim Protest," *Washington Post*, May 30, 2015, https://www.washingtonpost.com/news/post-nation/wp/2015/05/30 /hundreds-gather-in-arizona-for-armed-anti-muslim-protest/; Peter Holley, "The 'Unhinged' Oregon Protester That the FBI Has Been Tracking for Months," *Washington Post*, January 5, 2016, https://www.washingtonpost .com/news/morning-mix/wp/2016/01/05/why-a-notorious-anti-islam -radical-turned-on-the-federal-government-in-oregon/.

88. Aaron Ernst, "Meet the Anti-Islamic Organizer Who Set Off an FBI Manhunt," *Al Jazeera America*, December 2, 2015, http://america.aljazeera .com/watch/shows/america-tonight/articles/2015/12/2/jon-ritzheimer-anti

-islamic-muslim-fbi-manhunt.html; Graham Rayman, "FBI Warns NY Police About Anti-Islam Arizona Man," *New York Daily News*, November 27, 2015, http://www.nydailynews.com/news/crime/fbi-warns-ny-police-anti-islam-arizona-man-article-1.2448001.

89. Catherine Thompson, "Anti-Muslim Activist Says He Plans to Arrest Dem Sen. Debbie Stabenow," *Talking Points Memo*, September 23, 2015, http://talkingpointsmemo.com/muckraker/jon-ritzheimer-debbie-stabenow-threat.

90. Maxine Bernstein, "Oregon Refuge Occupier Jon Ritzheimer: 'I Am Extremely Sorry for This Entire Mess,'" *OregonLive.com*, November 30, 2017, http://www.oregonlive.com/oregon-standoff/2017/11/oregon_refuge_occupier_jon_rit.html.

91. Oath Keepers, "Oregon Standoff a Terrible Plan That We Might Be Stuck With," OathKeepers.org, January 4, 2016, https://www.oathkeepers.org/oregon-standoff-a-terrible-plan-that-we-might-be-stuck-with/; Oath Keepers, "Ammon Bundy—Martyr or Revolutionary?," OathKeepers.org, January 3, 2016, https://www.oathkeepers.org/ammon-bundy-martyr-or-revolutionary/.

92. Amanda Peacher, "There's Another Armed Group in Burns and They're Not the Bundys," Oregon Public Broadcasting, January 10, 2016, http://www.opb.org/news/series/burns-oregon-standoff-bundy-militia-news-updates/theres-another-armed-group-in-burns-and-theyre-not-the-bundys/.

93. Oath Keepers, "Historic 'Militia' Moment: Pacific Patriot Network (Including Oath Keepers) Calls on FBI," OathKeepers.org, January 10, 2016, https://www.oathkeepers.org/9435-2/.

94. Oath Keepers, "Historic 'Militia' Moment."

95. Daniel Kreiss, Joshua O. Barker, and Shannon Zenner, "Trump Gave Them Hope: Studying the Strangers in Their Own Land," *Political Communication* 34, no. 3 (2017): 470–78, https://doi.org/10.1080/10584609.2017.1330076.

96. For example, see Oath Keepers, "WikiLeaks: Murdered DNC Staffer Source of DNC Leaks . . . Not Russia," OathKeepers.org, August 10, 2016, https://www.oathkeepers.org/wikileaks-murdered-dnc-staffer-source-of-dnc-leaksnot-russia/.

97. Oath Keepers, Webinar—November 7, 2016, not available online, locally archived copy in possession of author; J. J. MacNab, "According to OK's Interpretation of 'Real Polls' Trump Will Win with 290+ Delegates, Unless There's 'Wide-Scale Fraud,'" @jjmacnab, November 6, 2016, https://twitter.com/jjmacnab/status/794362184276942848.

98. Oath Keepers, "Oath Keepers—a Sabot in the Machine to Stop Voter Fraud & Intimidation," OathKeepers.org, October 25, 2016, https://www

.oathkeepers.org/oath-keepers-sabot-machine-stop-voter-fraud
-intimidation/.

99. Oath Keepers, "Oath Keepers CALL TO ACTION to Spot, Document,
and Report Vote Fraud or Intimidation on Election Day, 2016," OathKeep-
ers.org, October 25, 2016, https://www.oathkeepers.org/oath-keepers-call
-action-spot-document-report-vote-fraud-intimidation-election-day-2016/.

100. Jennifer Williams, "The Oath Keepers, the Far-Right Group Answering
Trump's Call to Watch the Polls, Explained," Vox, November 7, 2016, http://
www.vox.com/policy-and-politics/2016/11/7/13489640/oath-keepers
-donald-trump-voter-fraud-intimidation-rigged; Peter Holley, "Race Riots,
Terrorist Attacks, and Martial Law: Oath Keepers Warn of Post-Election
Chaos," Washington Post, November 8, 2016, https://www.washingtonpost
.com/news/post-nation/wp/2016/11/08/race-riots-terror-attacks-and
-martial-law-oath-keepers-warn-of-post-election-chaos/.

101. Oath Keepers, "Oath Keepers CALL TO ACTION."

102. Tim Marcin, "Trump Voters Believe the President's False Claims That He
Won the Popular Vote," Newsweek, July 26, 2017, http://www.newsweek.com
/trump-won-popular-vote-half-voters-believe-poll-642284.

103. Christopher Mele and Annie Correal, "'Not Our President': Protests
Spread After Donald Trump's Election," New York Times, November 9,
2016, https://www.nytimes.com/2016/11/10/us/trump-election-protests.html;
Jon Swaine and Guardian Staff, "Anti-Trump Protesters Gear Up for Weekend Demonstrations Across the US," Guardian, November 12, 2016, http://
www.theguardian.com/us-news/2016/nov/11/anti-trump-protests-weekend
-new-york-trump-tower.

104. Michael Walsh, "Millions Sign Petition Urging Electoral College to Elect
Hillary Clinton," Yahoo.com, November 11, 2016, https://www.yahoo.com
/news/millions-sign-petition-urging-electoral-college-to-elect-hillary
-clinton-175038196.html.

105. Ian Simpson, "Anarchists Threaten to Disrupt Trump Inauguration, Police
Say Ready," Reuters, January 6, 2017, https://www.reuters.com/article/us-usa
-trump-inauguration/anarchists-threaten-to-disrupt-trump-inauguration
-police-say-ready-idUSKBN14Q2BG; Nicholas Fandos, "Trump Inauguration Security Planners Brace for Wave of Protesters," New York Times,
December 27, 2016, https://www.nytimes.com/2016/12/27/us/politics/donald
-trump-inauguration-security.html.

106. Oath Keepers, "NavyJack—Operation HYPO: Infiltrating Violent Protests
Against the President Elect," OathKeepers.org, November 11, 2016, https://
www.oathkeepers.org/navyjack-operation-hypo/.

107. Oath Keepers, "NavyJack—Communists Intend to Overthrow the United
States Before Inauguration Day (Updated 01/12/2017)," OathKeepers.org,

January 10, 2017, https://www.oathkeepers.org/navyjack-communists-intend
-overthrow-united-states-inauguration-day/.

108. Oath Keepers, "NavyJack—Operation HYPO."

109. Oath Keepers, "Oath Keepers Call to Action: Help Defend Free Speech
from Violent Thugs at Inauguration," OathKeepers.org, January 17, 2017,
https://www.oathkeepers.org/oath-keepers-call-action-help-defend-free
-speech-violent-thugs-inauguration/; Oath Keepers, "UPDATE: NavyJack—
The Presidential Inauguration (or Not) of Donald J. Trump," OathKeep-
ers.org, January 14, 2017, https://www.oathkeepers.org/navyjack-presidential
-inauguration-not-donald-j-trump/.

110. Oath Keepers, "Long Line to Get Thru Security at Deploraball. Cops
Pepper Spraying Disrupters Outside Pic.Twitter.Com/SF4DoPKjfw," @
Oathkeepers, January 6, 2017, https://twitter.com/Oathkeepers/status/8222
62877432250368; Lauren Gambino, "DeploraBall: Trump Lovers and Haters Clash at Washington DC Event," Guardian, January 20, 2017, http://
www.theguardian.com/world/2017/jan/20/deploraball-trump-lovers-and
-haters-clash-at-washington-dc-event.

111. Oath Keepers, "NavyJack—Oath Keepers at the Inauguration," OathKeep-
ers.org, January 21, 2017, https://www.oathkeepers.org/navyjack-oath
-keepers-inauguration/.

112. Peter Beinart, "The Rise of the Violent Left," The Atlantic, September 2017,
https://www.theatlantic.com/magazine/archive/2017/09/the-rise-of-the
-violent-left/534192/; Brenna Cammeron, "Antifa: Left-Wing Militants on
the Rise," BBC News, August 14, 2017, https://www.bbc.com/news/world
-us-canada-40930831; Elle Reeve, "We Camped Out with the Antifa
Activists Plotting to Disarm the Alt-Right," VICE News, May 9, 2018,
https://news.vice.com/en_us/article/7xmzmd/we-camped-out-with-the
-antifa-activists-plotting-to-disarm-the-alt-right.

113. Sarah Jaffe, "The Long History of Antifa," Progressive.org, September
13, 2017, http://progressive.org/api/content/fad7965e-9898-11e7-9332-121
bebc5777e/; Cammeron, "Antifa"; Anti-Defamation League, "Who Are
the Antifa?," Anti-Defamation League, https://www.adl.org/resources
/backgrounders/who-are-the-antifa. One particular confrontation stands
out. Richard Spencer, perhaps the most notorious figure in the alt-right,
known for saying inflammatory things like "Hail Trump, hail our people,
hail victory" (a clear allusion to the Nazi slogan "Heil Hitler"), was in
Washington, DC, for Donald Trump's inauguration. He was giving
an interview when a protestor dressed in black with his face covered ran
up, punched him in the face, and ran away. This conflict became a
meme, with hundreds of people setting the video of the punch to
music; others debated over whether punching a Nazi was acceptable in

contemporary America. Yoni Appelbaum and Daniel Lombroso, "'Hail Trump!': White Nationalists Salute the President-Elect," *The Atlantic*, November 21, 2016, https://www.theatlantic.com/politics/archive/2016/11 /richard-spencer-speech-npi/508379/; Kaitlyn Tiffany, "Right-Wing Extremist Richard Spencer Got Punched, but It Was Memes That Bruised His Ego," *The Verge*, January 23, 2017, https://www.theverge.com /2017/1/23/14356306/richard-spencer-punch-internet-memes-alt-right; Liam Stack, "Attack on Alt-Right Leader Has Internet Asking: Is It O.K. to Punch a Nazi?," *New York Times*, January 21, 2017, https://www.nytimes .com/2017/01/21/us/politics/richard-spencer-punched-attack.html.

114. Alan Feuer, "Antifa on Trial: How a College Professor Joined the Left's Radical Ranks," *Rolling Stone*, May 15, 2018, https://www.rollingstone.com /culture/features/antifa-activists-anti-fascist-movement-trial-college -professor-w519899; Reeve, "We Camped Out with the Antifa Activists"; Emma Grey Ellis, "White Supremacists Face a Not-so-New Adversary Online: The Antifa," *Wired*, February 4, 2017, https://www.wired.com/2017 /02/neo-nazis-face-new-foe-online-irl-far-left-antifa/.

115. Oath Keepers, "Oath Keepers Battle of Berkeley April 15 After Report," OathKeepers.org, April 21, 2017, https://www.oathkeepers.org/oath-keepers -battle-berkeley-april-15-report/; Oath Keepers, "Help Defend Free Speech in Berkeley," OathKeepers.org, April 26, 2017, https://www.oathkeepers.org /help-defend-free-speech-berkeley/; Oath Keepers, "CALL TO ACTION: Defend Free Speech in Boston on Saturday, May 13th!," OathKeepers.org, May 10, 2017, https://www.oathkeepers.org/call-action-defend-free-speech -boston-saturday-may-13th/.

116. Casey Michel, "How Militias Became the Private Police for White Suprem- acists," *Politico*, August 17, 2017, https://www.politico.com/magazine/story /2017/08/17/white-supremacists-militias-private-police-215498; Sam Jackson, "Don't Assume the Militias at the Charlottesville Rally Were White Supremacists. This Is What They Believe Now," *Washington Post*, Septem- ber 8, 2017, https://www.washingtonpost.com/news/monkey-cage/wp/2017 /09/08/remember-those-militias-at-the-charlottesville-unite-the-right -rally-heres-what-they-believe/.

117. Tom Gjelten, "'March Against Sharia' Planned Across the U.S.," NPR.org, June 10, 2017, https://www.npr.org/2017/06/10/532254891/march-against -sharia-planned-across-the-u-s.

118. Oath Keepers, "Help Support Defending ACT for America Marches Against Sharia This Saturday, June 10, Nationwide," OathKeepers.org, June 7, 2017, https://www.oathkeepers.org/help-support-defending-act -america-marches-sharia-saturday-june-10-nationwide/; Bill Morlin, "ACT's Anti-Muslim Message Fertile Ground for Oath Keepers," Southern

Poverty Law Center, June 12, 2017, https://www.splcenter.org/hatewatch /2017/06/12/act%E2%80%99s-anti-muslim-message-fertile-ground-oath -keepers.

119. Wiles, "Sugar Pine Mine, the Other Standoff."

120. Later, journalists found that groups similar to Oath Keepers used the aid they provided to communities near Houston, Texas, to coerce local communities into rejecting government aid. Michael Hardy, "How Far-Right Groups Took Over a Refugee Community After Harvey," *Texas Observer*, January 22, 2018, https://www.texasobserver.org/big-trouble-little -cambodia/.

121. Oath Keepers, "Oath Keepers Need Your Help in Puerto Rico!," Oath-Keepers.org, October 16, 2017, https://www.oathkeepers.org/oath-keepers -need-help-puerto-rico/; Oath Keepers, "UPDATE: Stewart Rhodes on Disaster Relief in Puerto Rico," OathKeepers.org, October 11, 2017, https:// www.oathkeepers.org/update-stewart-rhodes-disaster-relief-puerto-rico/.

122. Oath Keepers, "UPDATE," October 11, 2017.

123. Oath Keepers, "Call to Action: Church Security in Sutherland Springs, Texas," OathKeepers.org, November 11, 2017, https://oathkeepers.org/2017 /11/call-action-church-security-sutherland-springs-texas/.

124. Oath Keepers, "Call to Action: Church Security."

4. The Ongoing Struggle Over Natural Rights

1. Declaration of Independence (1776), http://www.archives.gov/exhibits /charters/declaration_transcript.html.

2. The idea of motivating frames comes from Robert D. Benford and David A. Snow, "Framing Processes and Social Movements: An Overview and Assessment," *Annual Review of Sociology* 26 (January 2000): 617, https:// doi.org/10.2307/223459.

3. This premise follows Charles R. Beitz, "Naturalistic Theories," in *The Idea of Human Rights* (New York: Oxford University Press, 2009), 48–72. Beitz elaborates on the distinction between these two understandings of natural rights, its lineage, and its significance.

4. There is ongoing debate in some communities over whether there is a difference between "unalienable" and "inalienable." Gregory Krieg, "Unalienable vs. Inalienable: A Centuries-Old Debate, Still Unresolved," *CNN*, http://www.cnn.com/2016/01/06/politics/barack-obama-unalienable -inalienable-gun-control/index.html. Some argue that the difference is vast: inalienable rights can be surrendered voluntarily, while unalienable rights cannot be surrendered under any circumstances. This difference

often follows from a tenuous parsing of differences between historical dictionaries. For example, Bo Perrin, "Unalienable vs. Inalienable," *Tea Party Tribune*, September 8, 2012, http://www.teapartytribune.com/2012/09/08/unalienable-vs-inalienable/; Susan Boskey, "How the Declaration of Independence Got Hijacked," *Beyond the National Myth* (blog), http://nationalmyth.org/how-the-declaration-of-independence-was-hijacked/; Alfred Adask, "'Unalienable' vs. 'Inalienable,'" *Adask's Law* (blog), July 15, 2009, https://adask.wordpress.com/2009/07/15/unalienable-vs-inalienable/. Both words appear in different drafts of the Declaration of Independence. On the Oath Keepers website and blog, both terms appear, but "unalienable" is far more common: "unalienable" appears in forty-one documents, and "inalienable" appears in nineteen. Of these documents, four contain both words. In this chapter, I treat the words as synonyms.

5. Oath Keepers, "Waco: A New Revelation," OathKeepers.org, January 18, 2016, https://www.oathkeepers.org/waco-a-new-revelation/.

6. Stewart Rhodes, "The First Fundamental Principle of Constitutional Interpretation: Your Rights Don't Come from Government," *Stewart Rhodes* (blog), February 18, 2009, http://stewart-rhodes.blogspot.com/2009/02/first-fundamental-principle-of.html. Italics here is underlining in the original.

7. Rhodes, "The First Fundamental Principle of Constitutional Interpretation"; D. J. Mulloy, *American Extremism: History, Politics, and the Militia Movement* (New York: Routledge, 2004), 128–31.

8. Rhodes, "The First Fundamental Principle of Constitutional Interpretation." Italics here is underlining in the original.

9. Stewart Rhodes, "The Bill of Rights: The Constitution's Built-In, Mandatory Manual of Constitutional Interpretation," *Stewart Rhodes* (blog), February 18, 2009, http://stewart-rhodes.blogspot.com/2009/02/bill-of-rights-constitutions-built-in.html. Italics here is underlining in the original.

10. Rhodes, "The Bill of Rights."

11. Rhodes, "The First Fundamental Principle of Constitutional Interpretation."

12. Declaration of Independence.

13. Oath Keepers, "Spending Bill Betrayal by Establishment Republicans Confirms Contempt for Base," OathKeepers.org, December 18, 2015, https://www.oathkeepers.org/establishment-republican-budget-betrayal-shows-contempt-for-america/.

14. Most political and legal theorists argue that natural rights have always been understood as subject to certain restrictions. For example, the right to free speech is not absolute, in that some speech can leave a speaker liable to sanction for their speech (for example, with defamation), based on the

competing natural right to one's reputation. Philip A. Hamburger, "Natural Rights, Natural Law, and American Constitutions," *Yale Law Journal* 102, no. 4 (January 1993): 907, https://doi.org/10.2307/796836.

15. Stewart Rhodes, "Don't Be Neoconned. Ron Paul on Understanding the Grave Threat to Our Constitutional Republic," *Stewart Rhodes* (blog), August 22, 2007, http://stewart-rhodes.blogspot.com/2007/08/dont-be -neoconned-ron-paul-on.html.

16. Oath Keepers, "Stewart Rhodes on Alex Jones Show 2-7-10 Part 3 of 3," 2010, YouTube video, https://www.youtube.com/watch?v=GoP-VnxtUGg.

17. Rhodes provides a fairly typical example of the conspiracism of Oath Keepers when he says: "We were never taught [about the Bill of Rights] in school, they intentionally dumb us down in public schools and don't teach us our own heritage and our own Constitution." His complaint about public schooling is not that it is inadequate but that "they" are using it as a weapon against the American people. Oath Keepers, "Alex Jones Round Table with Oath Keepers, Stewart Rhodes, Michael Boldin & Brandon Smith," 2011, YouTube video, https://www.youtube.com/watch?v=hdd9c _HTaq8.

18. Oath Keepers, "How to Be a Defender of the Republic—the Example of James Otis," *Oath Keepers* (blog), April 16, 2009, http://oath-keepers .blogspot.com/2009/04/how-to-be-defender-of-republic-example.html.

19. Rhodes, "The First Fundamental Principle of Constitutional Interpretation."

20. Oath Keepers, "Declaration of Orders We Will Not Obey," OathKeepers .org, https://www.oathkeepers.org/declaration-of-orders-we-will-not-obey/. This mirrors an argument from the National Rifle Association that the Second Amendment (which protects the right to keep and bear arms) is "America's First Freedom" (which is the name of one of their publications). The actor Charlton Heston, who was the ceremonial president of the NRA for five years, wrote that the right to keep and bear arms is "the one right that prevails when all others fail, the one right that allows rights to exist at all." Charlton Heston, "Our First Freedom," *Saturday Evening Post*, February 2000.

21. Oath Keepers, "Declaration Of Orders We Will Not Obey."

22. Oath Keepers, "How to Be a Defender of the Republic."

23. Oath Keepers, "Declaration of Orders We Will Not Obey."

24. Adam Weinstein has explained why arguments about gun confiscation during Hurricane Katrina are often mistaken, especially where they posit a government-orchestrated plot to disarm the residents of New Orleans. In short, gun confiscation was much less common than some reports suggest, and some law enforcement organizations proactively issued orders to law

enforcement on the ground that they were not to confiscate weapons except as part of criminal investigations. Adam Weinstein, "The NRA Twisted a Tiny Part of the Katrina Disaster to Fit Its Bigger Agenda," *The Trace*, August 31, 2015, https://www.thetrace.org/2015/08/nra-hurricane-katrina -gun-confiscation/.

25. "Seriously?," *This American Life*, https://www.thisamericanlife.org/radio -archives/episode/599/seriously.

26. David Sehat, *The Jefferson Rule: How the Founding Fathers Became Infallible and Our Politics Inflexible* (New York: Simon & Schuster, 2015); Saul Cornell, "Mobs, Militias, and Magistrates: Popular Constitutionalism and the Whiskey Rebellion," *Chicago-Kent Law Review* 81 (2006): 883.

5. The American Revolution Redux

1. Terry Bouton, *Taming Democracy: "The People," the Founders, and the Troubled Ending of the American Revolution* (New York: Oxford University Press, 2007).

2. For example, see Murray N. Rothbard, "Confiscation and the Homestead Principle," *Libertarian Forum*, June 15, 1969.

3. James Bamford, "Every Move You Make," *Foreign Policy*, September 7, 2016, https://foreignpolicy.com/2016/09/07/every-move-you-make-obama -nsa-security-surveillance-spying-intelligence-snowden/.

4. Oath Keepers, "Stewart Rhodes' Sixth Anniversary Essay," OathKeepers .org, April 20, 2015, https://www.oathkeepers.org/stewart-rhodes-sixth -anniversary-essay/.

5. Oath Keepers, "Stewart Rhodes' Sixth Anniversary Essay."

6. Oath Keepers, "Declaration of Orders We Will Not Obey," OathKeepers .org, https://www.oathkeepers.org/declaration-of-orders-we-will-not-obey/.

7. Oath Keepers, "Declaration Of Orders We Will Not Obey."

8. Oath Keepers, "Declaration Of Orders We Will Not Obey."

9. Oath Keepers, "Stewart Rhodes' Sixth Anniversary Essay."

10. Oath Keepers, "How the British Gun Control Program Precipitated the American Revolution," OathKeepers.org, August 17, 2015, https://www .oathkeepers.org/how-the-british-gun-control-program-precipitated-the -american-revolution/.

11. Oath Keepers, "How the British Gun Control Program Precipitated the American Revolution."

12. This mirrors an argument from the National Rifle Association that the Second Amendment protects "America's First Freedom." See chapter 4, note 20, in this volume.

13. Oath Keepers, "How the British Gun Control Program Precipitated the American Revolution."

14. Oath Keepers, "Stewart Rhodes on the 'Baldy & the Blonde Radio Show' Discussing Senate Bill 1867: Audio," 2011, YouTube video, https://www .youtube.com/watch?v=4IQnObVjLOo; Oath Keepers, "Stewart Rhodes on Alex Jones Radio Show: Jan. 11th 2012 Discussing NDAA," 2012, You-Tube video, https://www.youtube.com/watch?v=HTXN43Y5N6E. Else-where, Stewart Rhodes elaborates on this idea, rooting his discussion in the cases of Jose Padilla and Yaser Esam Hamdi. Padilla and Hamdi were American citizens who were designated as "unlawful enemy combatants" in the War on Terror and placed in military detention. Hamdi was cap-tured in Afghanistan in 2001 and accused of fighting with the Taliban. Padilla was arrested for allegedly plotting a terrorist attack in 2002; after his arrest, he was designated as an enemy combatant. Both men were held in a naval brig in South Carolina rather than in a civilian detention facil-ity. After legal challenges, the Supreme Court declared that the federal government can designate U.S. citizens as enemy combatants; individuals who have been designated as enemy combatants can be placed in military detention and do not need to face civilian trial. Rhodes vigorously con-demned this Supreme Court opinion, arguing that it bypassed the legal process for handling American citizens who are accused of treason as defined in Article III of the Constitution. According to Rhodes, "the Founders knew the sad English history of the abuse of special military and executive courts, such as the infamous Star Chamber . . . and endeavored to prevent their recurrence" in the United States. He argued that if the gov-ernment can charge and try American citizens under military law—even in times of emergency—then the government might use that power to declare "gun owners and tax protestors to be 'terrorists,'" using "enemy combatant status" to subject American citizens to military law. Thus, Oath Keepers declares that "any attempt to apply the laws of war to American civilians, under any pretext, such as against domestic 'militia' groups the government brands 'domestic terrorists,' is an act of war and an act of trea-son." Stewart Rhodes, "Understanding Enemy Combatant Status and the Military Commissions Act, Part I. Enemy Combatant Status: No More Per-nicious Doctrine," *Stewart Rhodes* (blog), October 28, 2006, http://www .stewart-rhodes.blogspot.com/2006/10/enemy-combatant-status-no-more .html; Hamdi v. Rumsfeld (Syllabus), 542 U.S. 507 (U.S. Supreme Court 2004); Rumsfeld v. Padilla (Syllabus), 542 U.S. 426 (U.S. Supreme Court 2004); Oath Keepers, "Declaration of Orders We Will Not Obey."

15. "One of the causes of the American Revolution was the attempt 'to ren-der the Military independent of and superior to the Civil Power' by

disbanding the Massachusetts legislature and appointing General Gage as 'military governor.'" Oath Keepers, "Declaration of Orders We Will Not Obey." The most prominent event that Oath Keepers points to in discussion of martial law is Jade Helm 15.

16. I come back to this point in the next chapter, in the context of the government's response to Hurricane Katrina.

17. A long-standing conspiracy among antigovernment extremists is that the federal government is complicit in a plot—usually led by the United Nations—to bring foreign troops to America to impose tyranny. See, for example, Jim Keith, *Black Helicopters Over America: Strikeforce for the New World Order* (Lilburn, GA: IllumniNet, 1994); Michael Janofsky, "'Militia' Man Tells of Plot to Attack Military Base," *New York Times*, June 25, 1995, http://www.nytimes.com/1995/06/25/us/militia-man-tells-of-plot-to -attack-military-base.html; Sam Jackson, "Conspiracy Theories in the Patriot/Militia Movement," GW Program on Extremism (May 2017), https://cchs.gwu.edu/sites/cchs.gwu.edu/files/downloads/Jackson%2 C%20Conspiracy%20Theories%20Final.pdf.

18. Oath Keepers, "Declaration of Orders We Will Not Obey."

19. Stewart Rhodes, "Reinstate the Draft! America's Youth Must Serve Their Country, One Way or Another—Sieg Heil!," *Stewart Rhodes* (blog), October 29, 2006, http://stewart-rhodes.blogspot.com/2006/10/reinstate-draft -americas-youth-must.html. Rhodes does not seem to recognize the incongruity of this argument with the widespread argument in the patriot/militia movement that militia service was mandatory for all able-bodied men in the early years of the country, an argument alluded to multiple times in documents written and shared by Oath Keepers. See, for example, Oath Keepers, "Is Martial Law Justified If ISIS Attacks?," OathKeepers.org, May 27, 2015, https://oathkeepers.org/2015/05/is-martial-law-justified-if-isis -attacks/; Oath Keepers, "Nelson Hultberg: Revitalization of the State Militias," OathKeepers.org, January 15, 2015, https://oathkeepers.org/2015/01 /nelson-hultberg-revitalization-of-the-state-militias/; Oath Keepers, "LCDR (Ret) Ernest G. Cunningham and Famous (Infamous) Survey," *Oath Keepers* (blog), April 15, 2009, http://oath-keepers.blogspot.com/2009 /04/lcdr-ret-ernest-g-cunningham-and-famous.html; Oath Keepers, "Stewart Rhodes and Oath Keepers of Josephine County, Oregon—Sugar Pine Mine," 2015, YouTube video, https://www.youtube.com/watch?v=XYm Vure11FA.

20. Michael More, "Urge Protection of States Rights," Pub. L. No. LC2235 (2009), http://laws.leg.mt.gov/legprd/LAW0203W$BSRV.ActionQuery? P_SESS=20091&P_BLTP_BILL_TYP_CD=HJ&P_BILL_NO=0026& P_BILL_DFT_NO=&P_CHPT_NO=&Z_ACTION=Find&P_ENTY

_ID_SEQ2=&P_SBJT_SBJ_CD=&P_ENTY_ID_SEQ=&P_PRNT
_FRNDLY_PG=Y. The resolution died in committee.

21. Stewart Rhodes, "Montana Introduces Resolution Asserting State
    Sovereignty—and Threatening Secession," *Stewart Rhodes* (blog), Feb-
    ruary 17, 2009, http://stewart-rhodes.blogspot.com/2009/02/montana-intro
    duces-resolution-asserting.html. Despite the title he gave to this post, Rhodes
    insists that this is *not* secession. Instead, this would be the federal gov-
    ernment taking action that would nullify the "compact between the
    states," which would result in states returning to their prior state of
    sovereignty.

22. "Armed civil disobedience" in this case refers to a rally held at the Wash-
    ington State Capitol where firearms activists openly carried firearms to pro-
    test state laws and rules for legislature visitors. Those activists also drew
    explicit parallels to the movement for independence, reminding the
    governor that the "founders outlined a list of grievances against King
    George III," then issuing their own list of grievances. Oath Keepers, "Kit
    Lange: Open Letter to Washington State Governor," OathKeepers.org,
    February 6, 2015, https://www.oathkeepers.org/kit-lange-open-letter-to
    -washington-state-governor/. See also Sam Jackson, "'Nullification Through
    Armed Civil Disobedience': A Case Study of Strategic Framing in the
    Patriot/Militia Movement," *Dynamics of Asymmetric Conflict* 12, no. 1 (2019):
    90–109, https://doi.org/10.1080/17467586.2018.1563904.

23. Oath Keepers, "Kit Lange: Open Letter to Washington State Governor."

24. Oath Keepers, "Declaration of Orders We Will Not Obey."

25. Oath Keepers, "Declaration of Orders We Will Not Obey."

26. D. J. Mulloy, *American Extremism: History, Politics, and the Militia Move-
    ment* (New York: Routledge, 2004), 3–54.

27. William Pencak, "Whittemore, Samuel (1696–1793), Farmer and Folk Hero
    of the American Revolution," in *American National Biography* (Oxford
    University Press, February 2000), https://www.anb.org/view/10.1093/anb
    /9780198606697.001.0001/anb-9780198606697-e-0101246.

28. Oath Keepers, "Oath Keepers Muster on Lexington Green 4/19/2009 1 of
    10," 2009, YouTube video, https://www.youtube.com/watch?v=7eactx2yX-w.

29. "Background of Selective Service," Selective Service System, https://www
    .sss.gov/About/History-And-Records/Background-Of-Selective-Service.

30. Some in and out of the movement, including the prominent media per-
    sonality Glenn Beck, framed this "tyrannical action" as double jeopardy.
    See chapter 3, note 81, in this volume.

31. Donald Trump would later pardon the Hammonds in July 2018. Eileen Sul-
    livan and Julie Turkewitz, "Trump Pardons Oregon Ranchers Whose
    Case Inspired Wildlife Refuge Takeover," *New York Times*, July 10, 2018,

https://www.nytimes.com/2018/07/10/us/politics/trump-pardon-hammond
-oregon.html.

32. Rebecca Hersher, "'It Was Time to Make a Hard Stand'; Closing Arguments Completed in Malheur Trial," NPR.org, October 19, 2016, http://
www.npr.org/sections/thetwo-way/2016/10/19/498526768/it-was-time-to
-make-a-hard-stand-closing-arguments-underway-in-malheur-trial.

33. "Protesters Led by Cliven Bundy's Son Occupy a Building at Oregon Wildlife Refuge," *Los Angeles Times*, January 2, 2016, http://www.latimes.com
/nation/nationnow/la-na-nn-oregon-ranchers-protest-20160102-story.html;
Les Zaitz, "Militiamen, Ranchers in Showdown for Soul of Burns," *Ore-
gonLive.com*, December 30, 2015, http://www.oregonlive.com/pacific
-northwest-news/index.ssf/2015/12/militiamen_ranchers_in_showdow
.html.

34. Oath Keepers, "Harney County Committee of Safety's Letter Asks Ammon
Bundy to Leave Refuge," OathKeepers.org, January 9, 2016, https://www
.oathkeepers.org/harney-county-committee-of-safety-letter-to-ammon
-bundy-asking-him-to-leave/. As the title of this webpage indicates, this
committee later wrote a letter to Bundy and the other occupiers asking
them to stop their occupation. Others in the patriot/militia movement have
also deployed the language of "Committee of Safety." Mulloy, *American
Extremism*, 71. On Committees of Safety, see Joshua Canale, "New York
Committee and Council of Safety," in *George Washington Digital Encyclopedia* (Mount Vernon Estate), https://www.mountvernon.org/library
/digitalhistory/digital-encyclopedia/article/new-york-committee-and
-council-of-safety/#1.

35. Oath Keepers, "Ammon Bundy—Martyr or Revolutionary?," OathKeep-
ers.org, January 3, 2016, https://www.oathkeepers.org/ammon-bundy-martyr
-or-revolutionary/. I discuss the Branch Davidians and Waco in more detail
in the next chapter.

36. Oath Keepers, "What Is the Best Method of Rebellion Against Tyranny?,"
OathKeepers.org, February 9, 2016, https://www.oathkeepers.org/what-is
-the-best-method-of-rebellion-against-tyranny/. Note here the reference to
"the *first* American Revolution." Oath Keepers is not shy about anticipating a second American Revolution, in which it expects to participate. The
group suggests in several places that a second revolution (which it sometimes calls a civil war) nearly broke out during the standoff at Bundy
Ranch in 2014. If anyone had fired a shot, the group says, "many or most
of the current serving trigger pullers in the Marine Corps would have
sided with the resistance—joining all of us pissed off veterans—in the
resulting civil war." Oath Keepers, "The Hammond Family Does NOT
Want an Armed Stand Off, and Nobody Has a Right to Force One on

Them," OathKeepers.org, January 1, 2016, https://www.oathkeepers.org/the-hammond-family-does/.

37. Jill Lepore, *The Whites of Their Eyes: The Tea Party's Revolution and the Battle Over American History* (Princeton, NJ: Princeton University Press, 2011), 60–64; Neil Longley York, *The Boston Massacre: A History with Documents* (New York: Routledge, 2010), 24–28.

38. David C. Rapoport, "Before the Bombs There Were the Mobs: American Experiences with Terror," *Terrorism and Political Violence* 20, no. 2 (2008): 167–94, https://doi.org/10.1080/09546550701856045.

39. John Rosman and Conrad Wilson, "FBI: Standoff Continues, Release Video of Finicum Death," Oregon Public Broadcasting, March 8, 2016, https://www.opb.org/news/series/burns-oregon-standoff-bundy-militia-news-updates/fbi-standoff-continues-release-video-of-finicum-death/.

40. Leah Sottile, "Chapter Three: The Widow's Tale," *Bundyville: The Remnant* (blog), July 2019, https://longreads.com/2019/07/17/bundyville-the-remnant-chapter-three-the-widows-tale/.

41. Oath Keepers, "What Is the Best Method of Rebellion Against Tyranny?"

42. Oath Keepers, "The Hammond Family Does NOT Want an Armed Stand Off."

43. Oath Keepers, "The Hammond Family Does NOT Want an Armed Stand Off."

44. This is not universally true, but it holds generally. For an exception, see a brief discussion of the role of conspiracy theories in justifications for independence in Joseph E. Uscinski and Joseph M. Parent, *American Conspiracy Theories* (New York: Oxford University Press, 2014), 2–3.

45. Mulloy makes a similar argument about the patriot/militia movement at large. He concludes that these references to the Founders and the American Revolution fall short because the conditions that would justify revolution (namely, a decision by the people at large rather than individuals or private groups, violations of core rights rather than "light or transient causes," and all other means of addressing the perceived problems falling short) have not been met. D. J. Mulloy, "'Liberty or Death': Violence and the Rhetoric of Revolution in the American Militia Movement," *Canadian Review of American Studies* 38, no. 1 (2008): 119–45.

46. David A. Snow et al., "Frame Alignment Processes, Micromobilization, and Movement Participation," *American Sociological Review* 51, no. 4 (1986): 464–81; David A. Snow and Robert D. Benford, "Ideology, Frame Resonance, and Participant Mobilization," in *From Structure to Action: Comparing Social Movement Research Across Cultures*, ed. Bert Klandermans, Hanspeter Kriesi, and Sidney G. Tarrow (Greenwich: JAI, 1988), 197–217; Robert D. Benford and David A. Snow, "Framing Processes and

Social Movements: An Overview and Assessment," *Annual Review of Sociology* 26 (January 2000): 611–39, https://doi.org/10.2307/223459.

47. I say this is likely rather than that this is certainly the case because there is no direct evidence to support (or contradict) this inference. The only possible direct evidence about thought processes that affect how individuals form arguments would be (1) observing those thought processes as they happen or (2) talking with the individuals who think those thoughts. Neither is possible in this case. The arguments already exist, so I cannot observe the thoughts that shape them, for example, through ethnography. I also have not spoken with the individuals who made the arguments, for two reasons. First, preliminary contact with Stewart Rhodes suggests that he would be unlikely to answer any questions that I would pose; he is distrustful of academics and journalists who do not have a track record of supporting his cause. Second, those individuals developing these arguments have an incentive to be dishonest if their framing choices were strategic rather than ideological. Members of the patriot/militia movement understand themselves to be driven by principled beliefs more than utilitarian calculation. As self-described patriots, they would not be likely to answer that they draw comparisons between their movement and the Founders because they think that will be an effective way to gain support from more Americans; they would be far more likely to answer that they draw these comparisons because they are accurate. In other words, if I asked Rhodes or others why they draw these comparisons, I would expect them to say that they believe the comparisons to be accurate and enlightening even if their primary reason was actually that they believed these comparisons to be an effective way for them to gain support.

48. "Americans have drawn Revolutionary analogies before. They have drawn them for a very long time. When in doubt, in American politics, left, right, or center, deploy the Founding Fathers." Lepore, *The Whites of Their Eyes*, 14.

49. David Sehat, *The Jefferson Rule: How the Founding Fathers Became Infallible and Our Politics Inflexible* (New York: Simon & Schuster, 2015).

50. "The Declaration of Sentiments, Seneca Falls Conference," 1848, https://sourcebooks.fordham.edu/halsall/mod/senecafalls.asp.

51. "Declaration of the Immediate Causes Which Induce and Justify the Secession of South Carolina from the Federal Union," Avalon Project, December 24, 1860, http://avalon.law.yale.edu/19th_century/csa_scarsec.asp; "Declaration of the Immediate Causes Which Induce and Justify the Secession of the State of Mississippi from the Federal Union," Avalon Project, 1861, http://avalon.law.yale.edu/19th_century/csa_missec.asp. For more, see Robert L. Tsai, *America's Forgotten Constitutions: Defiant Visions*

of Power and Community (Cambridge, MA: Harvard University Press, 2014), chap. 4.

52. Theda Skocpol and Vanessa Williamson, *The Tea Party and the Remaking of Republican Conservatism* (New York: Oxford University Press, 2012); Lepore, *The Whites of Their Eyes*; Ruth Braunstein, *Prophets and Patriots: Faith in Democracy Across the Political Divide* (Oakland: University of California Press, 2017), esp. chap. 3.

53. Mulloy, *American Extremism*, 75–87.

6. "No More Free Wacos"

1. Among many others, see D. J. Mulloy, *American Extremism: History, Politics, and the Militia Movement* (New York: Routledge, 2004), 12–16; Robert H. Churchill, *To Shake Their Guns in the Tyrant's Face: Libertarian Political Violence and the Origins of the Militia Movement* (Ann Arbor: University of Michigan Press, 2009), 13; 231–33; Mark Pitcavage, "Camouflage and Conspiracy: The Militia Movement from Ruby Ridge to Y2K," *American Behavioral Scientist* 44, no. 6 (February 2001): 957–81, https://doi.org /10.1177/00027640121956610; Lane Crothers, "The Cultural Foundations of the Modern Militia Movement," *New Political Science* 24, no. 2 (June 2002): 230–31, https://doi.org/10.1080/07393140220145225; Amy B. Cooter, "Americanness, Masculinity, and Whiteness: How Michigan Militia Men Navigate Evolving Social Norms," PhD diss., University of Michigan, 2013, 40–43, https://deepblue.lib.umich.edu/bitstream/handle /2027.42/98077/cooterab_1.pdf.

2. For an excellent journalistic perspective on this event, see Barak Goodman, "Ruby Ridge," *American Experience*, PBS, August 24, 2017, http://www .pbs.org/wgbh/americanexperience/films/ruby-ridge/. Mulloy also provides a good summary in Mulloy, *American Extremism*, 12–14.

3. For an excellent introduction to the Branch Davidians and the standoff at their Waco compound, including criticism of the FBI's actions, see James D. Tabor and Eugene V. Gallagher, "What Might Have Been," in *Why Waco? Cults and the Battle for Religious Freedom in America* (Berkeley: University of California Press, 1995), 1–22; Michael Barkun, "Millenarian Groups and Law Enforcement Agencies: The Lessons of Waco," *Terrorism and Political Violence* 6, no. 1 (1994): 75–95, https://doi.org/10.1080 /09546559408427245; Michael Barkun, "Appropriated Martyrs: The Branch Davidians and the Radical Right," *Terrorism and Political Violence* 19, no. 1 (January 2007): 117–24, https://doi.org/10.1080/09546550601054956; Mulloy, *American Extremism*, 14–16.

4. Associated Press, "Cameraman Recalls Conversation Said to Have Warned Waco Cult," *New York Times*, August 29, 1993, https://www.nytimes.com /1993/08/29/us/cameraman-recalls-conversation-said-to-have-warned -waco-cult.html.

5. Mulloy, *American Extremism*, 14–16; Tabor and Gallagher, "What Might Have Been," 21–22.

6. Barkun, "Appropriated Martyrs"; Mulloy, *American Extremism*, 14–16; Churchill, *To Shake Their Guns in the Tyrant's Face*, 231–33.

7. Stuart A. Wright, *Patriots, Politics, and the Oklahoma City Bombing*, Cambridge Studies in Contentious Politics (New York: Cambridge University Press, 2007), 164.

8. Barkun, "Millenarian Groups and Law Enforcement Agencies."

9. The group only mentions Ruby Ridge alongside Waco, never on its own. Most invocations of Waco do not also mention Ruby Ridge. Oath Keepers does not address why Ruby Ridge seems to be less important for the group, but it could be that the group does not want to draw too many parallels between itself and the Weaver family, given the family's ties to white supremacy.

10. Oath Keepers, "Waco: A New Revelation," OathKeepers.org, January 18, 2016, https://www.oathkeepers.org/waco-a-new-revelation/.

11. Oath Keepers, "Waco." Of course, criticism of police militarization is not limited to antigovernment extremists. For example, the American Civil Liberties Union (ACLU) has also condemned this tendency. American Civil Liberties Union, "Police Militarization," American Civil Liberties Union, https://www.aclu.org/issues/criminal-law-reform/reforming-police -practices/police-militarization.

12. Michael Vanderboegh, "No More Free Wacos: An Explication of the Obvious Addressed to Eric Holder, Attorney General of the United States," *Sipsey Street Irregulars* (blog), May 6, 2009, http://sipseystreetirregulars .blogspot.com/2009/05/no-more-free-wacos-explication-of.html.

13. Oath Keepers, "Oath Keeper in Delaware Arrested for Selling Guns," OathKeepers.org, March 8, 2015, https://www.oathkeepers.org/oath-keeper -in-delaware-arrested-for-selling-guns/; Oath Keepers, "Liberty Brothers Radio at Sugar Pine Mine in Oregon," OathKeepers.org, April 19, 2015, https://www.oathkeepers.org/liberty-brothers-radio-at-sugar-pine-mine-in -oregon-oath-keepers-welcome/.

14. Oath Keepers, "The Hammond Family Does NOT Want an Armed Stand Off, and Nobody Has a Right to Force One on Them," OathKeepers.org, January 1, 2016, https://www.oathkeepers.org/the-hammond-family-does/; Oath Keepers, "URGENT Warning on OR Standoff: Military Special OP Assets Have Been Assigned for Standoff. Keep Women and Children Out

of There," OathKeepers.org, January 5, 2016, https://www.oathkeepers.org/urgent-warning-on-or-standoff-military-special-op-assets-have-been-assigned-for-standoff-get-all-children-out-of-there-immediately/.

15. Oath Keepers, "Historic! Feds Forced to Surrender to American Citizens," *Oath Keepers* (blog), April 16, 2014, http://oath-keepers.blogspot.com/2014/04/historic-feds-forced-to-surrender-to.html.

16. Oath Keepers, "Stewart on Hammond Family Situation in Oregon," 2016, YouTube video, https://www.youtube.com/watch?v=b8HaFEPVJSA.

17. Oath Keepers, "The Hammond Family Does NOT Want an Armed Stand Off."

18. Oath Keepers, "The Hammond Family Does NOT Want an Armed Stand Off."

19. Oath Keepers, "Oregon Standoff a Terrible Plan That We Might Be Stuck With," OathKeepers.org, January 4, 2016, https://www.oathkeepers.org/oregon-standoff-a-terrible-plan-that-we-might-be-stuck-with/.

20. Oath Keepers, "URGENT Warning on OR Standoff."

21. Oath Keepers, "Friday Jan 9th Morning Press Briefing with III%, CFCF and PPN from the Oregon Refuge Center," 2016, YouTube video, https://www.youtube.com/watch?v=yKKaFvn69DY; Oath Keepers, "Historic 'Militia' Moment: Pacific Patriot Network (Including Oath Keepers) Calls on FBI," OathKeepers.org, January 10, 2016, https://www.oathkeepers.org/9435-2/.

22. Oath Keepers, "Warning to U.S. Military and Federal LEOs: Do Not Follow Orders to 'Waco' Ammon Bundy Occupation, or Risk Civil War," OathKeepers.org, January 15, 2016, https://www.oathkeepers.org/critical-warning-to-u-s-military-and-federal-leo-do-not-follow-orders-to-waco-ammon-bundy-occupation-in-oregon-or-you-risk-starting-a-civil-war/.

23. Oath Keepers, "Letter to U.S. Military from SGM Joseph A. Santoro (Ret), Oath Keepers Operations NCO, Writing from Burns, OR," OathKeepers.org, January 15, 2016, https://www.oathkeepers.org/letter-to-u-s-military-from-sgm-joseph-a-santoro-ret-oath-keepers-operations-nco-writing-from-burns-or/.

24. National Weather Service, "Hurricane Katrina—August 2005," November 2016, https://www.weather.gov/mob/katrina; "Hurricane Katrina Statistics Fast Facts," *CNN*, August 28, 2017, https://www.cnn.com/2013/08/23/us/hurricane-katrina-statistics-fast-facts/index.html.

25. Jed Horne, "Five Myths About Hurricane Katrina," *Washington Post*, August 31, 2012, https://www.washingtonpost.com/opinions/five-myths-about-hurricane-katrina/2012/08/31/003f4064-f147-11e1-a612-3cfc842a6d89_story.html.

26. Sabrina Shankman et al., "After Katrina, New Orleans Cops Were Told They Could Shoot Looters," *ProPublica*, July 24, 2012, https://www .propublica.org/article/nopd-order-to-shoot-looters-hurricane-katrina.

27. Mark Guarino, "Misleading Reports of Lawlessness After Katrina Worsened Crisis, Officials Say," *Guardian*, August 16, 2015, http://www .theguardian.com/us-news/2015/aug/16/hurricane-katrina-new-orleans -looting-violence-misleading-reports; Brian Thevenot and Gordon Russell, "Rumors of Deaths Greatly Exaggerated—Widely Reported Attacks False or Unsubstantiated—6 Bodies Found at Dome; 4 at Convention Center," *Times-Picayune*, September 26, 2005.

28. Carol Kopp, "The Bridge to Gretna," *CBS News*, December 15, 2005, https://www.cbsnews.com/news/the-bridge-to-gretna/.

29. Alex Berenson and John M. Broder, "Police Begin Seizing Guns of Civilians," *New York Times*, September 9, 2005, https://www.nytimes.com/2005 /09/09/us/nationalspecial/police-begin-seizing-guns-of-civilians.html; Adam Weinstein, "The NRA Twisted a Tiny Part of the Katrina Disaster to Fit Its Bigger Agenda," *The Trace*, August 31, 2015, https://www.thetrace .org/2015/08/nra-hurricane-katrina-gun-confiscation/.

30. Times-Picayune Staff, "Danziger Bridge Guilty Verdicts Are Another Strike Against New Orleans Police," *NOLA.com*, August 5, 2011, http://www .nola.com/crime/index.ssf/2011/08/danziger_jury_gives_new_orlean .html; Ken Daley and Emily Lane, "Danziger Bridge Officers Sentenced: 7 to 12 Years for Shooters, Cop in Cover-up Gets 3," *NOLA.com*, April 21, 2016, http://www.nola.com/crime/index.ssf/2016/04/danziger_bridge_offi- cers_sente.html.

31. Charles F. Parker et al., "Preventable Catastrophe? The Hurricane Katrina Disaster Revisited," *Journal of Contingencies and Crisis Management* 17, no. 4 (December 1, 2009): 206–20, https://doi.org/10.1111/j.1468–5973.2009 .00588.x; Arjen Boin, Christer Brown, and James A. Richardson, "Hurricane Katrina Revisited: Reflecting on Success and Failure," in *Managing Hurricane Katrina: Lessons from a Megacrisis* (Baton Rouge: Louisiana State University Press, 2019), 1–20. Boin and colleagues acknowledge this criticism and attempt to temper it somewhat by recognizing some aspects of the government's response to the storm that were successful.

32. Weinstein, "The NRA Twisted a Tiny Part of the Katrina Disaster to Fit Its Bigger Agenda."

33. Oath Keepers, "Oath Keepers Declaration of Orders We Will NOT Obey," 2009, YouTube video, https://www.youtube.com/watch?v=Zztaj2AFiy8.

34. This clip originally came from an episode of NBC News' *Meet the Press*, September 4, 2005, http://www.nbcnews.com/id/9179790/ns/meet_the _press/t/transcript-september/.

35. Elsewhere, the group states even more directly that the government "corrall[ed] people into camps where death was rampant." Oath Keepers, "Take These Steps Today to Survive an International Crisis," OathKeepers.org, March 20, 2014, https://www.oathkeepers.org/take-these-steps-today-to-survive-an-international-crisis/.

36. Oath Keepers, "Oath Keepers Declaration of Orders We Will NOT Obey" (video).

37. The Posse Comitatus Act prohibits the use of "any part of the Army or the Air Force as a posse comitatus or otherwise to execute the laws." This language does not prohibit the use of the military on U.S. soil for non–law enforcement purposes, though it is often portrayed that way. Eric V. Larson and John E. Peters, "Appendix D: Overview of the Posse Comitatus Act," in Preparing the U.S. Army for Homeland Security: Concepts, Issues, and Options (Santa Monica, CA: Rand, 2001), https://www.rand.org/pubs/monograph_reports/MR1251.html.

38. Oath Keepers, "Official Oath Keepers Speeches That July 4 Tea Party Events Can Use," Oath Keepers (blog), July 3, 2009, http://oath-keepers.blogspot.com/2009/07/official-oath-keepers-speeches-that.html.

39. Oath Keepers, "Bill O'Reilly Interviews Oath Keepers Founder Stewart Rhodes — 02-18-10," 2010, YouTube video, https://www.youtube.com/watch?v=Isd0FlGb_LY.

40. Oath Keepers, "Declaration of Orders We Will Not Obey," OathKeepers.org, https://www.oathkeepers.org/declaration-of-orders-we-will-not-obey/.

41. Oath Keepers, "Oath Keepers Muster on Lexington Green 4/19/2009 4 of 10," 2009, YouTube video, https://www.youtube.com/watch?v=t7sCHPU730w&list=PL5AE72FAE3DE00667&index=4.

42. Oath Keepers, "Oath Keepers Prove Some Troops Refused to Confiscate Guns During Katrina 1 of 5," 2010, YouTube video, https://www.youtube.com/watch?v=2HRZfvtYlCY; Oath Keepers, "Oath Keepers Prove Some Troops Refused to Confiscate Guns During Katrina 2 of 5," 2010, YouTube video, https://www.youtube.com/watch?v=ygeNzf__Gic; Oath Keepers, "Oath Keepers Prove Some Troops Refused to Confiscate Guns During Katrina 3 of 5," 2010, YouTube video, https://www.youtube.com/watch?v=UDryH9FKSoM; Oath Keepers, "Oath Keepers Prove Some Troops Refused to Confiscate Guns During Katrina 4 of 5," 2010, YouTube video, https://www.youtube.com/watch?v=I6aIcCJQoeY; Oath Keepers, "Oath Keepers Prove Some Troops Refused to Confiscate Guns During Katrina 5 of 5," 2010, YouTube video, https://www.youtube.com/watch?v=H_UvHalYKHM. Emphasis in the original.

43. Oath Keepers, "Oath Keepers Prove Some Troops Refused to Confiscate Guns During Katrina 1 of 5."

Conclusion: The Importance of Oath Keepers

1. Michael Calvin McGee, "The 'Ideograph': A Link Between Rhetoric and Ideology," *Quarterly Journal of Speech* 66, no. 1 (1980): 1–16, https://doi.org/10.1080/00335638009383499.

2. Oath Keepers, "Declaration of Orders We Will Not Obey," OathKeepers.org, https://www.oathkeepers.org/declaration-of-orders-we-will-not-obey/.

3. Amy B. Cooter, "Americanness, Masculinity, and Whiteness: How Michigan Militia Men Navigate Evolving Social Norms," PhD diss., University of Michigan, 2013, 10, 33, https://deepblue.lib.umich.edu/bitstream/handle/2027.42/98077/cooterab_1.pdf.

4. My usage of these terms follows the description by Endres and Senda-Cook, that "place" refers to the particular and "space" to the general. More concretely, I use "place" to refer to specific locations, whereas I use "space" to refer to types of locations or more abstract notions of location. For example, the Bundy Ranch is a place; the West (as a geographical subunit of the United States) is also a place, though a less specific one; and "the West" (as an imagined type of location that is connected with ideas of the frontier, rugged individualism, and independence) is a space. Danielle Endres and Samantha Senda-Cook, "Location Matters: The Rhetoric of Place in Protest," *Quarterly Journal of Speech* 97, no. 3 (August 2011): 259–60, https://doi.org/10.1080/00335630.2011.585167.

5. Priska Daphi, "'Imagine the Streets': The Spatial Dimension of Protests' Transformative Effects and Its Role in Building Movement Identity," *Political Geography* 56 (2017): 34–43, https://doi.org/10.1016/j.polgeo.2016.10.003.

6. Oath Keepers, "Wilderness Corridors: Agenda 21 Under a New Name," OathKeepers.org, July 7, 2015, https://www.oathkeepers.org/wilderness-corridors-agenda-21-under-a-new-name/.

7. Washington State Representative Matt Shea, who has ties to various antigovernment activists and was lauded on the Oath Keepers blog as being "on fire for [the] Constitution," has proposed splitting off the Eastern portion of Washington State from the coastal region to create a new state. He proposed naming that new state "Liberty." Oath Keepers, "Washington State Representative Matt Shea on Fire for Constitution," *Oath Keepers* (blog), December 22, 2014, http://oath-keepers.blogspot.com/2014/12/washington-state-representative-matt.html; Leah Sottile, "Chapter Four: The Preacher and the Politician," *Bundyville: The Remnant* (blog), July 18, 2019, https://longreads.com/2019/07/18/bundyville-the-remnant-chapter-four-the-preacher-and-the-politician/.

8. Scholarly discussion of the idea of a "frontier" in the United States often points back to Frederick Jackson Turner, "The Significance of the

Frontier in American History," in *The Significance of the Frontier in American History*, ed. Harold Peter Simonson (New York: Frederick Ungar, 1963); on the idealization of small farmers in early America, see, for example, Louis Hartz, *The Liberal Tradition in America: An Interpretation of American Political Thought Since the Revolution* (San Diego: Harcourt Brace Jovanovich, 1991), 119–28.

9. Oath Keepers, "Knoxville Tea Party: How's This for an April 19 Warm Up?," *Oath Keepers* (blog), April 15, 2009, http://oath-keepers.blogspot.com/2009 /04/knoxville-tea-party.html.

10. Oath Keepers, "CPT—Community Preparedness Teams," Oath-Keepers.org, https://www.oathkeepers.org/cpt-community-preparedness -teams/.

11. D. J. Mulloy, *American Extremism: History, Politics, and the Militia Movement* (New York: Routledge, 2004).

12. Robert H. Churchill, *To Shake Their Guns in the Tyrant's Face: Libertarian Political Violence and the Origins of the Militia Movement* (Ann Arbor: University of Michigan Press, 2009), 216–25.

13. For example, Oath Keepers, "Stewart on Hammond Family Situation in Oregon," 2016, YouTube video, https://www.youtube.com/watch ?v=b8HaFEPVJSA; Oath Keepers, "Stewart Rhodes Responds to the Hammond Family Situation," 2015, YouTube video, https://www.youtube.com /watch?v=yP5fklVoc54.

14. James D. Tabor and Eugene V. Gallagher, "What Might Have Been," in *Why Waco? Cults and the Battle for Religious Freedom in America* (Berkeley: University of California Press, 1995), 9.

15. Mike Blasky, Ben Botkin, and Colton Lochhead, "Rejected by the Revolution, Jerad and Amanda Miller Decided to Start Their Own," *Las Vegas Review-Journal*, June 14, 2014, http://www.reviewjournal.com/news/bundy -blm/rejected-revolution-jerad-and-amanda-miller-decided-start-their -own.

16. Nathan J. Russell, "An Introduction to the Overton Window of Political Possibilities," Mackinac Center for Public Policy, January 4, 2006, http:// www.mackinac.org/7504; Derek Robertson, "How an Obscure Conservative Theory Became the Trump Era's Go-To Nerd Phrase," *Politico*, February 25, 2018, http://politi.co/2FunqYx.

17. Russell, "An Introduction to the Overton Window of Political Possibilities"; David C. Atkinson, "Charlottesville and the Alt-Right: A Turning Point?," *Politics, Groups, and Identities* 6, no. 2 (April 2, 2018): 309–15, https://doi .org/10.1080/21565503.2018.1454330.

18. Ruth Braunstein, *Prophets and Patriots: Faith in Democracy Across the Political Divide* (Oakland: University of California Press, 2017).

19. Oath Keepers, Webinar, March 4, 2016, not available online, locally archived copy in possession of author; Oath Keepers, "Obama Suggests Mandatory Voting for U.S. Citizens," OathKeepers.org, March 19, 2015, https://www.oathkeepers.org/obama-suggests-mandatory-voting-for-u-s -citizens/; Oath Keepers, "The Elections Are Over!!!!," OathKeepers.org, November 5, 2014, https://www.oathkeepers.org/the-elections-are-over/.

20. Oath Keepers, "Border Rancher Warns of Cartel Border Takeover on U.S. Soil," 2014, YouTube video, https://www.youtube.com/watch?v=eE _Ix6OEaMI; Oath Keepers, "Border Rancher Overrun by Men with Gang Tattoos, Not 'Children,'" 2014, YouTube video, https://www.youtube .com/watch?v=sxnwYg7dMZI; Oath Keepers, "True Grit—An Interview with Tim 'Nailer' Foley of AZBR," 2015, YouTube video, https://www .youtube.com/watch?v=3pobe4ZPLzY; Oath Keepers, "Oath Keepers—a Sabot in the Machine to Stop Voter Fraud & Intimidation," OathKeepers .org, October 25, 2016, https://www.oathkeepers.org/oath-keepers-sabot -machine-stop-voter-fraud-intimidation/.

21. Oath Keepers National, "Oath Keepers Offer of Protection for Embattled Clerk Kim Davis," 2015, YouTube video, https://www.youtube.com/watch ?v=x2Z5e13hZzw.

22. Luke Darby, "Trump Warns of Civil War If He's Impeached and a Right-Wing Militia Cheers," GQ, September 30, 2019, https://www.gq.com/story /trump-civil-war-militia; Casey Michel, "The Oath Keepers Providing Volunteer Security at Trump's Minneapolis Rally Are Itching for a Civil War," Daily Beast, October 10, 2019, https://www.thedailybeast.com/the -oath-keepers-providing-volunteer-security-at-trumps-minneapolis-rally -are-itching-for-a-civil-war.

23. Mack Lamoureux, "Inside Canada's Armed, Anti-Islamic 'Patriot' Group," Vice, June 14, 2017, https://www.vice.com/en_us/article/new9wd/the-birth -of-canadas-armed-anti-islamic-patriot-group.

Appendix 1: Data and Methods

1. Hank Johnston, "A Methodology for Frame Analysis: From Discourse to Cognitive Schemata," in Social Movements and Culture, ed. Hank Johnston and Bert Klandermans (Minneapolis: University of Minnesota Press, 1995), 217–46.

2. David A. Snow et al., "Frame Alignment Processes, Micromobilization, and Movement Participation," American Sociological Review 51, no. 4 (1986): 464–81; David A. Snow and Robert D. Benford, "Ideology, Frame Resonance, and Participant Mobilization," in From Structure to Action:

Comparing Social Movement Research Across Cultures, ed. Bert Klandermans, Hanspeter Kriesi, and Sidney G. Tarrow (Greenwich: JAI, 1988), 197–217.

3. Katherine J. Cramer, *The Politics of Resentment: Rural Consciousness in Wisconsin and the Rise of Scott Walker* (Chicago: University of Chicago Press, 2016), 35.

4. For example, Justine Sharrock, "Oath Keepers and the Age of Treason," *Mother Jones*, April 2010, http://www.motherjones.com/politics/2010/03/oath-keepers; Jesse Bogan, "Police Shut Down Mysterious 'Oath Keepers' Guarding Rooftops in Downtown Ferguson," *St. Louis Post-Dispatch*, November 30, 2014, http://www.stltoday.com/news/local/crime-and-courts/police-shut-down-mysterious-oath-keepers-guarding-rooftops-in-downtown/article_f90b6edd-acf8-52e3-a020-3a78db286194.html; Brian Heffernan, "In Ferguson, Oath Keepers Draw Both Suspicion and Gratitude," *Al Jazeera America*, December 14, 2014, http://america.aljazeera.com/articles/2014/12/14/oath-keepers-fergusonprotests.html; Bethania Palma Markus, "Oath Keepers Put 'Boots on the Ground' to Guard Oath-Breaking Kim Davis from 'Dictator' Judge," *Raw Story*, September 10, 2015, https://www.rawstory.com/2015/09/oath-keepers-vow-to-defend-oath-breaking-kim-davis-with-guns-from-dictator-judge/; Peter Holley, "Race Riots, Terrorist Attacks, and Martial Law: Oath Keepers Warn of Post-Election Chaos," *Washington Post*, November 8, 2016, https://www.washingtonpost.com/news/post-nation/wp/2016/11/08/race-riots-terror-attacks-and-martial-law-oath-keepers-warn-of-post-election-chaos/; Jennifer Williams, "The Oath Keepers, the Far-Right Group Answering Trump's Call to Watch the Polls, Explained," *Vox*, November 7, 2016, http://www.vox.com/policy-and-politics/2016/11/7/13489640/oath-keepers-donald-trump-voter-fraud-intimidation-rigged; Casey Michel, "The Oath Keepers Providing Volunteer Security at Trump's Minneapolis Rally Are Itching for a Civil War," *Daily Beast*, October 10, 2019, https://www.thedailybeast.com/the-oath-keepers-providing-volunteer-security-at-trumps-minneapolis-rally-are-itching-for-a-civil-war.

5. Chip Berlet, "Who Is Mediating the Storm? Right-Wing Alternative Information Networks," in *Media, Culture, and the Religious Right* (Minneapolis: University of Minnesota Press, 1998), 249–73.

6. Kjerstin Thorson and Chris Wells, "How Gatekeeping Still Matters: Understanding Media Effects in an Era of Curated Flows," in *Gatekeeping in Transition*, ed. Timothy Vos and François Heinderyckx (New York: Routledge, 2015), 25–44.

7. Around this time, any attempt to save a page from the Oath Keepers website as an HTML file failed, whether collected using recursive download

tools or saved individually through the "Save As" function in a web browser. After being downloaded, these local HTML files infinitely reload. Eventually, I discovered that this problem was caused by several lines of Javascript code in each page. I removed these lines of Javascript from my local copies of the Oath Keepers website, which allows the pages to be viewed normally.

8. The Oath Keepers website includes comments on posts. The website generates a unique URL for each comment on each post. I filtered out files that were effectively duplicates corresponding to comments on posts.

9. The DA-RT (Data Access–Research Transparency) initiative in political science is a prominent example of this. See http://www.dartstatement.org.

10. Robert H. Churchill, *To Shake Their Guns in the Tyrant's Face: Libertarian Political Violence and the Origins of the Militia Movement* (Ann Arbor: University of Michigan Press, 2009).

11. Consultation with a copyright specialist at Syracuse University Libraries and with several lawyers confirms that this falls under fair use.

12. This software, called BeautifulSoup, is an html processing package available for the Python programming language. See https://www.crummy.com /software/BeautifulSoup/.

13. L. Dean Allen, "Promise Keepers and Racism: Frame Resonance as an Indicator of Organizational Vitality," *Sociology of Religion* 61, no. 1 (Spring 2000): 55–72.

14. Scholars have begun to find that characteristics of speech other than the words being used can be useful social science measures. For example, Bryce Dietrich, Ryan Enos, and Maya Sen found that the "emotional arousal" of Supreme Court justices can be measured by the pitch of their voices; emotional arousal in turn is a robust predictor of how the court will vote on a given case. Steven Mazie, "Supreme Court Justices May Give Away Their Votes with Their Voices," *The Economist*, December 21, 2017, https://www.economist.com/blogs/democracyinamerica/2017/12/pitch -perfect.

15. The list of keywords is available at https://github.com/sjacks26/PM-topic -dictionary. It is a living document; as such, the exact number of keywords may change over time.

Bibliography

OATH KEEPERS

Online Documents, Blog Posts, and Tweets

Oath Keepers. "About." OathKeepers.org. https://www.oathkeepers.org/about/.

——. "After Action Report—Operation Big Sky—Lincoln Montana." OathKeepers.org, September 18, 2015. https://www.oathkeepers.org/after-action-report-operation-big-sky-lincoln-montana/.

——. "Agenda 21 Primer." OathKeepers.org, January 14, 2016. https://www.oathkeepers.org/agenda-21-for-dummies/.

——. "Ammon Bundy—Martyr or Revolutionary?" OathKeepers.org, January 3, 2016. https://www.oathkeepers.org/ammon-bundy-martyr-or-revolutionary/.

——. "Board of Directors." OathKeepers.org. Accessed November 22, 2017. https://www.oathkeepers.org/board-of-directors/.

——. "Bylaws of Oath Keepers." OathKeepers.org. https://www.oathkeepers.org/bylaws/.

——. "Call to Action: Church Security in Sutherland Springs, Texas." OathKeepers.org, November 11, 2017. https://oathkeepers.org/2017/11/call-action-church-security-sutherland-springs-texas/.

——. "CALL TO ACTION: Defend Free Speech in Boston on Saturday, May 13th!" OathKeepers.org, May 10, 2017. https://www.oathkeepers.org/call-action-defend-free-speech-boston-saturday-may-13th/.

——. "A Century of American Figurehead Presidents Marching to the Beat of Wall Street and the New World Order." OathKeepers.org, February 23, 2015.

https://www.oathkeepers.org/a-century-of-american-figurehead-presidents
-marching-to-the-beat-of-wall-street-and-the-new-world-order/.

——. "CPT—Community Preparedness Teams." OathKeepers.org. https://www
.oathkeepers.org/cpt-community-preparedness-teams/.

——. "Critical Updates! Call to Action: March 2—Human Wall of Patriots on
Border to Support Trump's Emergency Declaration." OathKeepers.org, February 20, 2019. https://oathkeepers.org/2019/02/call-to-action-march-2-human
-wall-of-patriots-on-border-to-support-trumps-emergency-declaration/.

——. "Declaration of Orders We Will Not Obey." OathKeepers.org. https://www
.oathkeepers.org/declaration-of-orders-we-will-not-obey/.

——. "The Elections Are Over!!!!" OathKeepers.org, November 5, 2014. https://
www.oathkeepers.org/the-elections-are-over/.

——. "Find a Chapter Near You." OathKeepers.org. https://www.oathkeepers
.org/find-a-chapter-near-you/.

——. "The Hammond Family Does NOT Want an Armed Stand Off, and
Nobody Has a Right to Force One on Them." OathKeepers.org, January 1,
2016. https://www.oathkeepers.org/the-hammond-family-does/.

——. "Harney County Committee of Safety's Letter Asks Ammon Bundy to
Leave Refuge." OathKeepers.org, January 9, 2016. https://www.oathkeepers
.org/harney-county-committee-of-safety-letter-to-ammon-bundy-asking
-him-to-leave/.

——. "Help Defend Free Speech in Berkeley." OathKeepers.org, April 26, 2017.
https://www.oathkeepers.org/help-defend-free-speech-berkeley/.

——. "Help Support Defending ACT for America Marches Against Sharia This
Saturday, June 10, Nationwide." OathKeepers.org, June 7, 2017. https://www
.oathkeepers.org/help-support-defending-act-america-marches-sharia
-saturday-june-10-nationwide/.

——. "Historic! Feds Forced to Surrender to American Citizens." *Oath Keepers*
(blog), April 16, 2014. http://oath-keepers.blogspot.com/2014/04/historic-feds
-forced-to-surrender-to.html.

——. "Historic 'Militia' Moment: Pacific Patriot Network (Including Oath
Keepers) Calls on FBI." OathKeepers.org, January 10, 2016. https://www
.oathkeepers.org/9435-2/.

——. "How the British Gun Control Program Precipitated the American Revolution." OathKeepers.org, August 17, 2015. https://www.oathkeepers.org/how
-the-british-gun-control-program-precipitated-the-american-revolution/.

——. "HOW TO BE A DEFENDER OF THE REPUBLIC—THE EXAMPLE
OF JAMES OTIS." *Oath Keepers* (blog), April 16, 2009. http://oath-keepers
.blogspot.com/2009/04/how-to-be-defender-of-republic-example.html.

——. "Hundreds of Volunteers Needed at the Sugar Pine Mine Security Operation in Oregon." OathKeepers.org, May 1, 2015. https://www.oathkeepers.org

/hundreds-of-volunteers-needed-at-the-sugar-pine-mine-security-operation
-in-oregon/.

——. "Is Martial Law Justified If ISIS Attacks?" OathKeepers.org, May 27, 2015.
https://oathkeepers.org/2015/05/is-martial-law-justified-if-isis-attacks/.

——. "Jade Helm 15—To 'Operate Undetected Amongst Civilian Populations.'"
OathKeepers.org, March 30, 2015. https://www.oathkeepers.org/jade-helm-15
-to-operate-undetected-amongst-civilian-populations/.

——. "JADE HELM 2015: Questions and Reflections." OathKeepers.org, May 5,
2015. https://www.oathkeepers.org/jade-helm-2015-questions-and-reflections/.

——. "Kim Davis' Legal Team Declines Oath Keepers' Offer to Protect Her
Against Unlawful Arrrest [sic]." OathKeepers.org, September 11, 2015.
https://www.oathkeepers.org/kim-davis-legal-team-declines-oath-keepers
-offer-to-protect-her-against-unlawful-arrrest/.

——. "Kit Lange: Open Letter to Washington State Governor." OathKeepers
.org, February 6, 2015. https://www.oathkeepers.org/kit-lange-open-letter-to
-washington-state-governor/.

——. "Knoxville Tea Party: How's This for an April 19 Warm Up?" Oath Keepers
(blog), April 15, 2009. http://oath-keepers.blogspot.com/2009/04/knoxville-tea
-party.html.

——. "LCDR (Ret) Ernest G. Cunningham and Famous (Infamous) Survey."
Oath Keepers (blog), April 15, 2009. http://oath-keepers.blogspot.com/2009/04
/lcdr-ret-ernest-g-cunningham-and-famous.html.

——. "Letter to U.S. Military from SGM Joseph A. Santoro (Ret), Oath Keepers
Operations NCO, Writing from Burns, OR." OathKeepers.org, January 15,
2016. https://www.oathkeepers.org/letter-to-u-s-military-from-sgm-joseph-a
-santoro-ret-oath-keepers-operations-nco-writing-from-burns-or/.

——. "Liberty Brothers Radio at Sugar Pine Mine in Oregon." OathKeepers.org,
April 19, 2015. https://www.oathkeepers.org/liberty-brothers-radio-at-sugar
-pine-mine-in-oregon-oath-keepers-welcome/.

——. "Long Line to Get Thru Security at Deploraball. Cops Pepper Spraying
Disrupters Outside Pic.Twitter.Com/SF4D0PKjfw." Tweet. @Oathkeepers,
January 6, 2017. https://twitter.com/Oathkeepers/status/822262877432250368.

——. "NavyJack—Communists Intend to Overthrow the United States Before
Inauguration Day (Updated 01/12/2017)." OathKeepers.org, January 10, 2017.
https://www.oathkeepers.org/navyjack-communists-intend-overthrow
-united-states-inauguration-day/.

——. "NavyJack—Oath Keepers at the Inauguration." OathKeepers.org, January 21, 2017. https://www.oathkeepers.org/navyjack-oath-keepers-inauguration/.

——. "NavyJack—Operation HYPO: Infiltrating Violent Protests Against the
President Elect." OathKeepers.org, November 11, 2016. https://www
.oathkeepers.org/navyjack-operation-hypo/.

——. "Nelson Hultberg: Revitalization of the State Militias." OathKeepers.org, January 15, 2015. https://oathkeepers.org/2015/01/nelson-hultberg-revitalization -of-the-state-militias/.

——. "Oath Keeper in Delaware Arrested for Selling Guns." OathKeepers.org, March 8, 2015. https://www.oathkeepers.org/oath-keeper-in-delaware-arrested -for-selling-guns/.

——. "Oath Keepers—A Sabot in the Machine to Stop Voter Fraud & Intimida- tion." OathKeepers.org, October 25, 2016. https://www.oathkeepers.org/oath -keepers-sabot-machine-stop-voter-fraud-intimidation/.

——. "Oath Keepers Battle of Berkeley April 15 After Report." OathKeepers.org, April 21, 2017. https://www.oathkeepers.org/oath-keepers-battle-berkeley-april -15-report/.

——. "Oath Keepers Call to Action: Border Operation." OathKeepers.org, December 4, 2018. https://oathkeepers.org/2018/12/oath-keepers-call-to-action -border-operation/.

——. "Oath Keepers Call to Action: Help Defend Free Speech from Violent Thugs at Inauguration." OathKeepers.org, January 17, 2017. https://www .oathkeepers.org/oath-keepers-call-action-help-defend-free-speech-violent -thugs-inauguration/.

——. "Oath Keepers CALL TO ACTION to Spot, Document, and Report Vote Fraud or Intimidation on Election Day, 2016." OathKeepers.org, October 25, 2016. https://www.oathkeepers.org/oath-keepers-call-action-spot-document -report-vote-fraud-intimidation-election-day-2016/.

——. "Oath Keepers Guarding Businesses in Ferguson, Missouri: Calling on Volunteers to Assist." OathKeepers.org, November 25, 2014. https://www .oathkeepers.org/oath-keepers-guarding-businesses-in-ferguson-missouri -calling-on-volunteers-to-assist/.

——. "Oath Keepers Is Going 'Operational' by Forming Special 'Civilization Preservation' Teams." *Infowars*, October 1, 2013. http://www.infowars.com /oath-keepers-is-going-operational-by-forming-special-civilization -preservation-teams/.

——. "Oath Keepers National Call to Action: Help Us 'Protect the Protectors' by Guarding Recruiting and Reserve Centers." OathKeepers.org, July 21, 2015. https://www.oathkeepers.org/oath-keepers-national-call-to-action-help-us -protect-the-protectors-by-guarding-recruiting-and-reserve-centers/.

——. "Oath Keepers Need Your Help in Puerto Rico!" OathKeepers.org, Octo- ber 16, 2017. https://www.oathkeepers.org/oath-keepers-need-help-puerto -rico/.

——. "Oath Keepers Offers Kim Davis Protection from Further Imprisonment by Judge." OathKeepers.org, September 9, 2015. https://www.oathkeepers.org /oath-keepers-offer-of-protection-for-embattled-clerk-kim-davis/.

——. "Oath Keepers Pledges to Fight ISIS in U.S." OathKeepers.org, June 13, 2016. https://www.oathkeepers.org/oath-keepers-pledges-to-fight-isis/.

——. "Oath Keepers Update and SITREP." *Oath Keepers* (blog), March 11, 2009. http://oath-keepers.blogspot.com/2009/03/oath-keepers-update.html.

——. "Obama Suggests Mandatory Voting for U.S. Citizens." OathKeepers.org, March 19, 2015. https://www.oathkeepers.org/obama-suggests-mandatory -voting-for-u-s-citizens/.

——. "OFFICIAL OATH KEEPERS SPEECHES THAT JULY 4 TEA PARTY EVENTS CAN USE." *Oath Keepers* (blog), July 3, 2009. http://oath-keepers .blogspot.com/2009/07/official-oath-keepers-speeches-that.html.

——. "Open Letter of Warning to Governor Nixon from Missouri Oath Keepers." OathKeepers.org, August 22, 2014. https://www.oathkeepers.org/open -letter-of-warning-to-governor-nixon-from-missouri-oath-keepers-2/.

——. "Operation Big Sky: Protecting Rights of Miners in Montana." OathKeepers.org, August 6, 2015. https://www.oathkeepers.org/operation-big-sky -protecting-rights-of-miners-in-montana/.

——. "Oregon Standoff a Terrible Plan That We Might Be Stuck With." Oath-Keepers.org, January 4, 2016. https://www.oathkeepers.org/oregon-standoff-a -terrible-plan-that-we-might-be-stuck-with/.

——. "Principles of Our Republic Oath Keepers Are Sworn to Defend." *Oath Keepers* (blog), March 5, 2009. http://oath-keepers.blogspot.com/2009/03 /principles-of-our-republic-oath-keepers.html.

——. "Protect the Protectors—Update." OathKeepers.org, July 22, 2015. https:// www.oathkeepers.org/protect-the-protectors-update/.

——. "A Recommended Honorable Exit Strategy for Ammon Bundy." Oath-Keepers.org, January 6, 2016. https://www.oathkeepers.org/a-recommended -honorable-exit-strategy-for-ammon-bundy/.

——. "A Snowball Named Reuters." OathKeepers.org, August 12, 2015. https:// www.oathkeepers.org/a-snowball-named-reuters/.

——. "Spending Bill Betrayal by Establishment Republicans Confirms Contempt for Base." OathKeepers.org, December 18, 2015. https://www.oathkeepers.org /establishment-republican-budget-betrayal-shows-contempt-for-america/.

——. "State Chapters." OathKeepers.org, July 15, 2018. https://oathkeepers.org /state-chapters/.

——. "Stewart Rhodes' Sixth Anniversary Essay." OathKeepers.org, April 20, 2015. https://www.oathkeepers.org/stewart-rhodes-sixth-anniversary-essay/.

——. "Take These Steps Today to Survive an International Crisis." OathKeepers .org, March 20, 2014. https://www.oathkeepers.org/take-these-steps-today-to -survive-an-international-crisis/.

——. "Two Arizona State Legislators Will March with Oath Keepers and Speak in Quartzsite This Saturday, August 27, 2011!" August 24, 2011. https://myemail

.constantcontact.com/Two-Arizona-State-Legislators-Will-March-With
-Oath-Keepers-and-Speak-In-Quartzsite-this-Saturday—August-27—2011-
.html?soid=1102755758632&aid=FHVHi3BHDuw.

——. Untitled post. *Oath Keepers* (blog), April 16, 2014. http://oath-keepers
.blogspot.com/2014/04/note-first-at-moment-things-are-quiet.html.

——. "UPDATE: NavyJack—The Presidential Inauguration (or Not) of Donald J. Trump." OathKeepers.org, January 14, 2017. https://www.oathkeepers
.org/navyjack-presidential-inauguration-not-donald-j-trump/.

——. "UPDATE: Stewart Rhodes on Disaster Relief in Puerto Rico." OathKeep-
ers.org, October 11, 2017. https://www.oathkeepers.org/update-stewart-rhodes
-disaster-relief-puerto-rico/.

——. "Urge President Trump to Deploy U.S. Military to Secure ENTIRE Border and Build the Wall!" OathKeepers.org, January 8, 2019. https://oathkeepers
.org/2019/01/urge-president-trump-to-deploy-u-s-military-to-secure-entire
-border-and-build-the-wall/.

——. "URGENT Warning on OR Standoff: Military Special OP Assets Have
Been Assigned for Standoff. Keep Women and Children Out of There." Oath-
Keepers.org, January 5, 2016. https://www.oathkeepers.org/urgent-warning
-on-or-standoff-military-special-op-assets-have-been-assigned-for-standoff
-get-all-children-out-of-there-immediately/.

——. "U.S.-EU Statement Calls for Enforcement of UN Arms Treaty." Oath-
Keepers.org, March 30, 2014. https://www.oathkeepers.org/u-s-eu-statement
-calls-for-enforcement-of-un-arms-treaty/.

——. "WACO: A NEW REVELATION." OathKeepers.org, January 18, 2016.
https://www.oathkeepers.org/waco-a-new-revelation/.

——. "Warning to U.S. Military and Federal LEOs: Do Not Follow Orders to
'Waco' Ammon Bundy Occupation, or Risk Civil War." OathKeepers.org,
January 15, 2016. https://www.oathkeepers.org/critical-warning-to-u-s-military
-and-federal-leo-do-not-follow-orders-to-waco-ammon-bundy-occupation
-in-oregon-or-you-risk-starting-a-civil-war/.

——. "Washington State Representative Matt Shea on Fire for Constitution."
Oath Keepers (blog), December 22, 2014. http://oath-keepers.blogspot.com
/2014/12/washington-state-representative-matt.html.

——. "Welcome to Oath Keepers." *Oath Keepers* (blog), March 2, 2009. http://
oath-keepers.blogspot.com/2009/03/welcome-to-oath-keepers_02.html.

——. "What Is the Best Method of Rebellion Against Tyranny?" OathKeepers
.org, February 9, 2016. https://www.oathkeepers.org/what-is-the-best-method
-of-rebellion-against-tyranny/.

——. "WikiLeaks: Murdered DNC Staffer Source of DNC Leaks . . . Not Russia." OathKeepers.org, August 10, 2016. https://www.oathkeepers.org/wikileaks
-murdered-dnc-staffer-source-of-dnc-leaksnot-russia/.

——. "Wilderness Corridors: Agenda 21 Under a New Name." OathKeepers.org, July 7, 2015. https://www.oathkeepers.org/wilderness-corridors-agenda-21-under-a-new-name/.

YouTube Videos and Webinars

Oath Keepers. "4-16-09 Oath Keepers Stewart Rhodes on Alex Jones 1 of 2." 2009. https://www.youtube.com/watch?v=PdiXbSV21mk.

——. "Alex Jones Round Table with Oath Keepers, Stewart Rhodes, Michael Boldin & Brandon Smith." 2011. https://www.youtube.com/watch?v=hdd9c_HTaq8.

——. "Barricades Removed." 2013. https://www.youtube.com/watch?v=EorCtwFjXmQ.

——. "Bill O'Reilly Interviews Oath Keepers Founder Stewart Rhodes—02-18-10." 2010. https://www.youtube.com/watch?v=IsdoFlGb_LY.

——. "Border Rancher Overrun by Men with Gang Tattoos, Not 'Children.'" 2014. https://www.youtube.com/watch?v=sxnwYg7dMZI.

——. "Border Rancher Warns of Cartel Border Takeover on U.S. Soil." 2014. https://www.youtube.com/watch?v=eE_Ix6OEaMI.

——. "Bundys Cowboy Up and Get Cattle Back." 2014. https://www.youtube.com/watch?v=WQ_5b1z-HW4.

——. "Ernest Guy Cunningham Lexington Green April 19 2009." 2009. https://www.youtube.com/watch?v=5bSdtWfkiz4.

——. "Friday Jan 9th Morning Press Briefing with III%, CFCF and PPN from the Oregon Refuge Center." 2016. https://www.youtube.com/watch?v=yKKaFvn69DY.

——. "Oath Keepers Bundy Ranch Debrief." 2014. https://www.youtube.com/watch?v=4HkSAewoESg.

——. "Oath Keepers Declaration of Orders We Will NOT Obey." 2009. https://www.youtube.com/watch?v=Zztaj2AFiy8.

——. "Oath Keepers Muster on Lexington Green 4/19/2009 1 of 10." 2009. https://www.youtube.com/watch?v=7eactx2yX-w.

——. "Oath Keepers Muster on Lexington Green 4/19/2009 2 of 10." 2009. https://www.youtube.com/watch?v=osP45wNRD1w.

——. "Oath Keepers Muster on Lexington Green 4/19/2009 3 of 10." 2009. https://www.youtube.com/watch?v=NED1UJvXSRQ.

——. "Oath Keepers Muster on Lexington Green 4/19/2009 4 of 10." 2009. https://www.youtube.com/watch?v=t7sCHPU730w.

——. "Oath Keepers Muster on Lexington Green 4/19/2009 7 of 10." 2009. https://www.youtube.com/watch?v=Fcsousr6BR0.

——. "OATH KEEPERS PROVE SOME TROOPS REFUSED TO CONFIS-
CATE GUNS DURING KATRINA 1 of 5." 2010. https://www.youtube.com
/watch?v=2HRZfvtYlCY.

——. "OATH KEEPERS PROVE SOME TROOPS REFUSED TO CONFIS-
CATE GUNS DURING KATRINA 2 of 5." 2010. https://www.youtube.com
/watch?v=ygeNzf__Gic.

——. "OATH KEEPERS PROVE SOME TROOPS REFUSED TO CONFIS-
CATE GUNS DURING KATRINA 3 of 5." 2010. https://www.youtube.com
/watch?v=UDryH9FKSoM.

——. "OATH KEEPERS PROVE SOME TROOPS REFUSED TO CONFIS-
CATE GUNS DURING KATRINA 4 of 5." 2010. https://www.youtube.com
/watch?v=I6aIcCJQoeY.

——. "OATH KEEPERS PROVE SOME TROOPS REFUSED TO CONFIS-
CATE GUNS DURING KATRINA 5 of 5." 2010. https://www.youtube.com
/watch?v=H_UvHalYKHM.

——. "Oath Keepers Quartzsite Muster 8-27-2011." 2011. https://www.youtube
.com/watch?v=hpBCFgKRvdk.

——. "Oath Keepers Rally to Honor Jose Guerena and Oppose SWAT Searches."
2011. https://www.youtube.com/watch?v=S6NOx5Cx8Ws.

——. "Oath Keepers Remove Barricades from WW2 Memorial in DC." 2013.
https://www.youtube.com/watch?v=85FGRpg_5VE.

——. "Oath Keepers Tucson Memorial Day to Honor Jose Guerena and Our
War Dead." 2011. https://www.youtube.com/watch?v=dKrSQY_w34M.

——. "OK4TROOPS Constitutional Care Package Drive Promo Video." 2009.
https://www.youtube.com/watch?v=Spq1N8ELHj8.

——. "Removed Barricades from WW2 Memorial and Oath Keepers Talk to
Police." 2013. https://www.youtube.com/watch?v=ypTD8RIydmI.

——. "Stewart on Hammond Family Situation in Oregon." 2016. https://www
.youtube.com/watch?v=b8HaFEPVJSA.

——. "Stewart Rhodes and Oath Keepers of Josephine County, Oregon—Sugar
Pine Mine." 2015. https://www.youtube.com/watch?v=XYmVure11FA.

——. "Stewart Rhodes Interview—Senate Detention Bill Is Pure Treason—
Declares War on American People." 2011. https://www.youtube.com/watch
?v=stFsg-LQGlM.

——. "Stewart Rhodes on Alex Jones Radio Show: Jan. 11th 2012 Discussing
NDAA." 2012. https://www.youtube.com/watch?v=HTXN43Y5N6E.

——. "Stewart Rhodes on Alex Jones Show 2-7-10 Part 3 of 3." 2010. https://www
.youtube.com/watch?v=GoP-VnxtUGg.

——. "Stewart Rhodes on the 'Baldy & the Blonde Radio Show' Discussing
Senate Bill 1867: Audio." 2011. https://www.youtube.com/watch?v=4IQnObV
jLOo.

——. "Stewart Rhodes Responds to the Hammond Family Situation." 2015. https://www.youtube.com/watch?v=yP5fklVoc54.

——. "True Grit—An Interview with Tim 'Nailer' Foley of AZBR." 2015. https://www.youtube.com/watch?v=3pobe4ZPLzY.

——. Webinar—March 4, 2016. Not available online; locally archived copy in possession of author.

——. Webinar—November 7, 2016. Not available online; locally archived copy in possession of author.

Oath Keepers National. "Oath Keepers Offer of Protection for Embattled Clerk Kim Davis." 2015. https://www.youtube.com/watch?v=x2Z5e13hZzw.

——. "Urgent Message About Sam Andrews." 2015. https://www.youtube.com/watch?v=4tR-QoeoHxA.

Writings by Oath Keepers Members

Constitutional Sheriffs and Peace Officers Association (CSPOA). "About." http://cspoa.org/about/.

——. "Our Leadership." http://cspoa.org/about/our-leadership/.

——. "The Sheriff." http://cspoa.org/about/sheriff-mack/.

Liberty Brothers Radio Show. "If We Do Not Stop Jade Helm 15 There May Be No Future for Our Children!" 2015. YouTube video. https://www.youtube.com/watch?v=P_uLoGwpQEc.

——. "Stewart Rhodes on Jade Helm 15 on the Liberty Brothers." 2015. YouTube video. https://www.youtube.com/watch?v=8CC7c9a0KT8.

Rhodes, Stewart. "THE BILL OF RIGHTS: THE CONSTITUTION'S BUILT-IN, MANDATORY MANUAL OF CONSTITUTIONAL INTERPRETA-TION." *Stewart Rhodes* (blog), February 18, 2009. http://stewart-rhodes.blogspot.com/2009/02/bill-of-rights-constitutions-built-in.html.

——. "Don't Be Neoconned. Ron Paul on Understanding the Grave Threat to Our Constitutional Republic." *Stewart Rhodes* (blog), August 22, 2007. http://stewart-rhodes.blogspot.com/2007/08/dont-be-neoconned-ron-paul-on.html.

——. "THE FIRST FUNDAMENTAL PRINCIPLE OF CONSTITUTIONAL INTERPRETATION: YOUR RIGHTS DON'T COME FROM GOVERN-MENT." *Stewart Rhodes* (blog), February 18, 2009. http://stewart-rhodes.blogspot.com/2009/02/first-fundamental-principle-of.html.

——. "Montana Introduces Resolution Asserting State Sovereignty—And Threatening Secession." *Stewart Rhodes* (blog), February 17, 2009. http://stewart-rhodes.blogspot.com/2009/02/montana-introduces-resolution-asserting.html.

——. "Reinstate the Draft!: America's Youth Must Serve Their Country, One Way or Another—Sieg Heil!" *Stewart Rhodes* (blog), October 29, 2006. http://stewart-rhodes.blogspot.com/2006/10/reinstate-draft-americas-youth-must.html.

——. "Understanding Enemy Combatant Status and the Military Commissions Act, Part I. Enemy Combatant Status: No More Pernicious Doctrine." *Stewart Rhodes* (blog), October 28, 2006. http://www.stewart-rhodes.blogspot.com/2006/10/enemy-combatant-status-no-more.html.

REFERENCES

Abcarian, Robin, and Nicholas Riccardi. "Abortion Doctor George Tiller Is Killed; Suspect in Custody." *Los Angeles Times*, June 1, 2009. https://www.latimes.com/archives/la-xpm-2009-jun-01-na-tiller1-story.html.

Adask, Alfred. "'Unalienable' vs. 'Inalienable.'" *Adask's Law* (blog), July 15, 2009. https://adask.wordpress.com/2009/07/15/unalienable-vs-inalienable/.

Aho, James Alfred. *Far-Right Fantasy: A Sociology of American Religion and Politics*. New York: Routledge, 2016.

——. *The Politics of Righteousness: Idaho Christian Patriotism*. Seattle: University of Washington Press, 1990.

Allen, L. Dean. "Promise Keepers and Racism: Frame Resonance as an Indicator of Organizational Vitality." *Sociology of Religion* 61, no. 1 (Spring 2000): 55–72.

American Civil Liberties Union. "Police Militarization." https://www.aclu.org/issues/criminal-law-reform/reforming-police-practices/police-militarization.

Anti-Defamation League. "ACT for America." https://www.adl.org/resources/profiles/act-for-america.

——. "Defining Extremism: A Glossary of Anti-Government Extremist Terms, Movements and Philosophies." https://www.adl.org/education/resources/glossary-terms/defining-extremism-anti-government.

——. "Jewish 'Control' of the Federal Reserve: A Classic Anti-Semitic Myth." https://www.adl.org/education/resources/backgrounders/jewish-control-of-the-federal-reserve-a-classic-anti-semitic-myth.

——. "The Oath Keepers: Anti-Government Extremists Recruiting Military and Police." http://www.adl.org/combating-hate/domestic-extremism-terrorism/c/the-oath-keepers.html.

——. "The Sovereign Citizen Movement." 2016. https://www.adl.org/education/resources/reports/the-sovereign-citizen-movement.

——. "When Women Are the Enemy: The Intersection of Misogyny and White Supremacy." Anti-Defamation League Center on Extremism. 2018.

https://www.adl.org/resources/reports/when-women-are-the-enemy-the-inter
section-of-misogyny-and-white-supremacy.

——. "Who Are the Antifa?" https://www.adl.org/resources/backgrounders/who
-are-the-antifa.

Appelbaum, Yoni, and Daniel Lombroso. "'Hail Trump!': White Nationalists
Salute the President-Elect." *The Atlantic*, November 21, 2016. https://www
.theatlantic.com/politics/archive/2016/11/richard-spencer-speech-npi/508379/.

Appleton, Kirsten, and Veronica Stracqualursi. "Here's What Happened the Last
Time the Government Shut Down." *ABC News*, November 18, 2014. https://
abcnews.go.com/Politics/heres-happened-time-government-shut/story
?id=26997023.

Associated Press. "Cameraman Recalls Conversation Said to Have Warned
Waco Cult." *New York Times*, August 29, 1993. https://www.nytimes.com
/1993/08/29/us/cameraman-recalls-conversation-said-to-have-warned-waco
-cult.html.

——. "Protesters Led by Cliven Bundy's Son Occupy a Building at Oregon
Wildlife Refuge." *Los Angeles Times*, January 2, 2016. http://www.latimes
.com/nation/nationnow/la-na-nn-oregon-ranchers-protest-20160102-story
.html.

Atkinson, David C. "Charlottesville and the Alt-Right: A Turning Point?" *Politics, Groups, and Identities* 6, no. 2 (April 2, 2018): 309–15. https://doi.org/10
.1080/21565503.2018.1454330.

Backes, Uwe. "Meaning and Forms of Political Extremism in Past and Present."
Středo Evropské Politické Studie (2007): 242–62.

Bamford, James. "Every Move You Make." *Foreign Policy*, September 7, 2016.
https://foreignpolicy.com/2016/09/07/every-move-you-make-obama-nsa
-security-surveillance-spying-intelligence-snowden/.

Barkun, Michael. "Appropriated Martyrs: The Branch Davidians and the Radical Right." *Terrorism and Political Violence* 19, no. 1 (January 2007): 117–24.
https://doi.org/10.1080/09546550601054956.

——. *A Culture of Conspiracy: Apocalyptic Visions in Contemporary America*.
2nd ed. Berkeley: University of California Press, 2013.

——. "Millenarian Groups and Law Enforcement Agencies: The Lessons of
Waco." *Terrorism and Political Violence* 6, no. 1 (1994): 75–95. https://doi.org
/10.1080/09546559408427245.

——. "Purifying the Law: The Legal World of 'Christian Patriots.'" *Journal for
the Study of Radicalism* 1, no. 1 (April 2007): 57–70.

——. *Religion and the Racist Right: The Origins of the Christian Identity Movement*. Rev. ed. Chapel Hill: University of North Carolina Press, 1997.

——. "Violence in the Name of Democracy: Justifications for Separatism on the
Radical Right." *Terrorism and Political Violence* 12, no. 3–4 (2000): 193–208.

Beinart, Peter. "The Rise of the Violent Left." *The Atlantic*, September 2017. https://www.theatlantic.com/magazine/archive/2017/09/the-rise-of-the -violent-left/534192/.

Beitz, Charles R. "Naturalistic Theories." In *The Idea of Human Rights*, 48–72. New York: Oxford University Press, 2009.

Bekiempis, Victoria. "Oath Keepers Want to Arm Ferguson Protesters." *Newsweek*, August 19, 2015. https://www.newsweek.com/oath-keepers-ferguson -blacklivesmatter-michael-brown-black-lives-matter-second-363994.

Belanger, Christian. "What Is Jade Helm 15." *PolitiFact*, July 14, 2015. http://www .politifact.com/truth-o-meter/article/2015/jul/14/what-jade-helm-15/.

Benesch, Susan, Cathy Buerger, Tonei Glavinic, and Sean Manion. "Dangerous Speech: A Practical Guide." Dangerous Speech Project, December 31, 2018. https://dangerousspeech.org/guide/.

Benford, Robert D., and David A. Snow. "Framing Processes and Social Movements: An Overview and Assessment." *Annual Review of Sociology* 26 (January 2000): 611–39. https://doi.org/10.2307/223459.

Bennett, David H. *The Party of Fear: From Nativist Movements to the New Right in American History*. 2nd ed. New York: Vintage, 1995.

Berenson, Alex, and John M. Broder. "Police Begin Seizing Guns of Civilians." *New York Times*, September 9, 2005. https://www.nytimes.com/2005/09/09/us /nationalspecial/police-begin-seizing-guns-of-civilians.html.

Berger, J. M. *Extremism*. Cambridge, MA: MIT Press, 2018.

——. "The Hate List." *Foreign Policy*, March 12, 2013. http://www.foreignpolicy .com/articles/2013/03/12/the_hate_list.

——. "PATCON: The FBI's Secret War Against the 'Patriot' Movement, and How Infiltration Tactics Relate to Radicalizing Influences." New America Foundation. May 2012.

——. "The Patriot Movement's New Bestseller Tests Their Anti-Racism." *Daily Beast*, June 8, 2012. http://www.thedailybeast.com/articles/2012/06/08/the -patriot-movement-s-new-bestseller-tests-their-anti-racism.html.

——. "TASM 2019: J. M. Berger Keynote." 2019. YouTube video. https://www .youtube.com/watch?v=VfYuJR2z24U&feature=youtu.be&list=PLA9DF59 2615F3FCAD&t=756.

——. "The Turner Legacy: The Storied Origins and Enduring Impact of White Nationalism's Deadly Bible." International Centre for Counter-Terrorism—The Hague. 2016. https://icct.nl/publication/the-turner-legacy -the-storied-origins-and-enduring-impact-of-white-nationalisms-deadly -bible/.

——. "Without Prejudice: What Sovereign Citizens Believe." GW Program on Extremism, June 2016. https://extremism.gwu.edu/sites/extremism.gwu.edu /files/downloads/JMB%20Sovereign%20Citizens.pdf.

Berlet, Chip. "Who Is Mediating the Storm? Right-Wing Alternative Information Networks." In *Media, Culture, and the Religious Right*, 249–73. Minneapolis: University of Minnesota Press, 1998.

Bernstein, Maxine. "Oregon Refuge Occupier Jon Ritzheimer: 'I Am Extremely Sorry for This Entire Mess.'" *OregonLive.com*, November 30, 2017. http://www .oregonlive.com/oregon-standoff/2017/11/oregon_refuge_occupier_jon_rit .html.

Bjørgo, Tore. "Introduction: Terror from the Extreme Right." *Terrorism and Political Violence* 7, no. 1 (March 1995): 1–16. https://doi.org/10.1080/0954655950 8427283.

Blasky, Mike, Ben Botkin, and Colton Lochhead. "Rejected by the Revolution, Jerad and Amanda Miller Decided to Start Their Own." *Las Vegas Review-Journal*, June 14, 2014. http://www.reviewjournal.com/news/bundy-blm /rejected-revolution-jerad-and-amanda-miller-decided-start-their-own.

Blee, Kathleen M. *Inside Organized Racism: Women in the Hate Movement.* Berkeley: University of California Press, 2002.

Blee, Kathleen M., and Kimberly A. Creasap. "Conservative and Right-Wing Movements." *Annual Review of Sociology* 36, no. 1 (2010): 269–86. https://doi .org/10.1146/annurev.soc.012809.102602.

Blee, Kathleen M., and Elizabeth A. Yates. "The Place of Race in Conservative and Far-Right Movements." *Sociology of Race and Ethnicity* 1, no. 1 (2015): 127–36. https://doi.org/10.1177/2332649214555031.

Blinder, Alan, and Richard Pérez-Peña. "Kentucky Clerk Denies Same-Sex Marriage Licenses, Defying Court." *New York Times*, September 1, 2015. https:// www.nytimes.com/2015/09/02/us/same-sex-marriage-kentucky-kim-davis.html.

Bo Perrin. "Unalienable vs. Inalienable." *Tea Party Tribune*, September 8, 2012. http://www.teapartytribune.com/2012/09/08/unalienable-vs-inalienable/.

Bogan, Jesse. "Police Shut Down Mysterious 'Oath Keepers' Guarding Rooftops in Downtown Ferguson." *stltoday.com*, November 30, 2014. http://www .stltoday.com/news/local/crime-and-courts/police-shut-down-mysterious -oath-keepers-guarding-rooftops-in-downtown/article_f90b6edd-acf8–52e3 -a020–3a78db286194.html.

Boin, Arjen, Christer Brown, and James A. Richardson. "Hurricane Katrina Revisited: Reflecting on Success and Failure." In *Managing Hurricane Katrina: Lessons from a Megacrisis*, 1–20. Baton Rouge: Louisiana State University Press, 2019.

Boskey, Susan. "How the Declaration of Independence Got Hijacked." *Beyond the National Myth* (blog). http://nationalmyth.org/how-the-declaration-of -independence-was-hijacked/.

Bouton, Terry. *Taming Democracy: "The People," the Founders, and the Troubled Ending of the American Revolution.* New York: Oxford University Press, 2007.

Braunstein, Ruth. *Prophets and Patriots: Faith in Democracy Across the Political Divide*. Oakland: University of California Press, 2017.

Bravo López, Fernando. "Towards a Definition of Islamophobia: Approximations of the Early Twentieth Century." *Ethnic and Racial Studies* 34, no. 4 (April 2011): 556–73. https://doi.org/10.1080/01419870.2010.528440.

Breton, Albert, Gianluigi Galeotti, Pierre Salmon, and Ronald Wintrobe, eds. *Political Extremism and Rationality*. New York: Cambridge University Press, 2002.

Bundy Ranch. "DONATE." *Bundy Ranch* (blog), April 6, 2014. http://bundyranch .blogspot.com/2014/04/you-have-been-asking-what-you-can-do_6.html.

——. "Facts & Events in the Hammond Case." *Bundy Ranch* (blog), November 12, 2015. http://bundyranch.blogspot.com/2015/11/facts-events-in -hammond-case.html.

Cammeron, Brenna. "Antifa: Left-Wing Militants on the Rise." *BBC News*, August 14, 2017. https://www.bbc.com/news/world-us-canada-40930831.

Canale, Joshua. "New York Committee and Council of Safety." In *George Washington Digital Encyclopedia*. Mount Vernon Estate. https://www .mountvernon.org/library/digitalhistory/digital-encyclopedia/article/new -york-committee-and-council-of-safety/#1.

Carter, David, Steve Chermak, Jeremy Carter, and Jack Drew. "Understanding Law Enforcement Intelligence Processes." Report to the Office of University Programs, Science and Technology Directorate, U.S. Department of Homeland Security. START, 2014. https://www.start.umd.edu/pubs/START_Understanding LawEnforcementIntelligenceProcesses_July2014.pdf.

Chermak, Steven M. *Searching for a Demon: The Media Construction of the Militia Movement*. Boston: Northeastern University Press, 2002.

Chokshi, Niraj. "The Federal Government Moved Some Cattle and Nevada's Governor Isn't Happy About It." *Washington Post*, April 9, 2014. https://www .washingtonpost.com/blogs/govbeat/wp/2014/04/09/the-federal-government -moved-some-cows-and-nevadas-governor-isnt-happy-about-it/.

Churchill, Robert H. *To Shake Their Guns in the Tyrant's Face: Libertarian Political Violence and the Origins of the Militia Movement*. Ann Arbor: University of Michigan Press, 2009.

CNN. "Hurricane Katrina Statistics Fast Facts." *CNN*, August 28, 2017. https:// www.cnn.com/2013/08/23/us/hurricane-katrina-statistics-fast-facts/index .html.

Cooter, Amy B. "Americanness, Masculinity, and Whiteness: How Michigan Militia Men Navigate Evolving Social Norms." PhD diss., University of Michigan, 2013. https://deepblue.lib.umich.edu/bitstream/handle/2027.42 /98077/cooterab_1.pdf.

Cornell, Saul. "Mobs, Militias, and Magistrates: Popular Constitutionalism and the Whiskey Rebellion." *Chicago-Kent Law Review* 81 (2006): 883.

Cramer, Katherine J. *The Politics of Resentment: Rural Consciousness in Wisconsin and the Rise of Scott Walker.* Chicago: University of Chicago Press, 2016.

Crothers, Lane. "The Cultural Foundations of the Modern Militia Movement." *New Political Science* 24, no. 2 (June 2002): 221–34. https://doi.org/10.1080/07393140220145225.

Cunningham, Ernest Guy. "The 29 Palms Survey." https://www.29palmssurvey.com/survey.html.

Cush, Andy. "Whose Side Are the Oath Keepers in Ferguson On?" *Gawker*, August 18, 2015. http://gawker.com/whose-side-are-the-oath-keepers-in-ferguson-on-1723917237.

Daley, Ken, and Emily Lane. "Danziger Bridge Officers Sentenced: 7 to 12 Years for Shooters, Cop in Cover-up Gets 3." *NOLA.com*, April 21, 2016. http://www.nola.com/crime/index.ssf/2016/04/danziger_bridge_officers_sente.html.

Daniszewski, John. "Writing About the 'Alt-Right.'" *Definitive Source* (blog), Associated Press, November 28, 2016. https://blog.ap.org/behind-the-news/writing-about-the-alt-right.

Daphi, Priska. "'Imagine the Streets': The Spatial Dimension of Protests' Transformative Effects and Its Role in Building Movement Identity." *Political Geography* 56 (2017): 34–43. https://doi.org/10.1016/j.polgeo.2016.10.003.

Darby, Luke. "Trump Warns of Civil War If He's Impeached and a Right-Wing Militia Cheers." *GQ*, September 30, 2019. https://www.gq.com/story/trump-civil-war-militia.

"Declaration of Sentiments, Seneca Falls Conference." 1848. https://sourcebooks.fordham.edu/halsall/mod/senecafalls.asp.

"Declaration of the Immediate Causes Which Induce and Justify the Secession of South Carolina from the Federal Union," December 24, 1860. Avalon Project. http://avalon.law.yale.edu/19th_century/csa_scarsec.asp.

"Declaration of the Immediate Causes Which Induce and Justify the Secession of the State of Mississippi from the Federal Union," 1861. Avalon Project. http://avalon.law.yale.edu/19th_century/csa_missec.asp.

Delreal, Jose. "Memorial Circus Outrages Visitors." *Politico*, October 5, 2013. https://www.politico.com/story/2013/10/government-shutdown-wwii-memorial-97875.html.

Dizard, Wilson. "Oath Keepers Armed Group Offers to Protect Kim Davis from Arrest." *Al Jazeera America*, September 11, 2015. http://america.aljazeera.com/articles/2015/9/11/oath-keeper-davis-rowan-county-clerk.html.

Durham, Martin. *The Christian Right, the Far Right, and the Boundaries of American Conservatism.* New York: Manchester University Press, 2000.

——. *White Rage: The Extreme Right and American Politics.* New York: Routledge, 2007.

Ellis, Emma Grey. "White Supremacists Face a Not-so-New Adversary Online: The Antifa." *Wired,* February 4, 2017. https://www.wired.com/2017/02/neo-nazis-face-new-foe-online-irl-far-left-antifa/.

Endres, Danielle, and Samantha Senda-Cook. "Location Matters: The Rhetoric of Place in Protest." *Quarterly Journal of Speech* 97, no. 3 (August 2011): 257–82. https://doi.org/10.1080/00335630.2011.585167.

Ernst, Aaron. "Meet the Anti-Islamic Organizer Who Set Off an FBI Manhunt," *Al Jazeera America,* December 2, 2015. http://america.aljazeera.com/watch/shows/america-tonight/articles/2015/12/2/jon-ritzheimer-anti-islamic-muslim-fbi-manhunt.html.

Esparza, Andre' Gabriel. "Civil Unrest, Militia on Alert as Government Attempts Double Jeopardy by Imprisoning Ranchers." *DontComply.Com* (blog), January 1, 2016. https://www.dontcomply.com/civil-unrest-militia-alert-government-attempts-double-jeopardy-imprisoning-ranchers/.

Fandos, Nicholas. "Trump Inauguration Security Planners Brace for Wave of Protesters." *New York Times,* December 27, 2016. https://www.nytimes.com/2016/12/27/us/politics/donald-trump-inauguration-security.html.

Fausset, Richard, Alan Blinder, and Michael S. Schmidt. "Gunman Kills 4 Marines at Military Site in Chattanooga." *New York Times,* July 16, 2015. https://www.nytimes.com/2015/07/17/us/chattanooga-tennessee-shooting.html.

Fernandez, Manny. "Conspiracy Theories Over Jade Helm Training Exercise Get Some Traction in Texas." *New York Times,* May 6, 2015. https://www.nytimes.com/2015/05/07/us/conspiracy-theories-over-jade-helm-get-some-traction-in-texas.html.

Feuer, Alan. "Antifa on Trial: How a College Professor Joined the Left's Radical Ranks." *Rolling Stone,* May 15, 2018. https://www.rollingstone.com/culture/features/antifa-activists-anti-fascist-movement-trial-college-professor-w519899.

——. "The Oath Keeper Who Wants to Arm Black Lives Matter." *Rolling Stone,* January 3, 2016. http://www.rollingstone.com/politics/news/the-oath-keeper-who-wants-to-arm-black-lives-matter-20160103.

Fuller, Jaime. "The Long Fight Between the Bundys and the Federal Government, from 1989 to Today." *Washington Post,* January 4, 2016. https://www.washingtonpost.com/news/the-fix/wp/2014/04/15/everything-you-need-to-know-about-the-long-fight-between-cliven-bundy-and-the-federal-government/.

Gambino, Lauren. "DeploraBall: Trump Lovers and Haters Clash at Washington DC Event." *Guardian,* January 20, 2017. http://www.theguardian.com/world/2017/jan/20/deploraball-trump-lovers-and-haters-clash-at-washington-dc-event.

Gjelten, Tom. "'March Against Sharia' Planned Across the U.S." *NPR.org*, June 10, 2017. https://www.npr.org/2017/06/10/532254891/march-against-sharia -planned-across-the-u-s.

Goins-Phillips, Tré. "Glenn Beck: Re-Sentencing Oregon Ranchers Is 'Double Jeopardy.'" *TheBlaze*, January 4, 2016. http://www.theblaze.com/news/2016/01 /04/glenn-beck-re-sentencing-oregon-ranchers-is-double-jeopardy/.

Goodman, Barak. "Ruby Ridge." *American Experience*. PBS, August 24, 2017. http://www.pbs.org/wgbh/americanexperience/films/ruby-ridge/.

Griffin, Tamerra, Stephanie McNeal, Michelle Broder Van Dyke, Mike Hayes, and Tasneem Nashrulla. "New Details in Chattanooga Shooting Reveal How Unarmed Marines Fled from Shooter." *BuzzFeed*, July 23, 2015. https://www .buzzfeed.com/tamerragriffin/officer-involved-shooting-at-a-military-center -in-tennessee.

Guarino, Mark "Misleading Reports of Lawlessness After Katrina Worsened Crisis, Officials Say." *Guardian*, August 16, 2015. http://www.theguardian.com /us-news/2015/aug/16/hurricane-katrina-new-orleans-looting-violence -misleading-reports.

Hamburger, Philip A. "Natural Rights, Natural Law, and American Constitutions." *Yale Law Journal* 102, no. 4 (January 1993): 907. https://doi.org/10.2307 /796836.

Hamdi v. Rumsfeld (Syllabus). 542 U.S. 507 (U.S. Supreme Court 2004).

Hardy, Michael. "How Far-Right Groups Took Over a Refugee Community After Harvey." *Texas Observer*, January 22, 2018. https://www.texasobserver.org/big -trouble-little-cambodia/.

Hartz, Louis. *The Liberal Tradition in America: An Interpretation of American Political Thought Since the Revolution*. San Diego: Harcourt Brace Jovanovich, 1991.

Hawley, George. *Making Sense of the Alt-Right*. New York: Columbia University Press, 2017.

Heffernan, Brian. "In Ferguson, Oath Keepers Draw Both Suspicion and Gratitude." *Al Jazeera America*, December 14, 2014. http://america.aljazeera.com /articles/2014/12/14/oath-keepers-fergusonprotests.html.

Hegeman, Roxana. "Militia Member Sentenced to 25 Years in Kansas Bomb Plot." *US News & World Report*, January 25, 2019. https://www.usnews.com /news/us/articles/2019–01–25/3-militia-members-face-sentencing-in-kansas -bomb-plot.

Hersher, Rebecca. "'It Was Time to Make a Hard Stand'; Closing Arguments Completed in Malheur Trial." *NPR.org*, October 19, 2016. http://www.npr.org /sections/thetwo-way/2016/10/19/498526768/it-was-time-to-make-a-hard -stand-closing-arguments-underway-in-malheur-trial.

Heston, Charlton. "Our First Freedom." *Saturday Evening Post*, February 2000.

Holley, Peter. "Race Riots, Terrorist Attacks, and Martial Law: Oath Keepers Warn of Post-Election Chaos." *Washington Post*, November 8, 2016. https://www.washingtonpost.com/news/post-nation/wp/2016/11/08/race-riots-terror-attacks-and-martial-law-oath-keepers-warn-of-post-election-chaos/.

——. "The 'Unhinged' Oregon Protester That the FBI Has Been Tracking for Months." *Washington Post*, January 5, 2016. https://www.washingtonpost.com/news/morning-mix/wp/2016/01/05/why-a-notorious-anti-islam-radical-turned-on-the-federal-government-in-oregon/.

"Honor Flight Network." https://www.honorflight.org/.

Horne, Jed. "Five Myths About Hurricane Katrina." *Washington Post*, August 31, 2012. https://www.washingtonpost.com/opinions/five-myths-about-hurricane-katrina/2012/08/31/003f4064-f147-11e1-a612-3cfc842a6d89_story.html.

IN THE MATTER OF: ELMER S. RHODES, An Attorney at Law, Respondent, No. PR 14-0698 (Montana Supreme Court December 8, 2015).

Jackman, Tom. "National Sheriffs' Group, Opposed to Federal Laws on Guns and Taxes, Calls for Defiance." *Washington Post*, April 28, 2016. https://www.washingtonpost.com/news/true-crime/wp/2016/04/28/national-group-of-sheriffs-opposed-to-federal-government-overreach-gains-size-momentum/.

Jackson, Sam. "Conspiracy Theories in the Patriot/Militia Movement." GW Program on Extremism. May 2017. https://cchs.gwu.edu/sites/cchs.gwu.edu/files/downloads/Jackson%2C%20Conspiracy%20Theories%20Final.pdf.

——. "Don't Assume the Militias at the Charlottesville Rally Were White Supremacists. This Is What They Believe Now." *Washington Post*, September 8, 2017. https://www.washingtonpost.com/news/monkey-cage/wp/2017/09/08/remember-those-militias-at-the-charlottesville-unite-the-right-rally-heres-what-they-believe/.

——. "Non-Normative Political Extremism: Reclaiming a Concept's Analytical Utility." *Terrorism and Political Violence* 31, no. 2 (2019): 244–59. https://doi.org/10.1080/09546553.2016.1212599.

——. "'Nullification Through Armed Civil Disobedience': A Case Study of Strategic Framing in the Patriot/Militia Movement." *Dynamics of Asymmetric Conflict* 12, no. 1 (2019): 90–109. https://doi.org/10.1080/17467586.2018.1563904.

——. "A Schema of Right-Wing Extremism in the United States." Policy Briefs. International Centre for Counter-Terrorism—The Hague (November 4, 2019). https://icct.nl/publication/a-schema-of-right-wing-extremism-in-the-united-states/.

——. "'We Are Patriots:' Uses of National History in Legitimizing Extremism." *Europe Now*, October 2, 2018. https://www.europenowjournal.org/2018/10/01/we-are-patriots-uses-of-national-history-in-legitimizing-extremism/.

Jaffe, Sarah. "The Long History of Antifa." *Progressive.org*, September 13, 2017. http://progressive.org/api/content/fad7965e-9898-11e7-9332-121bebc5777e/.

Janofsky, Michael. "'Militia' Man Tells of Plot to Attack Military Base." *New York Times*, June 25, 1995. http://www.nytimes.com/1995/06/25/us/militia-man-tells -of-plot-to-attack-military-base.html.

Johnston, Hank. "A Methodology for Frame Analysis: From Discourse to Cognitive Schemata." In *Social Movements and Culture*, ed. Hank Johnston and Bert Klandermans, 217–46. Minneapolis: University of Minnesota Press, 1995.

Juergensmeyer, Mark. *Terror in the Mind of God: The Global Rise of Religious Violence*. Berkeley: University of California Press, 2003.

Keith, Jim. *Black Helicopters Over America: Strikeforce for the New World Order*. Lilburn, GA: IllumniNet, 1994.

"Kim Davis Declines Offer from Oath Keepers to Protect Her from the Feds." *Talking Points Memo*. September 14, 2015. http://talkingpointsmemo.com /livewire/kim-davis-declines-oath-keepers.

Koerner, Claudia. "Here's the Story of the Ranchers Whose Case Sparked a Militia Standoff in Oregon." *BuzzFeed*, January 5, 2016. https://www.buzzfeed .com/claudiakoerner/heres-the-story-of-the-ranchers-whose-case-sparked-a -militia.

Kopp, Carol. "The Bridge to Gretna." *CBS News*, December 15, 2005. https:// www.cbsnews.com/news/the-bridge-to-gretna/.

Kreiss, Daniel, Joshua O. Barker, and Shannon Zenner. "Trump Gave Them Hope: Studying the Strangers in Their Own Land." *Political Communication* 34, no. 3 (July 3, 2017): 470–78. https://doi.org/10.1080/10584609.2017 .1330076.

Krieg, Gregory. "Unalienable vs. Inalienable: A Centuries-Old Debate, Still Unresolved." *CNN*. http://www.cnn.com/2016/01/06/politics/barack-obama -unalienable-inalienable-gun-control/index.html.

LaCapria, Kim. "Jade Helm Concludes." *Snopes*, September 15, 2015. http://www .snopes.com/2015/09/15/jade-helm-over/.

Lamoureux, Mack. "Inside Canada's Armed, Anti-Islamic 'Patriot' Group." *Vice*, June 14, 2017. https://www.vice.com/en_us/article/new9wd/the-birth-of -canadas-armed-anti-islamic-patriot-group.

Larson, Eric V., and John E. Peters. "Appendix D: Overview of the Posse Comitatus Act." In *Preparing the U.S. Army for Homeland Security: Concepts, Issues, and Options*. Santa Monica, CA: Rand, 2001. https://www.rand.org /pubs/monograph_reports/MR1251.html.

"LaVoy Finicum's Death, One Year Later." *KOIN* 6 (blog), January 25, 2017. http:// koin.com/2017/01/25/lavoy-finicums-death-one-year-later/.

Lenz, Ryan. "Montana Moves to Strip Oath Keepers' Founder of License to Practice Law." Southern Poverty Law Center, November 4, 2015. https://www .splcenter.org/hatewatch/2015/11/04/montana-moves-strip-oath-keepers%E 2%80%99-founder-license-practice-law.

——. "Oath Keepers Group Takes on 'Pivot Point' Arizona Town." Southern Poverty Law Center, August 29, 2011. https://www.splcenter.org/hatewatch /2011/08/29/oath-keepers-group-takes-%E2%80%98pivot-point%E2%80%99 -arizona-town.

Lepore, Jill. *The Whites of Their Eyes: The Tea Party's Revolution and the Battle Over American History*. Princeton, NJ: Princeton University Press, 2011.

Levin, Sam. "'I Still Don't Believe It': Hammond Family Feels Forgotten in Oregon Standoff." *Guardian*, January 17, 2016. http://www.theguardian.com/us -news/2016/jan/17/oregon-militia-standoff-occupation-dwight-steven -hammond.

Lewis, Helen. "To Learn About the Far Right, Start with the 'Manosphere.'" *The Atlantic*, August 7, 2019. https://www.theatlantic.com/international/archive /2019/08/anti-feminism-gateway-far-right/595642/.

Lind, Dara. "Unite the Right, the Violent White Supremacist Rally in Charlottesville, Explained." *Vox*, August 12, 2017. https://www.vox.com/2017/8/12 /16138246/charlottesville-nazi-rally-right-uva.

Lowery, Wesley. "Black Lives Matter: Birth of a Movement." *Guardian*, January 17, 2017. http://www.theguardian.com/us-news/2017/jan/17/black-lives -matter-birth-of-a-movement.

Luibrand, Shannon. "How a Death in Ferguson Sparked a Movement in America." *CBS News*, August 7, 2015. https://www.cbsnews.com/news/how-the -black-lives-matter-movement-changed-america-one-year-later/.

MacNab, J. J. "According to OK's Interpretation of 'Real Polls' Trump Will Win with 290+ Delegates, Unless There's 'Wide-Scale Fraud.'" Tweet. @jjmacnab, November 6, 2016. https://twitter.com/jjmacnab/status/794362184276942848.

Marcin, Tim. "Trump Voters Believe the President's False Claims That He Won the Popular Vote." *Newsweek*, July 26, 2017. http://www.newsweek.com/trump -won-popular-vote-half-voters-believe-poll-642284.

Markus, Bethania Palma. "Oath Keepers Put 'Boots on the Ground' to Guard Oath-Breaking Kim Davis from 'Dictator' Judge." *Raw Story*, September 10, 2015. https://www.rawstory.com/2015/09/oath-keepers-vow-to-defend-oath -breaking-kim-davis-with-guns-from-dictator-judge/.

Mattheis, Ashley. "Understanding Digital Hate Culture." *Centre for Analysis of the Radical Right* (blog), August 19, 2019. https://www.radicalrightanalysis .com/2019/08/19/understanding-digital-hate-culture/.

Matthews, Dylan. "All 20 Previous Government Shutdowns, Explained." *Vox*, January 19, 2018. https://www.vox.com/policy-and-politics/2018/1/19/16905584 /government-shutdown-history-clinton-obama-explained.

Mazie, Steven. "Supreme Court Justices May Give Away Their Votes with Their Voices." *The Economist*, December 21, 2017. https://www.economist.com /blogs/democracyinamerica/2017/12/pitch-perfect.

McGee, Michael Calvin. "The 'Ideograph': A Link Between Rhetoric and Ideology." *Quarterly Journal of Speech* 66, no. 1 (February 1, 1980): 1–16. https://doi.org/10.1080/00335638009383499.

McManus, John F. "Twenty-Nine Palms Survey: What Really Motivated Its Author?" Jews for the Preservation of Firearms Ownership, October 2, 1995. http://jpfo.org/articles-assd/29palms-mcmanus.htm.

McVeigh, Rory. "What's New About the Tea Party Movement?" In *Understanding the Tea Party Movement*, ed. Nella Van Dyke and David S. Meyer, 15–34. Burlington, VT: Ashgate, 2014.

Medina, Jennifer. "Arizona Town's Mayor at Center of Dispute." *New York Times*, July 15, 2011. https://www.nytimes.com/2011/07/16/us/16quartzsite.html.

Meet the Press. "Transcript for September 4." September 4, 2005. http://www.nbcnews.com/id/9179790/ns/meet_the_press/t/transcript-september/.

Mele, Christopher, and Annie Correal. "'Not Our President': Protests Spread After Donald Trump's Election." *New York Times*, November 9, 2016. https://www.nytimes.com/2016/11/10/us/trump-election-protests.html.

Michel, Casey. "Former CIA Director Says Russian Bots Amplified Jade Helm Conspiracies." *Think Progress*, May 3, 2018. https://thinkprogress.org/russian-bots-amplified-jade-helm-conspiracies-6caa41073c08/.

——. "How Militias Became the Private Police for White Supremacists." *Politico*, August 17, 2017. https://www.politico.com/magazine/story/2017/08/17/white-supremacists-militias-private-police-215498.

——. "The Oath Keepers Providing Volunteer Security at Trump's Minneapolis Rally Are Itching for a Civil War." *Daily Beast*, October 10, 2019. https://www.thedailybeast.com/the-oath-keepers-providing-volunteer-security-at-trumps-minneapolis-rally-are-itching-for-a-civil-war.

——. "Opinion: How the Russians Pretended to Be Texans—and Texans Believed Them." *Washington Post*, October 17, 2017. https://www.washingtonpost.com/news/democracy-post/wp/2017/10/17/how-the-russians-pretended-to-be-texans-and-texans-believed-them/.

Midlarsky, Manus I. *Origins of Political Extremism: Mass Violence in the Twentieth Century and Beyond.* New York: Cambridge University Press, 2011.

More, Michael. Urge protection of states rights, Pub. L. No. LC2235 (2009). http://laws.leg.mt.gov/legprd/LAW0203W$BSRV.ActionQuery?P_SESS=20091&P_BLTP_BILL_TYP_CD=HJ&P_BILL_NO=0026&P_BILL_DFT_NO=&P_CHPT_NO=&Z_ACTION=Find&P_ENTY_ID_SEQ2=&P_SBJT_SBJ_CD=&P_ENTY_ID_SEQ=&P_PRNT_FRNDLY_PG=Y.

Morlin, Bill. "ACT's Anti-Muslim Message Fertile Ground for Oath Keepers." Southern Poverty Law Center, June 12, 2017. https://www.splcenter.org/hatewatch/2017/06/12/act%E2%80%99s-anti-muslim-message-fertile-ground-oath-keepers.

——. "Ex-Marine and Fugitive Tied to Oath Keepers Arrested." *Southern Poverty Law Center*, August 25, 2011. https://www.splcenter.org/hatewatch/2011/08/25/ex-marine-and-fugitive-tied-oath-keepers-arrested.

Mudde, Cas. "Introduction: Political Extremism—Concepts, Theories, and Democratic Responses." In *Political Extremism*, ed. Cas Mudde, 1:xxiii–xxix. Los Angeles: SAGE, 2014.

Mulloy, D. J. *American Extremism: History, Politics, and the Militia Movement.* New York: Routledge, 2004.

——. "'Liberty or Death': Violence and the Rhetoric of Revolution in the American Militia Movement." *Canadian Review of American Studies* 38, no. 1 (2008): 119–45.

Murphy, Andrew R. "Longing, Nostalgia, and Golden Age Politics: The American Jeremiad and the Power of the Past." *Perspectives on Politics* 7, no. 1 (2009): 125–41. https://doi.org/10.1017/S1537592709090148.

——. "Two American Jeremiads: Traditionalist and Progressive Stories of American Nationhood." *Politics and Religion* 1, no. 1 (2008): 85–112. https://doi.org/10.1017/S1755048308000059.

Nagourney, Adam. "A Defiant Rancher Savors the Audience That Rallied to His Side." *New York Times*, April 23, 2014. https://www.nytimes.com/2014/04/24/us/politics/rancher-proudly-breaks-the-law-becoming-a-hero-in-the-west.html.

National Weather Service. "Hurricane Katrina—August 2005." November 2016. https://www.weather.gov/mob/katrina.

Neiwert, David. "After Dyer's Rape Arrest, 'Oath Keepers' Disavow Any Association with Onetime Key Figure." *Crooks and Liars*, January 21, 2010. https://crooksandliars.com/david-neiwert/after-dyers-rape-arrest-oath-keepers.

——. *Alt-America: The Rise of the Radical Right in the Age of Trump.* New York: Verso, 2017.

——. "Back at the Bundy Ranch, It's Oath Keepers vs. Militiamen as Wild Rumors Fly." *Southern Poverty Law Center*, April 30, 2014. https://www.splcenter.org/hatewatch/2014/04/30/back-bundy-ranch-its-oath-keepers-vs-militiamen-wild-rumors-fly.

——. "Oath Keepers Descend Upon Oregon with Dreams of Armed Confrontation Over Mining Dispute." *Southern Poverty Law Center*, April 22, 2015. https://www.splcenter.org/hatewatch/2015/04/23/oath-keepers-descend-upon-oregon-dreams-armed-confrontation-over-mining-dispute.

Ortiz, Erik, Gabe Gutierrez, and Daniella Silva. "Kim Davis, Kentucky Clerk Blocking Gay Marriages, Held in Contempt." *NBC News*, September 3, 2015. https://www.nbcnews.com/news/us-news/kentucky-clerk-kim-davis-held-contempt-court-n421126.

Padilla, Vivian. "Jon Ritzheimer, Organizer of Various Anti-Islam Rallies, Appears in Oregon Protest Videos." *ABC News*, January 4, 2016. http://www .abc15.com/news/national/jon-ritzheimer-organizer-of-various-anti-islam -rallies-appears-in-oregon-protest-videos.

Parker, Charles F., Eric K. Stern, Eric Paglia, and Christer Brown. "Preventable Catastrophe? The Hurricane Katrina Disaster Revisited." *Journal of Contingencies and Crisis Management* 17, no. 4 (December 1, 2009): 206–20. https:// doi.org/10.1111/j.1468–5973.2009.00588.x.

Peacher, Amanda. "There's Another Armed Group in Burns and They're Not the Bundys." Oregon Public Broadcasting, January 10, 2016. http://www.opb .org/news/series/burns-oregon-standoff-bundy-militia-news-updates/theres -another-armed-group-in-burns-and-theyre-not-the-bundys/.

Pencak, William. "Whittemore, Samuel (1696–1793), Farmer and Folk Hero of the American Revolution." In *American National Biography*. Oxford University Press, February 2000. https://www.anb.org/view/10.1093/anb/9780198606 697.001.0001/anb-9780198606697-e-0101246.

Perliger, Arie. "Identifying Three Trends in Far Right Violence in the United States." *CTC Sentinel* 5, no. 9 (September 2012): 5–7.

Pierce, Scott Masters. "Kim Davis Turned Down the Oath Keepers' Offer of Armed Security." *Vice*, September 15, 2015. https://www.vice.com/en_au /article/nn93g8/kim-davis-turned-down-the-oath-keepers-offer-of-armed -security-vgtrn-915.

Pitcavage, Mark. "Camouflage and Conspiracy: The Militia Movement from Ruby Ridge to Y2K." *American Behavioral Scientist* 44, no. 6 (February 2001): 957–81. https://doi.org/10.1177/00027640121956610.

Pogue, James. "The Oath Keepers Are Ready for War with the Federal Government." *Vice*, September 14, 2015. http://www.vice.com/read/miner-threat -0000747-v22n9.

Potok, Mark. "The Year in Hate and Extremism." Southern Poverty Law Center, February 15, 2017. https://www.splcenter.org/fighting-hate/intelligence -report/2017/year-hate-and-extremism.

Powers, Ashley. "The Renegade Sheriffs." *New Yorker*, April 23, 2018. https://www .newyorker.com/magazine/2018/04/30/the-renegade-sheriffs.

Printz v. United States. https://www.oyez.org/cases/1996/95-1478.

Purdue, Simon. "Toxic Masculinity and Lone Wolf Radicalization." *Centre for Analysis of the Radical Right* (blog), November 21, 2019. https://www .radicalrightanalysis.com/2019/11/21/toxic-masculinity-and-lone-wolf -radicalization/.

Rapoport, David C. "Before the Bombs There Were the Mobs: American Experiences with Terror." *Terrorism and Political Violence* 20, no. 2 (2008): 167–94. https://doi.org/10.1080/09546550701856045.

Rayfield, Jillian. "Oath Keeper-Backed AZ Mayor Says His Recall Election Was Rigged Thanks to 'Nazi' Police Force." *Talking Points Memo*, September 2, 2011. https://talkingpointsmemo.com/muckraker/oath-keeper-backed-az-mayor-says-his-recall-election-was-rigged-thanks-to-nazi-police-force.

Rayman, Graham. "FBI Warns NY Police About Anti-Islam Arizona Man." *New York Daily News*, November 27, 2015. http://www.nydailynews.com/news/crime/fbi-warns-ny-police-anti-islam-arizona-man-article-1.2448001.

Reeve, Elle. "We Camped Out with the Antifa Activists Plotting to Disarm the Alt-Right." *Vice*, May 9, 2018. https://news.vice.com/en_us/article/7xmzmd/we-camped-out-with-the-antifa-activists-plotting-to-disarm-the-alt-right.

Rivinius, Jessica. "Sovereign Citizen Movement Perceived as Top Terrorist Threat." *START*, July 30, 2014. https://www.start.umd.edu/news/sovereign-citizen-movement-perceived-top-terrorist-threat.

Robertson, Derek. "How an Obscure Conservative Theory Became the Trump Era's Go-To Nerd Phrase." *Politico*, February 25, 2018. http://politi.co/2FunqYx.

Robin, Corey. *The Reactionary Mind: Conservatism from Edmund Burke to Sarah Palin*. New York: Oxford University Press, 2011.

Rosman, John, and Conrad Wilson. "FBI: Standoff Continues, Release Video of Finicum Death." Oregon Public Broadcasting, March 8, 2016. https://www.opb.org/news/series/burns-oregon-standoff-bundy-militia-news-updates/fbi-standoff-continues-release-video-of-finicum-death/.

Rothbard, Murray N. "Confiscation and the Homestead Principle." *Libertarian Forum*, June 15, 1969.

Rumsfeld v. Padilla (Syllabus). 542 U.S. 426 (U.S. Supreme Court 2004).

Russell, Nathan J. "An Introduction to the Overton Window of Political Possibilities." Mackinac Center for Public Policy, January 4, 2006. http://www.mackinac.org/7504.

Russell-Kraft, Stephanie. "The Rise of Male Supremacist Groups." *New Republic*, April 4, 2018. https://newrepublic.com/article/147744/rise-male-supremacist-groups.

Sainato, Michael. "Ferguson Oath Keepers Leader Sam Andrews Forms Splinter Group." *Observer* (blog), August 30, 2015. http://observer.com/2015/08/ferguson-oath-keepers-leader-sam-andrews-forms-splinter-group/.

Schwinn, Steven D. "It's Time to Abandon Anti-Commandeering (but Don't Count on This Supreme Court to Do It)." *SCOTUSblog*, August 17, 2017. https://www.scotusblog.com/2017/08/symposium-time-abandon-anti-commandeering-dont-count-supreme-court/.

Sehat, David. *The Jefferson Rule: How the Founding Fathers Became Infallible and Our Politics Inflexible*. New York: Simon & Schuster, 2015.

Selective Service System. "Background of Selective Service." https://www.sss.gov/About/History-And-Records/Background-Of-Selective-Service.

Shankman, Sabrina, Tom Jennings, Brendan McCarthy, Laura Maggi, and A. C. Thompson. "After Katrina, New Orleans Cops Were Told They Could Shoot Looters." *ProPublica*, July 24, 2012. https://www.propublica.org/article/nopd-order-to-shoot-looters-hurricane-katrina.

Shapira, Harel. *Waiting for José: The Minutemen's Pursuit of America*. Princeton, NJ: Princeton University Press, 2013.

Sharrock, Justine. "Oath Keepers and the Age of Treason." *Mother Jones*, April 2010. http://www.motherjones.com/politics/2010/03/oath-keepers.

Simpson, Ian. "Anarchists Threaten to Disrupt Trump Inauguration, Police Say Ready." *Reuters*, January 6, 2017. https://www.reuters.com/article/us-usa-trump-inauguration/anarchists-threaten-to-disrupt-trump-inauguration-police-say-ready-idUSKBN14Q2BG.

Skocpol, Theda, and Vanessa Williamson. *The Tea Party and the Remaking of Republican Conservatism*. New York: Oxford University Press, 2012.

Smith, Mitch. "Kansas Trio Convicted in Plot to Bomb Somali Immigrants." *New York Times*, September 10, 2018. https://www.nytimes.com/2018/04/18/us/kansas-militia-somali-trial-verdict.html.

Sneed, Tierney. "Oath Keepers on Their Way to 'Protect' KY Clerk Kim Davis from US Marshals." *Talking Points Memo*, September 10, 2015. http://talkingpointsmemo.com/livewire/kim-davis-oath-keepers.

Snow, David A., and Robert D. Benford. "Ideology, Frame Resonance, and Participant Mobilization." In *From Structure to Action: Comparing Social Movement Research Across Cultures*, ed. Bert Klandermans, Hanspeter Kriesi, and Sidney G. Tarrow, 197–217. Greenwich: JAI, 1988.

Snow, David A., E. Burke Rochford Jr., Steven K. Worden, and Robert D. Benford. "Frame Alignment Processes, Micromobilization, and Movement Participation." *American Sociological Review* 51, no. 4 (1986): 464–81.

Snow, David A., Rens Vliegenthart, and Pauline Ketelaars. "The Framing Perspective on Social Movements: Its Conceptual Roots and Architecture." In *The Wiley Blackwell Companion to Social Movements*, 2nd ed., ed. David A. Snow, Sarah Anne Soule, Hanspeter Kriesi, and Holly J. McCammon, 392–410. Hoboken, NJ: Wiley, 2019.

Somin, Ilya. "Federalism, the Constitution, and Sanctuary Cities." *Washington Post*, November 26, 2016. https://www.washingtonpost.com/news/volokh-conspiracy/wp/2016/11/26/federalism-the-constitution-and-sanctuary-cities/.

Sottile, Leah. "Chapter Four: The Preacher and the Politician." *Bundyville: The Remnant* (blog), July 18, 2019. https://longreads.com/2019/07/18/bundyville-the-remnant-chapter-four-the-preacher-and-the-politician/.

——. "Chapter Three: The Widow's Tale." *Bundyville: The Remnant* (blog), July 2019. https://longreads.com/2019/07/17/bundyville-the-remnant-chapter-three-the-widows-tale/.

Southern Poverty Law Center. "Antigovernment Movement." https://www
.splcenter.org/fighting-hate/extremist-files/ideology/antigovernment.

——. "Michael Brian Vanderboegh." https://www.splcenter.org/fighting-hate
/extremist-files/individual/michael-brian-vanderboegh-0.

——. "The Second Wave: Return of the Militias." August 2009. https://www
.splcenter.org/20090731/second-wave-return-militias.

Stack, Liam. "Attack on Alt-Right Leader Has Internet Asking: Is It O.K. to Punch
a Nazi?" New York Times, January 21, 2017. https://www.nytimes.com/2017/01
/21/us/politics/richard-spencer-punched-attack.html.

Stanglin, Doug, and Kyle Jahner. "Controversial Jade Helm Military Exercise
Opens in Texas." USA Today, July 15, 2015. http://www.usatoday.com/story
/news/nation/2015/07/15/operation-jade-helm-texas/30191795/.

Stern, Jessica. Terror in the Name of God: Why Religious Militants Kill. 1st ed.
New York: Ecco, 2003.

Sullivan, Eileen, and Julie Turkewitz. "Trump Pardons Oregon Ranchers Whose
Case Inspired Wildlife Refuge Takeover." New York Times, July 10, 2018.
https://www.nytimes.com/2018/07/10/us/politics/trump-pardon-hammond
-oregon.html.

Swaine, Jon, and Guardian Staff. "Anti-Trump Protesters Gear Up for Weekend
Demonstrations Across the US." Guardian, November 12, 2016. http://www
.theguardian.com/us-news/2016/nov/11/anti-trump-protests-weekend-new
-york-trump-tower.

Sweeney, Matthew. "What Is the Sovereign Citizen Movement, What Do They
Believe, and How Are They Spreading?" Radicalisation Research, June 19, 2018.
https://www.radicalisationresearch.org/guides/sweeney-sovereign-citizen
-movement/.

Tabor, James D., and Eugene V. Gallagher. "What Might Have Been." In Why
Waco? Cults and the Battle for Religious Freedom in America, 1–22. Berkeley:
University of California Press, 1995.

Talwani, Sanjay. "Lincoln Remains Quiet as Oath Keepers Continue 'Operation Big Sky.'" August 21, 2015. KRTV 3. http://www.krtv.com/story/29762011
/lincoln-remains-quiet-as-oath-keepers-continue-operation-big-sky.

——. "'Patriot' Groups Protecting White Hope Mine near Lincoln in 'Operation Big Sky.'" August 15, 2015. KRTV 3. http://www.krtv.com/story/29731505
/patriot-groups-protecting-white-hope-mine-near-lincoln-in-operation-big
-sky.

Thevenot, Brian, and Gordon Russell. "Rumors of Deaths Greatly
Exaggerated—Widely Reported Attacks False or Unsubstantiated—6 Bodies Found at Dome; 4 at Convention Center." Times-Picayune, September 26, 2005.

This American Life. "Seriously?" https://www.thisamericanlife.org/radio-archives /episode/599/seriously.

Thompson, Catherine. "Anti-Muslim Activist Says He Plans to Arrest Dem Sen. Debbie Stabenow." *Talking Points Memo,* September 23, 2015. http:// talkingpointsmemo.com/muckraker/jon-ritzheimer-debbie-stabenow -threat.

——. "Oath Keepers Founder: Traitor McCain Should Be 'Hung by the Neck Until Dead.'" *Talking Points Memo,* May 13, 2015. http://talkingpointsmemo .com/livewire/stewart-rhodes-hang-john-mccain.

Thorson, Kjerstin, and Chris Wells. "How Gatekeeping Still Matters: Understanding Media Effects in an Era of Curated Flows." In *Gatekeeping in Transition,* ed. Timothy Vos and François Heinderyckx, 25–44. New York: Routledge, 2015.

Tiffany, Kaitlyn. "Right-Wing Extremist Richard Spencer Got Punched, but It Was Memes That Bruised His Ego." *The Verge,* January 23, 2017. https://www .theverge.com/2017/1/23/14356306/richard-spencer-punch-internet-memes -alt-right.

Times-Picayune Staff. "Danziger Bridge Guilty Verdicts Are Another Strike Against New Orleans Police." *NOLA.com,* August 5, 2011. http://www.nola .com/crime/index.ssf/2011/08/danziger_jury_gives_new_orlean.html.

Tsai, Robert L. *America's Forgotten Constitutions: Defiant Visions of Power and Community.* Cambridge, MA: Harvard University Press, 2014.

——. "The Troubling Sheriffs' Movement That Joe Arpaio Supports." *Politico,* September 1, 2017. http://politi.co/2er3E3M.

Tumposky, Ellen. "Arizona SWAT Team Defends Shooting Iraq Vet 60 Times." *ABC News,* May 20, 2011. https://abcnews.go.com/US/tucson-swat-team -defends-shooting-iraq-marine-veteran/story?id=13640112.

Turner, Frederick Jackson. "The Significance of the Frontier in American History." In *The Significance of the Frontier in American History,* ed. Harold Peter Simonson. New York: Frederick Ungar, 1963.

Uscinski, Joseph E., and Joseph M. Parent. *American Conspiracy Theories.* New York: Oxford University Press, 2014.

Van Dyke, Nella, and Sarah A. Soule. "Structural Social Change and the Mobilizing Effect of Threat: Explaining Levels of Patriot and Militia Organizing in the United States." *Social Problems* 49, no. 4 (2002): 497–520. https://doi .org/10.1525/sp.2002.49.4.497.

Vanderboegh, Michael. "A Brief Three Percent Catechism—a Discipline Not for the Faint-Hearted." *Sipsey Street Irregulars* (blog), June 29, 2014. http:// sipseystreetirregulars.blogspot.com/2014/06/a-brief-three-percent-catechism .html.

——. "No More Free Wacos: An Explication of the Obvious Addressed to Eric Holder, Attorney General of the United States." *Sipsey Street Irregulars* (blog), May 6, 2009. http://sipseystreetirregulars.blogspot.com/2009/05/no-more-free -wacos-explication-of.html.

——. "What Is a 'Three Percenter'?" *Sipsey Street Irregulars* (blog), February 17, 2009.   http://sipseystreetirregulars.blogspot.com/2009/02/what-is-three -percenter.html.

Walker, Jesse. "Oath Keeper Who Called for #BlackOpenCarry March in Ferguson Leaves the Group, Plans His Own March; Oath Keepers Say the Original March Will Proceed—Hit & Run." *Reason.com*, August 27, 2015. http://reason.com/blog/2015/08/27/oath-keeper-who-called-for-blackopen carr.

Walsh, Michael. "Millions Sign Petition Urging Electoral College to Elect Hillary Clinton." *Yahoo*, November 11, 2016. https://www.yahoo.com/news /millions-sign-petition-urging-electoral-college-to-elect-hillary-clinton -175038196.html.

Weinstein, Adam. "The NRA Twisted a Tiny Part of the Katrina Disaster to Fit Its Bigger Agenda." *The Trace*, August 31, 2015. https://www.thetrace.org/2015 /08/nra-hurricane-katrina-gun-confiscation/.

Wiles, Tay. "Sugar Pine Mine, the Other Standoff." *High Country News*, February 2, 2016. http://www.hcn.org/issues/48.2/showdown-at-sugar-pine -mine.

Williams, Jennifer. "The Oath Keepers, the Far-Right Group Answering Trump's Call to Watch the Polls, Explained." *Vox*, November 7, 2016. http://www.vox .com/policy-and-politics/2016/11/7/13489640/oath-keepers-donald-trump -voter-fraud-intimidation-rigged.

Wintrobe, Ronald. *Rational Extremism: The Political Economy of Radicalism*. New York: Cambridge University Press, 2006.

Wright, Stuart A. *Patriots, Politics, and the Oklahoma City Bombing*. Cambridge Studies in Contentious Politics. New York: Cambridge University Press, 2007.

Wyler, Grace. "The Bundy Ranch Standoff Was Only the Beginning for America's Right-Wing Militias." *Vice*, April 16, 2014. https://www.vice.com/en_us /article/dpwykw/an-armed-standoff-in-nevada-is-only-the-beginning-for -americas-right-wing-militias.

Wyloge, Evan. "Hundreds Gather in Arizona for Armed Anti-Muslim Protest." *Washington Post*, May 30, 2015. https://www.washingtonpost.com/news/post -nation/wp/2015/05/30/hundreds-gather-in-arizona-for-armed-anti-muslim -protest/.

York, Neil Longley. *The Boston Massacre: A History with Documents*. New York: Routledge, 2010.

Zaitz, Les. "Militiamen, Ranchers in Showdown for Soul of Burns." *OregonLive*
.*com*, December 30, 2015. http://www.oregonlive.com/pacific-northwest-news
/index.ssf/2015/12/militiamen_ranchers_in_showdow.html.

Zeskind, Leonard. *Blood and Politics: The History of the White Nationalist Movement from the Margins to the Mainstream*. New York: Farrar Straus Giroux,
2009.

Index